THE DIRTY THIRTIES

by
William H. Hull, M.A.

Tales of the Nineteen Thirties During Which
Occurred a Great Drought, a Lengthy Depression and
the Era Commonly Called The Dust Bowl Years.

Other books by William H. Hull

All Hell Broke Loose
Aunt Zettie's Wonderful Salve
Prayers for Healing
Public Relations for Pharmacists

D1023720

Second Printing

Copyright 1989 William H. Hull
6833 Creston Road
Edina, Minnesota 55435

ISBN 0-939330-03-2

Production by Stanton Publication Services, Inc., Minneapolis

CONTENTS

INTRODUCTION

Our World Is Crazy
The Drought Of The Thirties
The Good Old Days
The Year Is 1936
Adolph Hitler Solved Our Depression Problems

OUR WORLD IS CRAZY

The other day someone told me that Michael and Mary are very uptight and so tense these days that they're having difficulty getting along. They can't cope.

Why? Because Mary's mother is ill. Because they have two young children. Because both parents work, bringing in about fifty thousand a year, and having lots of difficulty.

In contrast to their world, full of television, frozen food, unlimited fresh food at the groceries, a huge buying capability, I can only think of the people who have told me of their troubles in the thirties — the people whose stories are included in this book. Of people like some I know who cut the maggots out of the meat so they could use it. Of people like my own dear mother who could perform miracles with food that today's woman wouldn't know how to handle. Flake hominy, for example.

Stop. Think for a moment. What would it have meant to the young people of the thirties to have airconditioning at home and in their auto — much less in two autos? What would it have been like not to have to burn corncobs because they couldn't afford coal, much less have automatic gas heat? What would it have meant to have money and checking accounts, instead of not having a spare nickle? Five cents, that is. Five measly pennies.

When I hear the stories these dear people tell of the thirties, when I hear the pathetic situations where people went to bed hungry, when they lived off potatoes and lard, when they couldn't eat their chickens because the meat was so greasy and distasteful because the fowl lived on grasshoppers. Help us, Lord, for our affluence. Help us for our lack of appreciation of how far we have come in fifty years. Help us to appreciate.

When we go to the grocery store and buy a hundred dollars worth of groceries so casually, when we go out for a simple dinner and are pleased to do it for thirty dollars for two people, we should stop and consider how that money would have changed the lives of an entire family back in the Dirty Thirties. Let us consider. Let us think. Let us appreciate. Let us thank God.

— WHH

THE DROUGHT OF THE THIRTIES

The Crash. The Depression. Hard Times. They (It) had come in twenty-nine and was still very much with us. People were poor. Modern day people at the close of the century don't have any idea what it was to be poor—not like it was then.

And it was hot. And dry. Oh, Lord, how hot and dry it was. That's what we'll examine in this book, particularly human experiences.

The situation didn't happen all at once. People didn't simply wake up one day in 1934 or 1936 and say 'Good gosh, it's about the hottest it has ever been.' It came about gradually.

It was so dry in 1933 that on Sunday, November 12 a duststorm occurred that involved a vast territory stretching from the Canadian line—Lake Superior to Montana—southward to the western Ohio and lower Missouri valleys, a region greater than the combined areas of France, Italy and Hungary. It was a straight line wind that created more dust in South Dakota than ever before in the memories of old settlers and weather observers. In Iowa those winds blew corn from the stalks, visibility was low and artifical lights were required during the daytime. Flying schedules into the Dakotas and Manitoba were cancelled.[1] That was some storm.

Signs of 'Extreme Drought' began to appear in 1933 and worsened. That is the highest (worst) category used by the National Climatic Data Center and it was applied to Kansas, South Dakota and Minnesota in June 1933. By April 1934 it applied to huge areas of the country, yet East Texas, part of Oklahoma, most of Arkansas, Louisiana and Florida were at near normal conditions. By August 1934 the situation was so severe and so widespread that practically all of the midwest, the upper midwest and the west were either categorized as being in 'Extreme Drought' or 'Severe drought' conditions—either being very serious.[2]

During 1935 the situation improved but by August 1936 the central and north central states again were in those 'Extreme Drought' classifications.

Texas, for example, was in worse drought conditions in 1956 (twenty years later) than in 1934–1936.

Drought has been cited as a scourge of mankind since biblical times. It still is a menace to world food supplies. Insect plagues, with which it ranks as a crop threat, can be fought by modern means but drought still remains unconquered. Of course drought doesn't mean the same to each of us. To the farmer it means a shortage of moisture in the root zone of his crops. To the hydrologist it suggests below average water levels in streams, lakes and reservoirs. To the economist it means a water shortage which adversely affects the established economy. All have a concern which depends on the effects of a fairly prolonged weather situation.

At this time we must compliment and laud Wayne C. Palmer, Chief, Bio-climatology Section, Office of Climatology, United States Department of Commerce, Weather Bureau, Washington, D.C. Palmer made a bold new presentation in a paper[3] prepared and delivered at the Fourth Conference on Agricultural Meteorology of a combined meeting of the American Meteorological Society and the American Society of Agronomy in St. Louis on November 28, 1961.

In that paper, Palmer presented a whole new way of analyzing statistically the water needs based on a very involved formula including many factors. It has become a standard technique and, for example, is the basis by which the National Climatic Center could prepare many charts showing visually the affects of the various droughts in this country. (See footnote #2).

The Palmer Drought Severity Index (PDSI) was designed for drought computations for monthly averages data using the principles of a balance between moisture supply and demand. Man-made changes such as increased irrigation, new reservoirs and added industrial water use are not considered. Apparently the National Weather Service uses the PDSI monthly in forecasting.(2-page IV)

In his presentation Palmer said: 'The underlying concept of the paper is that the amount of precipitation required for the near-normal operation of the established economy of an area, is dependent on the average climate of the area and on the meteorological conditions which prevailed both during and preceding the month or period in question. The paper demonstrates a method for computing this required precipitation. The difference between the actual precipitated and computed precipitation represents a fairly direct measure of the departure of the moisture aspect of the weather from normal. When these departures are weighted according to the local ratio between average moisture demand and average moisture supply, the resulting index numbers appear to be of reasonably comparable economic significance both in space and time.'

It is important that his procedures enabled researchers thereafter to work with data for specific somewhat narrow geographical areas and thus be more pertinent. For that we thank him as citizens.

Now let's take a look at people's experiences during these years. How did they live? What were their problems?

(1) As reported by M.R.Hovde, Weather Bureau Office, Huron, S.D., in the *Monthly Weather Review*, United States Department of Agriculture, Weather Bureau, January, 1934 issue, page 12. Not copyrighted.

(2) *Atlas of Monthly Palmer Hydrological Drought Indices (1931–1983) For The Contiguous United States*, by Thomas R. Karl and Richard W. Knight, National Climatic Data Center, Federal Building, Asheville, N.C. 28801–2696. Not copyrighted.

(3) *Meteorological Drought: It's Measurement and Classification*, Wayne C. Palmer, Department of Commerce, Weather Bureau, Washington, D.C., 1961. Not copyrighted.

THE GOOD OL' DAYS

Oh, yes, indeed, I remember the good ol' days.

When I remember as a boy walking down that dusty country road with the dust puffing up between my toes, I get slightly homesick. When I remember how much fun it was to kick that warm dust and forget that it stuck to the bottom of my pants, I want to do it again. I forget the rocks that were hidden in the dust, the stubbed and bloody toes that really hurt when you ripped back a toenail.

I think of my grandfather's farm and my tangential mind quickly jumps back to the new barn. Well, it was new then. There always seemed to be a mule tethered in the lower level; to one side, on the slope, was this wonderful-tasting well water. Of course the adults didn't like it because it had too much iron in it. Maybe I liked it because they didn't. Maybe that taste of iron was directly related to the mule. But Grandpa knew it was safe or he wouldn't have let me drink from it. Oh, that good ol' well! But it was one just like it, or a cistern, from which I picked up the typhoid fever that ravaged my childhood body.

It may be that some younger reader may not know that a cistern is really an underground storage tank for rain water. That rainwater washed off the roof of the house, down the gutters into a drainpipe going into the cistern. But Grandfather threw a by-pass lever so the first waters went onto the ground. Then when the roof was clean, he threw the switch to direct that water into the cistern. There are parts of the world, like in Bermuda, where there is no water except for cistern or hauled in water.

But those cisterns had to be cleaned or the drinking, cooking, batheing water became contaminated. Oh, for the good ol' days.

The farmer didn't have it so bad. He had at least one good team, if he were lucky, and he could stroll across the field while the team pulled the plow turning the soil, or pulled a wagon that automatically scattered the winter's accumulation of manure onto the field. Of course he did walk mostly and he did get tired. But today's farmer doesn't have that thrill. He must sit in an airconditioned cab of a sixty thousand dollar tractor, listening to his choice of music, spending huge amounts of money for machine and fuel. What's that about the good ol' days?

It certainly was a different kind of gamble back then.

Town life was simple, too. We kids didn't know we were having a tough time when we walked to grade school—and later to high school. We walked from McRoberts street, down a long hill, across the railroad tracks, up another hill, all the way into downtown, out main street forever, past interesting things like service stations, garages, morning stores being opened, flirting with girls. Man, I tell you, it was tough. And it was like 35 miles each way. Well, maybe two miles maximum. Today's kids miss all that. They have to get into a busfull of screaming kids, all determined to wreck the driver's eardrums and have to punch each other all the way to school. Things are tough. Or course today they don't get to fall on that icy hill and get a hernia. They don't get the chance to be switched by the man at the service station if he hears bad language. Poor kids.

Many of us didn't have electricity. That and the radio probably changed the world more than everything else put together. Millions of us knew nothing about all the devices we take for granted today. Like the toaster that sat atop the stove. And the radio brings news almost before it happens. Wouldn't it have been superb to have had an announcer with Teddy Roosevelt at San Juan hill?

And heat! We had the good old advantage of burning corncobs or wood that we got to split ourselves, or coal or kerosene — in a hot summer kitchen as well as in the winter. Many of us remember mother cooking on a big kitchen range, heated with wood from the woodlot, water boiling on the side, biscuits kept in the warmer halfway up the stovepipe. And we had the pleasure of having coal buckets. They were nasty, dirty things to bring in coal and have it near an indoor stove. They had a handle affixed to the bucket by knifelike appendages sticking up from the bucket itself. I say knifelike because this five or six year old kid fell down on one and has the chin scar yet today to prove it.

Oh, yes, they were good ol' days. We had such wonderful things as doctors making housecalls and tacking quarantine cards on our front door, of good fresh milk from our own Bossy (sometimes it had a weird taste), home butchered meat that sometimes came from our own pet calf or the little shoat that our sisters thought were so cute and grew to love. And we had cats — sometimes like thousands of cats. But they were helpful. They killed mice in the barn and eradicated all the new bunnies we were trying to protect.

And it goes on and on — but I won't. It's perfectly obvious that much of the apeal of the good ol' days is a yearning for the simple life which has escaped most seniors today. We remember the simplicity but forget the dangers and the uncertainties. Perhaps it's just as well.

THE YEAR IS 1936

The year is 1936. In its 20th day Britain's George V dies; his son Edward would give up the throne at year's end for American divorcee Wallis Warfield Simpson. Hitler reoccupies the Rhineland. The Spanish Civil War begins in Spanish Morocco and President Roosevelt wins election to a second term with 61 percent of the vote. John Maynard Keynes publishes his "The General Theory of Employment, Interest and Money," William Faulkner comes out with "Absalom, Absalom," Margaret Mitchell with "Gone with the Wind," Irma Rombauer with "The Joy of Cooking." H.L. Hunt founds his oil company.

Boulder Dam is completed on the Colorado River and Life magazine begins publication, as do England's Penguin Books, which will start a revolution in paperback publishing. "Ethan Frome" opens at the National Theatre with Ruth Gordon, Raymond Massey and Tom Ewell. Robert Sherwood's "Idiot's Delight," starring Alfred Lunt and Lynn Fontanne, wins the Pulitzer for drama. Bob Feller signs with the Indians, Joe DiMaggio with the Yankees.

In the Upper Midwest, Minnesota Valley Canning adds asparagus to its line of Green Giant canned vegetables and General Mills introduces fictitious food authority Betty Crocker.

And on a soon-to-be drought-stricken farm in Western Wisconsin is born David Charles Wood, who would one day come to write a column about self-publishing.

Dave Wood
Minneapolis, MN

Reprinted with special permission from the Star-Tribune, Minneapolis, MN, Nov. 8, 1987.
Referenced to James Trager's "The People's Chronology" (Holt, Rinehart and Winston 1979).

IT WAS ADOLPH HITLER WHO SOLVED OUR DEPRESSION PROBLEMS

Join me in a trip down memory lane with eighty years of turbulent and confusing economic and political events. My personal life has never been too exciting but, as a historian, I've been on a roller coaster. Four wars, two serious depressions, two catastrophic Black October market crashes, an about-face economic revolution during the thirties, the rise of the Russian superpower intent on controlling the world, communism established in Cuba and central America, a large American force in the Persian gulf, and much, much more.

But let's discuss the Hoover days and his effort to stop our national economic decline. Between 1929 and '32 there were 85,000 business failures. Much of our great industrial plant in this country shut down. Our national income fell from 81 billion dollars in 1929 to 41 billion in the mid nineteen-thirties. From riches to rags—the age of apple vendors, soup kitchens, bread lines, rising unemployment figures. From promises of two cars in every garage we declined to no cars in no garage.

Hoover attempted through the Agricultural Marketing Act to help the farmer with the Federal Reserve Board to stimulate business; a public works program was passed to speed up work on public buildings and to spend more on the construction trades. The Reconstruction Finance Corporation was de-

signed to pump monies into private business as well as some direct unemployment relief. Most of this was the application of the Republican philosophy of
subsidized industry and business, on the trickle-down theory.

Relief was too slow and the voter turned to the new promises of the Demo-
cratic party. When FDR was elected and inaugurated on March 4, 1933, he
called a special session of congress on March 9. He had no panacea for the depression but was not afraid to experiment and a remarkable hundred-days followed during which action was taken to meet the needs of a discouraged and
destitute people.

The Emergency Banking Act of March 1933 reorganized insolvent national
banks. The FERA (Federal Emergency Relief Administration) was created to
assist states in distributing aid to the jobless. The CCC (Civilian Conservation
Corps) planned work for unemployed young men. The NRA (National Recovery Act) was passed to prepare codes and eliminate competition, to strengthen
unions, to establish minimum wages and maximum hours. Later declared un-
constitutional. The Agricultural Adjustment Act, also declared unconstitu-
tional, was passed to control production with a cash subsidy for crop reduction.
A long range reform came soon after. The TVA (Tennessee Valley Authority).
Control of banking through the Federal Deposit Insurance Corporation. By
1934 the spirit of the nation improved but little if any economic recovery appeared. The repeal of the eighteenth amendment did some good as new liquor
taxes helped to pay the increasing expenditures.

Considerable changes were made in gold and silver programs but had little
effect on the depression. CWA, the Civil Works Administration, was a program of direct federal aid to unemployed, in the hopes of stimulating private
industry. One of the most important permanent acts was Social Security which,
in the years following, has been expanded far beyond its original intent. A
Wages and Hour Act, a Fair Labor Standards Act, placed a heavy hand over the
employer and industry by the federal government. The help given to the labor
unions by the federal government during this period led to widespread increase
in union power—splits in the unions themselves, sit-down strikes, violence and
the use of force. Despite all efforts unemployment and need continued and a
new WPA (Works Progress Administration) was passed in which local projects
were directly paid for by the federal government.

By the early 1940s 11 billion dollars had been spent on temporary make-work
jobs. The NYA (National Youth Administration) was passed to give part time
work to high school and college students to subsidize their education. The Re-
settlement Administration resettled people and gave help relocating them as
far away as Alaska. A large increase in taxes had to be passed to pay for these
many programs. As it turned out the great depression was not defeated, the
economy was still suffering in 1938.

Strange as it sounds it was Adolph Hitler who changed the entire situation when his army invaded Poland and England and France entered the war. At that moment our entire farm, industrial, banking, maritime, railroad, transportation, shipbuilding couldn't find enough employees and all funds originally intended for farm subsidies and make-work programs were rediverted to business and industry. Our economy came alive thanks to Hitler and his legions.

I taught school during these years (1932–1973). During the depression we had 190 people on the faculty and 210 on the janitorial staff, plus hiring a thousand extra men part time year around. I received just over a hundred dollars per month and our school board spent the surplus funds as a relief agency. Our town got new sidewalks, paved alleys, built a stone fence around the golf course. And men stood about with shovels and brooms waiting for the snow to fall. The city would buy no mechanical equipment to remove snow because it took less labor. Teachers were fired if they worked in the summer. No miners worked during the summer because the mines were all closed. Hitler reopened every iron mine in the area and all men and women were hired to fuel the war effort. Soon afterwards our young men ended up in the armed services of the United States.

This now raises a question or a series of questions. Do we try to subsidize only the poor on a dole to increase purchasing power? Or do we give only to business and industry on a trickle-down basis? Or do we enter a war situation to solve economic problems? I've seen it all but I can find no completely acceptable answer.

Einer A. Anderson
Virginia, Minnesota

COUNTRY LIFE

It Made Us Better People
Fire On The Farm
Corn Crop Totalled Five Gallons Of Nubbins
Atlas Sorgo—Know What That Is?
Moonlight Plowing Beat The Heat
We Got Lights
Bees Ruined A Damned Good Team
I play In A Band—Not A Kitchen Band
Nothing But Choring All Day Long
The Cream Separator
We Called Tumbleweeds "Russian Thistles"
I'll Hear Those Shots Forever
Truckloads Of Dead Animals
A Horseback Trip Across South Dakota
Uncle Had Electricity and a Kerosene Refrigerator
Shattered Dreams
When One Died A Thousand Came To His Funeral
Barn Was Better Building Than Our House
Those Sand Hills Winds
Our Purebred Holstein Bull Calf
Brother's Funeral Service In Front Yard
The Lost Art Of Soapmaking
Nothing But Hard Work And Do Without
Six Bucks For Hundred Pound Hog
Who Is That Woman With The Gray Hair And Wrinkles?
Oil Trash Came In—We Locked Our Doors
The Ol' Swimmin' Hole
All His Life In One County
I Saw A Grown Man Cry
One End Always Fell Short
I Went Through The Thirties With Nothing
Moving Out of Nebraska
Black Sunday's Wind Broke Wind Guages
Can't Remember Any Green Grass
The Dirty Thirties In Happy, Texas
Dry-Land Farming
There Were Chiselers Then Too
In Praise Of My Father
North Carolina Revisited
As If You Were Stricken Blind

IT MADE US BETTER PEOPLE

The summer of 1936 followed one of the worst winters northeast Iowa had experienced in many years. It seems sometimes one weather extreme will follow another extreme.

It seemed as if everything stood still after the depression. We had just started to farm in 1931 with not much money and no family finances to help us out. It wasn't easy. Prices farmers received were terribly low and the unemployed had no income with which to buy anything. We sold corn for ten cents a bushel, sometimes having to burn it to keep warm, even though we had some wood.

Butterfat brought twenty-five cents a pound, eggs five and six cents a dozen, prime hogs for $2.55 a hundred weight (I still have the sales slips.) We sold a thousand pound bull for $16, minus a dollar for hauling him. He made a lot of hamburger which sold for three pounds for a quarter. Steak was twenty-five cents a pound.

We had milk, eggs, meat, a garden and fruit trees to help out. We never went hungry but we had no money to buy even Jello for two or three cents a box. or any other luxury. All we bought was flour at seventy-five cents a forty-nine pound sack, sugar for five cents a pound, coffee for twenty-five cents a pound. I baked our own bread, made starter yeast to save buying it, churned our own butter, even made our own soap and washed all of our clothes by hand on a washboard.

We didn't have much but we didn't go in debt. We patched and repatched our clothes so much there wasn't much left of the original garment.

Our recreation was visiting our neighbors and friends, not even a ten cents admission to the local show. I can't remember that we felt slighted because all of our friends were in the same financial bind.

There wasn't much of a welfare program then. The government began buying staple commodities like flour, rice, beans, oatmeal and fruit to distribute to the needy. The big golden oranges the welfare children brought to school for lunch were looked at with envy by those children whose families weren't on welfare. Their folks had to buy the small cheaper ones or none at all.

How good the fresh lettuce, oranges and bananas looked in the stores in the early spring. We went home, searched for and dug up the first dandelion greens — that were so tasty. But we survived.

About Christmas eve 1935 it started snowing lightly and every day it got a little colder and stormier, until by New Years eve we had blizzard conditions. It seemed as if it snowed every day in January and into February; it seldom got above zero during the day and, of course, was much colder at night. Trains were snowbound and cars with coal couldn't get through; when coal did arrive they would only sell eight or ten gunnysacks full so everyone could get a little. We kept thinking that hopefully another train would get through.

There weren't snowplows on the dirt roads then, just on the main gravelled roads. There were no blacktopped farm to market roads. The road crews were fortunate if they could get the main roads open, which would fill in about as soon as plowed.

We had two bachelor brother neighbors who helped keep a road open through the fields over a mile to the main gravelled road. One brother had an old touring car with a cut-off back seat and a box thereon. It had no top or windshield but he bucked the snow to go in and out; he also hauled our coal for us as well as cut some wood for us. In return we gave them a meal each day and I did their washing because by now I had a washing machine. We were eternally grateful for their help.

We were fortunate on the farm. The people in town didn't have any place to live unless their families took them in. Single men worked as hired men for their room and board all winter just to have a place to stay.

When the banks closed the people who might have had a little money in them, couldn't draw it out. We lived on Park's folk's farm so that year we gave them all the money from the hogs and my husband borrowed all the could on his life insurance policies to help pay taxes and interest. Many people lost their farms because they couldn't pay.

By the forepart of March, 1936, it began to warm up. I hadn't been off the place since Christmas. With five small children I couldn't get away. On the first of March I left the four boys and our oldest daughter with my husband and walked a half mile to see an older neighbor lady in snow at least hip deep all the way. My daughter, Delores, could stay atop the snow but I fell through every step but how nice to get away, to see someone else again. We were totally exhausted and very wet when we got home.

There were times during those months when I would go to the barn and clean calf pens or do other chores, just to get outside.

That summer, 1936, was dry and hot. We had lots of hay to make and not much machinery with which to make it. There were no balers, just hay loaders which didn't work too well and still required a lot of hand labor.

There was no electricity on the farm then; we used lamps in the house and carried lanterns around the outside building to do chores every evening.

Through that hot summer we had no refrigeration. No cool drinks. No place to keep perishable food. When we butchered in the winter I canned meat enough for the summer. During the summer I canned 500 to 600 quarts of vegetables and sauce to keep us through the winter.

That fall of 1936 we had our first good corn crop in spite of the hot, dry weather. The depression was easing up a bit but we still worked very hard through long hours.

My husband is deceased, dying at age 82. He loved visiting with the older folks talking of the days of hardship. They all felt they had been better people because of it, with more love for their neighbors and the unfotunate ones. We made our own way with no government handouts to make us lazy.

The Lord saw fit to help us through the hard times and He's richly blessed us since.

Mrs. Park Cowles
West Union, Iowa

FIRE ON THE FARM

1936 was a memorable year for me, Trudi Brucker, age ten, living on a farm in central Illinois. There wasn't another year in my young life that I remember more vividly.

My baby brother was born on January 19, the only one of a family of seven children born in a hospital, twenty miles away. On this particular, super-cold day while my father was at the hospital, the temperature dropped below zero, the wind grew stronger and suddenly it turned into a full-scale blizzard. The doctor and my father, with much difficulty, managed to drive the seventeen miles back to the doctor's office in our small town but Dad still had over two miles to our home. Roads were drifted amd it was impossible to make it by car so my dad started walking. How he ever made it was a miracle. When he arrived, his face was ghostly white and he was covered with snow. Luckily, he only suffered frostbite of the ears.

Our family was spread out. My older brother had gone to the high school to pick up my two sisters and a neighbor girl. He managed to drive two miles before getting stuck in a snow drift. He and the three girls walked one half mile in the blinding snow, none being dressed warmly enough for sub-zero weather. When they finally reached our house they had to break a bathroom window to get inside. Believe me, that was a co-o-o-ld room for days until father was able to fix the window. Even though they walked such a short distance my sister's friend had frost-bitten one hand. (Editor: sounds like experiences from my book ALL HELL BROKE LOOSE, about the Armistice Day 1940 blizzard in Minnesota.)

My younger brother and I were in a one-room grade school one-half mile east of home. A neighbor saw the storm getting worse and came to pick up the children and the teacher; he managed to drop the teacher and us off at our house since there was no chance of getting her to town. Soon a truck driver, stuck in a nearby drift, sought refuge with us. The house was getting crowded! Imagine 17 and 15 year old girls cooking dinner for a group of ten people that night and finding places for everyone to sleep. We felt warm and cozy crowding around the pot-bellied stove in our dining room and listening to the wind howling outside. We were all thankful that we were safely inside.

It was a big jump, from one extreme to another, when summer came. It was unbearably hot, dry and windy. Many farmers worked in the fields at night to escape the daytime heat. I remember my father coming in after dark and, since the house hadn't cooled off much, taking a pillow and blanket and sleeping in the yard.

With temperatures over one hundred, farmers still had to thresh the oats as usual in July. One time my father and oldest brother were away from home threshing at a neighbor's farm, tossing bundles of oats onto the hayrack, as were other men in the threshing run. The men had eaten their noon meal in the church basement where women and girls served at least 175 threshers, so they could eat well and get back to work. My two sisters had spent most of the day there and at about two o'clock returned home. They sat down with a big sigh of relief to talk to my mother; my older sister took off her dress and shoes and sat there in her slip, fanning and trying to cool herself.

For some reason, my fifteen year old sister stepped outside and smelled smoke. Looking upstairs she saw smoke billowing from a window, then ran back into the house screaming "Fire"! She hurried to the telephone and rang for the operator, but no answer. We were all frantically looking for my five-year old brother and a visiting friend, while she tried to reach the operator. So my sister, minus her dress, jumped into the car, told me to come along with the baby, and we raced to the neighbor's a mile away. No one was home so we raced on to another neighbor's, placed the call, and rushed back home. Mother had found the two small boys outside but the whole upper story of the house was ablaze and the wind was fanning the flames. Some men had arrived to help carry out downstairs furnishings but nobody could get to the upstairs bedrooms or closets, so all the family clothing was destroyed, as well as the 200 quarts of canned food in the basement, which my mother had laboriously canned earlier.

Nobody can understand the horror of a farm fire unless they have gone through it. Here we were in the midst of a depression and a drought and we had lost all we owned, or so it seemed.

The men of the neighborhood tried to save the barn, not too far from the house. Hot embers were flying toward it because of the wind and it would have been disastrous if all the hay therein would have gone up in smoke too. They started a bucket brigade and soon the fire department arrived. The rig's water pressure wasn't strong enough to reach the top of the barn so the men threw ropes over the top and passed up buckets of water to the men atop the building. Other men were inside the haymow throwing water as it smoldered from the embers that burned through the roof. Also, by this time, the heat from the huge house fire was now in danger of causing combustion in the barn. An explosion was definitely possible. But, those courageous men did manage to save our barn.

I had a great view of all this action because I had taken refuge in our car, along with my baby brother which mother had given me to care for. It was parked at the end of the driveway and about the only safe place for a ten-year old. I sat there and watched my sister help carry out the dining room buffet filled with dishes. To this day she can't explain how she was able to lift and carry one end of this buffet, because she tried later and couldn't budge it.

There wasn't much humor to this terrible event. Well, perhaps a little when my older sister discovered she didn't have on her dress or shoes; she had been so busy she had forgotten and was very embarrassed. Everyone assured her they hadn't even noticed.

The real hardship started the next day. With our house a total loss, my parents fixed up a large tool shed as a place to live until a new house could be built. They put wooden planks on the dirt floor, brought in tables and chairs, a kerosene stove for cooking, a kitchen cupboard. etc. Of course the good people of the community had a household shower for us and brought quilts, clothes and other needed articles. We had no electricity, no running water, no ice box, no windows, no insulation, no screens. Talk about roughing it! I know the Lord was watching over us because none of us got sick even though we lived this way for three months while carpenters built a new house for us. I remember my mother having the two carpenters in for lunch and now wonder how she managed to have food to feed them.

Not only was it a hundred or more degrees every day that summer, we also had one electrical storm after another at night. You can imagine how the thunderstorms sounded in that building with the low roof. I was scared to death. One night a neighbor's barn was struck by lightning and it burned to the ground. The huge fire lit up the sky for miles around and even the pouring rain didn't put it out.

Another thing I feared was mice. Oh, yes, we had them in that building we called home that summer and they liked to climb up and down the walls at night. At least, I thought they did. I can't imagine how I kept from suffocating every night because I slept with the summer quilt over my head no matter how hot it was. We three girls were furnished with a double bed and a cot but, because of our fear of mice, all three slept in the double bed with poor little me in the middle.

Looking back on that long, hot, miserable summer I know how lucky I was to be only ten years old. I didn't have the work load of the adults. I'm sure I carried lots of water from the well and did other necessary errands or tasks asked of me — and I did a lot of baby sitting of my baby brother. I rather enjoyed the job of pushing the buggy around the yard, putting mosquito netting over his buggy when he was napping and watching him sleep under the big tree, while I tried to read a book.

About the middle of October we moved into the basement of our new house. There we lived for a couple of months, still camping out but a little warmer than in the other building. Now we needed some of that extra warmth because it does get cold in central Illinois in November.

We had our first meal in our new kitchen, on the main level of course, on Christmas day. It was not a huge traditional meal, which we enjoyed later, but it seemed just wonderful to us. That was a very merry Christmas, I can tell you, on December 25, 1936.

Mrs. Robert Kluever
Bentonville, Arkansas

CORN CROP TOTALLED FIVE GALLONS OF NUBBINS

We lived in Union county, South Dakota, north of Elk Point and near Spink, in 1936.

I remember that year very well, even though I am now 88 years old and that was 52 years ago.

It was the only year we never picked corn. There wasn't any. My husband walked up the hollow in the field and all he got was nubbins to fill a five-gallon pail. So that was our entire corn harvest.

It was so dry and we had such bad dust storms. I can remember one Sunday we went to church and it wasn't bad yet. But by the time we got home it was so dusty that it got dusk and when I went to gather the eggs after dinner the chickens had gone to roost. That was the worst day, I think.

Even if all the windows were shut we could write our name on any piece of furniture or the window sills, which had little piles of dust on them.

That year we didn't have much to feed the chickens, let alone corn, but, as my husband had a corn sheller outfit, he would get a job to shell the previous year's corn. It wasn't long before the chickens learned that's where the corn came from after he swept the corn off the sheller when he came home. After a few times they flew up on the sheller and soon there was no corn left to sweep away.

But we lived through it like the chickens did. We farmed over fifty years and that was the only year with no corn crop. My husband is gone now and I live in a Care Center.

Mrs. Emil Klemme
Akron, Iowa

ATLAS SORGO-KNOW WHAT THAT IS?

As I remember it the drought of 1934 was the worst of the two (1934 vs 1936) and the worst in my memory. The things I remember about 1936 were the winter blizzards. Beginning in early January we had one snow storm after another.

I was born on August 29, 1924 so on my birthday in 1936 I was twelve years old. In that winter of 1936 there was a stretch of over thirty days when the temperature didn't rise above zero. By our own thermometer on our farm nine miles southwest of Anamosa, it went down to 36 below zero once. It reached 30 below several times. The coldest temperature I remember being reported was 57 below at International Falls.

I was attending a country school 1¼ miles from home and it was closed for six weeks that winter. Of course the county didn't have enough snow removal equipment to clean out all the roads in a hurry so most farmers banded together to shovel out their own roads.

We were milking about 20 cows, plus about 200 hogs and 400 laying hens, plus a flock of 20 sheep. After the cream and eggs accumulated for a week or so we would get the roads partly open and with four horses on a bobsled we would head for the nearest town, which was Olin. We'd sell these things and buy livestock feed, groceries, coal and other supplies. Then hurry back home before another storm started.

After school started again I cut across our fields and there was a bunch of Atlas sorgo in shocks that were surplus to our silo. These shocks were food and shelter to several hundred pheasants through this bad weather we had been having.

We got through this bad time a lot better than some other people in our neighborhood. We had a big wood pile in our back yard as well as in the basement behind the furnace. The coal was burned through the late night so the fire wouldn't go out and let the house get cold. As a result of the ground having not been frozen under the snow, the moisture went down and was available next spring.

In this area farmers who got their crops in early had good crops, because of the available moisture. The first cuttings of hay were pretty fair but the second crop of clover and alfalfa were both lighter. The oats were fair and the third crop of alfalfa was almost nothing. My father was planting hybrid corn so it took the dry weather far better than that of the neighbors who had planted the old open polinated corn. This year our corn yielded 50 bushels per acre.

As I said, the dryest year as I remember it was 1934. During January and February I was carrying in firewood. One evening I looked up and saw clouds of dust and soil blowing high overhead. This was from western Iowa and the great plains states. There wasn't much snow that winter and there was no spring rain that year. Dad planted his first hybrid corn in 1935 so, with the dry weather, our corn only went about 25 to 30 bushels per acre. The hay was almost non-existent and the oats made a little better than their seed back.

We plowed up some hay ground and put in Atlas sorgo for silage, so we had some feed. One thing that saved us was a large acreage of river bottom pasture that had plenty of grass for the milk cows. On July 4, that year, the Wapsipinicon river was running only ankle deep. At about 4 P.M. I went across it but when we had finished all our evening chores and supper a big storm hit us. It rained hard, thundered and lightning was everywhere from about 8 PM until daylight. The river was then out of its banks and nearly a mile wide. By the next day it was down to waist deep so I could wade across again to check out the fences so we could turn out the cows. It didn't rain again until the 5th of August.

That August 5 was my Dad's birthday and we had to stay in the house, not have our picnic as planned. That year Dad cut way back on the hogs in order to save grain for the milk cows. We could get back into the hog business easily but it took years to build up a good dairy herd.

As I said, my Dad planted his first hybrid corn that spring of 1935. He planted two bushels, each in three foot, six inch rows, cross checked both ways. Each bushel planted seven acres so this put in fourteen acres out of thirty possible. The hybrid out-yielded the other corn by 25 or 30 bushels so it was all hybrid from then on. From 1937 we had good crops.

We haven't had a crop failure since those years. Just south of here, below I-80, they had a failure a few years ago. In the thirties the drought was much worse and lasted much longer in the great plains states from Texas to the Dakotas and Montana and up into the Canadian prairie provinces. Of course I remember they had terrible conditions from Kentucky down to the gulf coast. Last summer that area looked as bad as 1934 did in our area.

There were also some very bad years in Nebraska and Kansas in the 1950s. My wife's uncle in southeast Nebraska didn't even pick all his corn because it wouldn't pay for the gasoline to pick it. He just turned his cattle in and let them eat it as it was.

I'll never forget some other years too...like 1932...when things *were really bad* in this country.

Joseph C. Glenn
Anamosa, Iowa

MOONLIGHT PLOWING BEAT THE HEAT

I farmed my entire life in Green county, Iowa, near Jefferson and I remember well the summer of thirty-six. One of the strange things about the 1936 drought was that it followed such a wet and terrible winter.

I lived on a farm not far from a coal mine; the snow became so deep so early that people who went to the mine for coal, as well as the coal miners, became snowbound there with no food. A man from Jefferson, about fifteen miles from the mine, put together a dog train to carry food to those stranded people.

My father and I had several head of cattle we were trying to feed. He went to mow some short foxtail hay and the team nearly had to run with the mower so the short hay would fall off the sickle. It didn't amount to much but it was the best we could find.

The corn crop all burned up from the heat and dry weather. We would pick corn all day in the same wagon and barely see the corn in the wagon by nightfall. We had 80 acres of corn to pick and never moved the spout from the elevator for the entire season. The seed corn in those days was very shallow rooted and didn't have much chance.

It was so hot that some of us farmers went to the fields after dark when there was a beautiful full moon and plowed as long as the moon was shining.

I don't see how we made it but can remember that everything turned out okay.

The year 1934 was nearly as bad in our neighborhood. That year we lived south of highway 30. North of this road the corn made 40 bushels per acre while ours was just fodder.

I also lived through another dry year—1977. This was the last year I farmed. My corn made about 60 bushels but many of my neighbors didn't even combine their corn. Had I used the same kind of seed corn I used in 1936 this would also have been a total failure.

To the modern farmer this seems unreal but it is true. Things were very different then.

Hamilton Wheeler
Churdan, Iowa

WE GOT LIGHTS

That's the expression that farmers all over the country were using proudly —
'We got lights.' What they meant, in today's vernacular, was that the power
line had finally come down the road and into their farm. In the middle of their
kitchen, their living room, their bedroom, they had a pendant wire with a light
bulb. For the first time they weren't dependent upon the coal oil lamp or even
that modern gasoline lamp. They had power.

The Rural Electrification Administration (REA) was passed May 11, 1935,
to supply loans and help to rural cooperatives to take electric power to the farms.
After all "rural" was the key word in the act, passed during FDR's administration.

It is almost impossible to realize the impact of electricity coming to the farm,
unless you experienced it. Here, for the first time, was the open sesame to permit the farmer to power his cream separator, to provide light in the barn for
early morning milking, to give his wife some household tools to make her life
easier. These things all cost money and, remember, money was in very short
supply, but they were available if one could afford them.

Rural Americans were in the dark — sometimes both day and night. The
nights were dark as pitch, dented slightly by the pale, flickering light of kerosene lamps. The days, sometimes, were dark brown with dust, a darkness unsuccessfully challenged by those same lamps.

The change did not happen overnight, of course. Before REA could become
a familiar household presence on millions of isolated farmsteads and ranches,
there was a war to be fought; in the aftermath of the war there were shortages
of both manpower and materials to overcome; and there was, besides, opposi-
tion in some quarters to settle... The project originally mandated a ratio of two
consumers per mile of line. Later the coverage was extended to serve areas with
only one and one-fourth consumers per mile. The scope of the blueprint was
immense — so immense that some saw the venture as pure folly. . . .The doubt-
ers were to be confounded, however, by the knockout success of REA.

It was so exciting that Carl Stahl of Redfield, South Dakota, couldn't wait
for dark to come, so he could put on the yard light. His wife, Rosa, remembers
the day well, when lights finally got to their farm. Their wiring was done by
November, 1946 but the power didn't actually get there until March 2. She well
remembers how they went through the house throwing switches. Their daughter, Rosalie, said she'd never forget the day she came home from school and put
on the lights and ran upstairs to see if her room had lights.

I remember that big yard light, Rosa continues, the children played under
so much. What a relief it was when I went out to milk and didn't have to get the
old kerosene lantern lit. If it was in the other end of the barn, you needed an-

other light to see it. Sometimes we had to look twice to see which cows had been milked. . . .Oh, for the good old days, says who?

Mainly taken from a story originally written by Winnie Vophees of Hitchcock, SD, for The Redfield SD Press and reprinted by special permission of the publisher.

BEES RUINED A DAMNED GOOD TEAM

I worked on a farm in Wayne County, Iowa, which borders Missouri. Watering cattle on the flat lands of this area three miles west of Seymour, Iowa, was a big job. Windmills did most of the pumping because there was no electricity for power pumps in the rural area.

I went to work one summer morning and my boss, Henry Donald, was at the top of a windmill oiling it. He caught his hand in the gears and cut off three fingers but he finished the job before he came down. He was taken to the doctor but he didn't lose a day's work because of the injury.

He had eighty acres about seven miles from the home place, forty of which were in wheat and forty in pasture. He lost several calves because of water shortage.

Those were busy days for us. Daily chores during the summer months included feeding the cattle twice daily, plowing corn, cutting hay and stacking or baling it, cutting oats or wheat.

Henry's son and I cut wheat and shocked it, ready for threshing. We used four head of horses on the binder; when the job was done we started home. I had one team and the hayrack and the son had one team and the binder. This was in July.

We were about two miles toward home and suddenly I thought a cloud had come over me on the hayrack. I looked up and it was a swarm of honey bees. They completely covered the team's heads until I couldn't see their heads. The horses went into a fence and went down.

I ran off the back of the hayrack and saw a full watertank at a nearby windmill. I headed for it and thought I'd jump in if the bees got on me. I was stung a few times on the head but that was all.

I then went to a nearby farm home and told the people what happened. The farmer got his bee net and smoker and smoked the bees off the horses. We cut the harness off them and got them on their feet again, put them in a barnyard and called the veterinarian. The vet tapped their jugular veins and the first blood was actually blue. This was a team of three and four-year olds and I had broken them myself that spring. But after that episode they were not worth a damn.

I worked for five dollars a week and paid nine cents a pound for bacon and bought three gallons of gasoline for fifty cents. This all happened when I was about 28 or 29 years old. I now am past 80.

Emmett Philby
Centerville, Iowa

I PLAY IN A BAND (NOT A "KITCHEN" BAND)

As I think back on my life, I have really had an interesting one.

At four years of age I danced on a stage for a prize at a medicine show. I remember seeing Halley's comet in 1910. I marched in the first Armistice Day parade at 2 A.M. in 1918. I listened to Dutch Reagan broadcast ball games in the twenties over WHO in Des Moines. I sang on radio from a station in Fairmont, Minnesota, in the days when folks would call in and say "Program coming in fine" and then request a number. As I say, my life has not always been easy, but not dull either.

I can talk much better than I can write and my mind is so full of these interesting stories about the old days which I managed to live through that it's a pleasure to tell them to some one who's truly interested.

I was born on a farm in 1902 in Davis county, Iowa. My parents moved to Marshalltown about 1910 where my father worked on the railroad; that made it nice because we could ride free.

Before I was married and moved from Marshalltown, I worked at Woolworth's for four dollars a week; they paid us in cash every Saturday night at 9 P.M.

I guess we were what you call middle class folks, not wealthy and not poor. Never had to have help from the state or government as so many do now. We always worked hard, always paid cash for what we bought, or we didn't buy it. We always had plenty of good food to eat. Our home was rented but I grew up in a home with running water, a bathroom, and electric lights.

But this is what happened. I fell in love and married a farm boy in 1921. He had just returned from France and World War I. Farms were hard to find so we decided to go farther north to Emmet county to live. We shipped our ten head of horses, a few cows and some crates of chickens, a green farm wagon and a few pieces of furniture. My husband rode in the box-car with the horses because they had to be fed and watered. My mother and I went a few days later by passenger train.

The farm we rented had 300 acres and we had to do everything the hard way. There were no tractors—we used horses. We were about ten miles south of the

Minnesota state line and we didn't realize that the climate was a little different. Three times in five years our crops were completely ruined by hail and we had no hail insurance. Times were not getting any better.

The house was fine in the spring and summer with beautiful trees and lots of small lakes close by with plenty of fish. But the winters were another story. We had never even heard of such a thing as insulation. We didn't have electricity or gas so, of course, no bathroom, or electric lights, no electric irons, washers, refrigerator or furnace. Water had to be carried in a bucket from the wind-mill, which was down the hill close to the barn.

It was not unusual to get up in the morning and find the tea-kettle frozen solid as well as the baby's diapers which I had changed during the night. My husband would start a roaring fire in the two stoves, using the cobs the children had carried in the night before. Many times we thanked God for our wonderful neighbors. We all worked together as a team and needed each other.

As the years went on, the depression came upon us and times grew harder; we still had the cows but we could sell a ten gallon can of cream and the money wouldn't even buy the basic necessities. I'm thinking of sugar, flour, matches, oil for lamps, vinegar and even the Prince Albert tobacco my husband had to smoke. All that saved us was that we had our own meat, canned and dried vegetables, and home-made butter from our own cream.

There were also nice times, such as card parties, house and barn dances, school activities and home talent plays. One good thing about winter was the home-made ice cream. All I had to do was beat up a few eggs, put in the milk, cream, vanilla and some lemon extract—things of which we always had plenty. My husband would get ice from the water tank, crush it and, using some of the coarse salt, he would pack the freezer, sit it on the warm oven door and turn the crank; I would get on the phone and tell the closest neighbors to walk over because the ice cream is freezing. And they never came empty handed, always bringing cookies or cakes.

Some times we were shut in for weeks and the only way we could get around was by foot. Our nearest store was three miles away. School was sometimes closed for six weeks at a time; we had terrible drifts—much higher than the car. I remember the time I nearly lost my life riding in an old Model-T Ford before cars had safe heaters.

Summers were bad. We had a very dry 1935 but I had never lived in Emmet county where the dust storms shut out the sun like they did that year. My husband was caught in the field and didn't realize what was going on until it was too late. One horse dropped dead on the spot and the other one died later from breathing the dust.

It was almost impossible to eat because the dirt and chaff came inside the house around the windows and doors. I would set the table and within five minutes the dishes would be covered with dirt and straw. There were days when we would pin wet bed sheets to the windows to keep out the dust. My one and only rug was a beautiful wine color but it was so covered with dust the true color was impossible to identify.

We paid our hired hand thirty dollars a month, plus room and board and furnished him a horse to ride to town, just three miles away.

We lived in Emmet county for fifteen years. We decided we were never going to get any place there so we left in March, 1936. We went there out of debt with a nice start and left in debt. We came back home.

We did go broke but we started over. My husband had advertised our farm for sale but ended doing it three times because the roads had been closed for weeks. No one could get in or out.

We were looking out of the window about nine P.M. one night and saw this very bright light down the road about a mile; we knew it had to be a large snowplow coming to dig us out. Being a good farm wife, I got busy, opened up a quart jar of home-canned chicken, made a batch of noodles, mashed potatoes, hot biscuits and chicken gravy, home-canned apple sauce and coffee. It took them until midnight to get to us—and did that food look good to them. That was fifty-one years ago and here is the end of that story: that nice young man who drove that snowplow was later married and moved to Marshalltown; he lives at a nursing home there and I get to visit with him once a month when my musical group goes there to entertain.

Yes, we lived through hard times and good. We raised three children. We both worked to pay off the bank and managed to buy a few acres of land; prices went up and we built a lovely home and retired in 1960. We sold out, my husband passed away in 1977. Now I'm trying to do all the things I never had time to do before. I took up oil painting, I play in a band (not a "kitchen" band) at nursing homes, the State Soldiers home, churches, the state fair and the Waterloo Cattle Congress. I collect musical instruments, now having three table organs, one large organ, four guitars, two banjos, two ukes, five harmonicas, one piano accordian, two tambourines, Lawrence Welk spoons and seven grandchildren, some of whom I hope will take after Grandma.

I was eighty-five last July 9 and people tell me I don't look it (Editor: I agree) so I guess that hard work didn't hurt me too much.

When I tell these things to this generation, I think they don't believe it, but everything I have said here is truth indeed.

Audrey McLeland
Marshalltown, Iowa

NOTHING BUT CHORING ALL DAY LONG

We were married the first day of 1936—January 1. A beautiful, sunny day and the weather remained calm until the middle of the month. Then heavy snow and high winds made six foot drifts all over the place. My father and mother, having been born in the 1860s, had often told of farmsteads being entirely isolated in such heavy drifts in the early prairie years. There had been nothing but prairie grass to hold the heavy snows but that grass was soon flattened. Farmsteads with groves caught the brunt of the drifts to the point of not being visible from any distance. Often people got lost in those storms; my father had experienced that. He was given up for lost but he found a farm and stayed there for safety.

Even in our day we had no modern snow removal machinery; this was still in the days of horsepower for farming. We did have a heavy duty county snowplow which finally aided us in April. We spent a lot of time trying to keep roads passable, at least with tunnels for horse and wagons or for walking. Neighbors took down fences so we could get out for necessary staples. Occasionally the grocer would deliver to places on the highway, perhaps within walking distance of a farm a mile away.

It was nothing but choring all day long. Wells had to be thawed. Drinking founts to be kept operating and feeding the best we could. Cattle and horses were let out twice daily for water but there was no need to coax them back into shelter. Lots of stall cleaning and bedding and scooping out the snow that blew in. Stockyards had to be scooped along the fences to keep cattle from getting out.

We cut down the few trees which were accessible, for fuel to warm our ancient, unprotected house. Once I got to town, four and a half miles away, for coal, but it was sold on a limited basis. They allowed me only five hundred pounds. Several farmers banded together with bobsleds and went over twenty miles to the Fansler coal mine near Bagley and had to stay for days with little supplies.

We couldn't deliver our produce, so we had an over-supply of eggs and cream.

We had ordered baby chicks which arrived in early April. Unable to ready the brooder house, we were saved when the hatchery man loaned us a chick battery and we put the babies in our sun porch for a few weeks where we had an oil heater.

It was ten years later before we had electricity. Our radio batteries had lapsed so our only communication with the outside world was through the country telephone line, when it wasn't shorted out.

There was no mail for weeks at a time—when a neighbor would get to town and bring mail and newspapers for his neighbors. That would be a great day.

The wash was all done by hand, mostly from melted snow and was draped to dry on lines strung throughout the house.

The following summer — 1936 — was a disaster. There was no rain, 103 to 111 degrees of temperature. My 110 acres of corn, which I picked by myself, was of low yield and poor quality. One forty acre field made only five bushels to the acre. It was much harder to pick these nubbins than average size ears.

We have recently celebrated our 52 years together. We have a son and daughter, six grandchildren and seven great-grandchildren. I will soon be eighty and my wife seventy-six. We retired from the farm near Scranton in the late seventies and now live in Jefferson in fairly good health.

Cleo F. Gibson
Jefferson, Iowa

THE CREAM SEPARATOR

I never thought I'd forget the manufacturer's name of that cream separator I sometimes turned at Uncle Seb's farm when I was a boy. I visited him and Aunt Flora, both now gone, God rest their souls, at their place at Lamine, Missouri, just atop the hill over the Lamine river.

The separator was a tool that separated the cream from the milk, so the valuable cream could be sent to market for butter-making purposes. It was a rather large piece of equipment with a bowl on top for the raw milk and funnels coming out for the cream and the residue — the skim milk so to speak.

I just shared a bit of nostalgia with friends recently at the Kanabec County Historical Society and Museum in Mora, Minnesota, where I saw one of these old machines on display. Both George (last name unknown) and I remembered how you turned these things until they reached a certain pitch. If it weren't being turned fast enough, all the cream wasn't being removed and someone would yell at you to turn faster. Rev it up, it isn't screaming loudly enough.

But there were lots of memories of Aunt Flora and Uncle Seborn. There was the blacksnake in the cottonwood over the lawn swing, that Uncle Seb disposed of by proper application of the twelve gauge shotgun. Also there was the self-sown watermelon seed that sprouted and grew near the cistern by the back door. With it being so hot and dry, Aunt Flora sustained it by throwing her dishwater on it, so it could live. After many weeks, it came harvest time for the melon and I was so fortunate to be there. One bite and — ugh — it tasted of soapy dishwater. So it was destroyed.

William H. Hull
Edina, Minnesota

WE CALLED TUMBLEWEEDS RUSSIAN THISTLES

Anyone who writes about the dust storms in South Dakota will describe the huge black clouds that looked like rain clouds, but rain clouds never seemed to appear.

I wasn't allowed to stay outdoors when the wind started blowing. It seemed the clouds were rolling along the ground but probably the rolling effect was from the Russian thistles—which was the local term for tumbleweeds—because they seemed to arrive first.

After the storm we'd make a huge pile of thistles next to the garage and then climb on the roof and jump into the pile. The Chamber of Commerce had a contest on at least one occasion to give a prize for the largest thistle.

I was nine years old when these storms were prevalent and I remember seeing the distant clouds and watching them approach. The plains of South Dakota are much different than the land of trees here in Michigan. My mother would make sure doors and windows were tightly closed and she tucked towels in every crevice. She ran around our home covering all the furniture with sheets, even the kitchen table. The dust was so fine it still sifted into the home. It took many hours of sweeping and dusting after the winds had calmed just to clear out that dust and to shake the sheets outdoors.

My grandparents lived on a farm and the farm machinery would be buried in dust and the fence posts nearly covered with the soil There was no harvest due to the lack of rain and temperatures running over a hundred degrees daily for so many weeks. There was no cooling off at night either.

We lived on Main street in De Smet, South Dakota and, although my parents viewed the storms with dismay, I anticipated receiving twenty-five cents for sweeping the front sidewalk. There would be several inches of powdery fine dust to sweep away so no one would track it into the house. As I swept I would also have a huge pile of grasshoppers; most of them would jump away because they seemed to survive any kind of weather.

I hated the required bath after the cleanup but that quarter seemed like a huge sum of money. At least it was the type of storm that everyone survived and provided a conversation topic at the corner cafe where everyone gathered to sip their five-cent cup of coffee.

These depression memories are part of my childhood in South Dakota; it was a happy time for me and I have benefited from those hard times.

Helen Jean (Whyte) Carroll
Wyoming, Michigan

I'LL HEAR THOSE SHOTS FOREVER

That night after Mother read the Bible, Dad announced that our young stock would be purchased by the government and sent east to greener pastures. How hard that hit we girls. The soft-eyed calves we had petted so often had to go. At least they would not be shot. The next day we said goodbye to the calves and went to school heartsick.

Other cattle were not so fortunate. With both feed and water being nearly non-existent drastic measures had to be taken.

The very next day at the far end of our pasture officials set up a city dump ground, actually a slaughtering area. Many vehicles were going fast past our gate on the way to that area. There the bony, old sick cattle would be hauled out in any kind of vehicle, lined up beside the deep trenches to fall therein when shot. I shall forever hear the echo of those shots from inside our house even though we tightly closed the doors and windows. Dad came in late in the day and said "They're shooting the bulls now. It will be over soon."

The evening was like any other one on the dusty South Dakota farm. From the cattle herding to the green spots in the ditches on the perimeter of the farm, work was over for the day. The large eyed bony cattle had given enough milk to fill the pails, the ten of them giving enough milk for a two dollar plus check on Saturday night. That would buy a ring of bologna and a few other items: I might be lucky to have five cents left over.

Our shoes need to be shined for school the next day. There wasn't any money for such luxuries as shoe polish for my one and only pair of shoes so egg white would keep them presentable for a day if I walked on the harder tracks of the dusty road.

Breakfast was over quickly because chores came first and usually took longer than expected. With an abundance of grasshoppers for the chicken feed, perhaps there were enough eggs laid to have two eggs for breakfast. The hens had to be watered well if there were enough water in the well that day; maybe it had filled some during the night, seeping upwards.

School began at nine o'clock, with the usual formalities except in grade rooms three and four on the south side of our wooden building. Just before noon, it suddenly became so dark that everyone on that side was startled.

Our teacher told us to put on our wraps because everyone was going home. Dad soon drove up in the Model T Ford with its lights burning brightly. As I ran to the car my eyes filled with dirt and it was like a snowstorm only different and choking. Everything was filthy.

Many other cars were lined up like a funeral procession, waiting for their children, too.

Once home we were surprised at how things had changed. Our shiny hardwood floor was the color of the garden. Dirt was thick between the windows and screens. Our faces were blackened as if we were of another race and our hair was full of grit.

In the garden, the vines were black. Peas and cucumbers looked like some strange new weed. No one wasted water to clean them because living animals were short of water. Plants had to go without. The eyes of my puppies were filled with dirt and as I petted the cat it was like shaking a dusty rug.

It was just one more day but even worse than the one before. The cream separator and milk pails had to be rewashed and rinsed because we had placed them outside the milk house to dry and, hopefully, sterilize in the hot sun's rays.

The herd came up from the brown, bare pasture with dust in their mouths, noses and eyes. No one could herd them in that wind.

The pigs didn't seem to object. As long as the separator worked they'd be fed, but their tanks resembled a dirty creek.

At a supper of potatoes, balogna and fresh bread no one did much talking. This was a special meal Mother had prepared, hoping to cheer us. Cream and sugar poured over freshly cut slices of bread was a delicacy. We were lucky. Many went to bed hungry. The hoboes that came to our door a few blocks from the tracks thought that Mother gave them a banquet.

The one redeeming feature for some of us was that we hadn't known any other life except depression. For my sister, ten years older, it was more of a blow. She had known the days when Mother and Dad were comfortably well off.

As I look back and see how bravely my parents faced taxes, bills, expenses with nothing in sight but hope, I often see that worn leather-covered Bible which was the rock of their existence—and this oft-quoted verse: "In all thy ways acknowledge Him and He will direct thy path." Yes, He surely did. Our farm did not go for taxes. We scrimped and paid off the mortgage. How great He is—the one who directed our path through the great depression.

Phyllis Hills Brantl
Madison, Minnesota

TRUCKLOADS OF DEAD ANIMALS

I worked in the telephone office at Buffalo above Beutner's drug store. There was no air conditioning, just one large fan which blew at us relentlessly; after several hours we felt dried out and dull. Some of us became ill from the excessive heat, from no rest at night and from drinking too much water. Also, loss of salt was a factor.

Northwest Bell headquarters issued salt tablets and ginger ale. No water was to be consumed, only what was necessary for medication. The chief operator was to give each girl a small sip (and it ws small indeed) of the ginger ale every half hour. Not chilled either but at room temperature.

Then a large tub was brought into the room and a huge chunk of ice placed therein. The fan was directed to blow across the ice and cool us. It surely did help — at least one side of us was cooled a bit.

Many farm animals succumbed to the excessive heat. Our switchboard was flooded with calls to the rendering plant near the cities. Because animals were dying everywhere, not just in Buffalo, our manager started taking the pick-up information at our offices. Every day a man came to use the long list we assembled of farmers who had dead animals. So many sad events. I remember that one farmer's team fell dead in their harness while they were working in the field. Many farmers stayed in the fields daytime while others worked only in the evenings and nights.

The heat was hard on hogs too. Many farmers tried hosing them and making holes in which they could lay and wallow. Since hogs don't perspire or pant as many animals do, they just suffered and died.

The rendering trucks, with their sideboards were always passing with animal legs sticking above the truck sides; working where I did, I always knew what that meant.

The driver came at noon to pick up the list and he felt that he should do something in gratitude to us for handling these calls. Our service was just our duty and no charge was ever made. Anyway, he started bring me an over-sized ice cream cone. It was so hot that the cream was always melting and running down the cone. He always brought the cone in his bare hands, with no napkin, and I could only imagine seeing those same hands handling those dead creatures. I would try to lick a few slurps off the top and, as soon as he was gone, I would hurry to the rest room to dispose of the cone.

One day he came without a cone, thank goodness. He said "I didn't bring you a cone today but I have something else I'm sure you'll like." He reached into his pocket and handed me a tiny bit of fluff, a baby owl. It was so cute. He said it was sitting in the gravel road rut and he feared it would be run over. Well, I could flush the cone in the toilet but what could I do with a tiny baby owl? I called the school and someone came for it.

Everyone at the telephone office became ill, except me. Maybe the ice cream cone protected me. Those were very frightening and sad times for everyone. I was young and soon mended but I always remembered how badly the farmers were hurt by the terrible loss of their animals. Plus that never ending pressing heat — which one day reached 105 degrees. How I remember the howling wind, the blowing dust and Dad's face black from the dust when he came in from the field.

Kathryn U. Clark
Monticello, Minnesota

A HORSEBACK TRIP ACROSS SOUTH DAKOTA

My uncle Dave Kinghorn owned a ranch on Two-top Butte which is north of Nisland, South Dakota. He was an old time cattle man but the grass had gotten so scarce that he sold all his cattle and bought a few hundred head of sheep. He didn't know much about sheep so he hired me, an experienced sheep herder at age nineteen, to work for him. He and Aunt Grace lived at the main ranch on the south side of Two-top and the hired man, Joe Shroyer, and I, were staying at the old ranch on the north side. A cousin had been living there but at this time lived in Montana.

During prohibition my cousin had made moonshine liquor and had several stills destroyed by the Feds. At the end of prohibition he stored the still in the attic of the ranch house and that is the only still I've ever seen. While herding sheep, I had discovered the location of one of the destroyed stills in a cave in a deep canyon. I told the hired man, Joe, about it and he informed there was a more recent one that the Feds had never found and that it was within one hundred yards of the house, but he wouldn't tell me where it was.

A few days later while corraling the sheep I rode my horse over an old manure pile and almost fell into a trap-door that led to an underground room. That was the still. My cousin would make whiskey at night, then cover the opening with heavy planks, hitch the team to the fresno (Editor: a fresno is a type of horse-drawn scoop) and dump a load of manure from the shed on top of it. Joe told a story of one time the Feds, while looking for the still, had hit a rock and ripped a hole in the oil-pan and had to spend the night with my cousin; he had to take them to Belle Fourche the next day to get help.

Another cousin, Maurice Brengle, owned a ranch near Redig, South Dakota, which his grandson lives on now. Maurice is retired and lives in Buffalo. In 1936 there was no grass left on his range so he leased some land on the Pine Ridge Indian reservation and had his sheep trucked down there for the winter.

Maurice wanted me to trail his ten head of horses down there so I took a temporary leave from Uncle Dave's because a horseback trip across the state of South Dakota sounded like a lot of fun. The first day on the trail I travelled the twenty-five miles to the Kinghorn ranch and spent the night with Joe. I intended to ride a different horse each day, and rode Rabbit, a little grey, the first day. The morning of the second day I saddled Paint, a tall skittish pinto. I managed to get on him but only stayed about twenty seconds because he bucked me off in two jumps. I then caught Red and changed off between him and Rabbit the rest of the way on the trip.

I stayed the second night at Nisland, about another twenty-five miles on the trail. There I kept the horses in a livery stable and had to pay a dollar for the hay they ate. The next day I had lunch in a cafe at Vale, which cost me seventy cents, then proceeded to a ranch just east of Sturgis. The first ranch at which I stopped couldn't let me stay because his horses had distemper, but he directed me to another house where he was sure I'd be welcomed.

I'd heard about this family and really didn't want to stay there and, sure enough, it was as bad as rumors said. They were very friendly people but so dirty it was unbelievable. The mother volunteered to get me some supper, even though it was well past supper time, but I lied and said I had already eaten up the road. She had a cold and would blow her nose without using a handkerchief — just blew and let the mucous fly where it would. Then I had to sleep with their retarded son whose underwear was so filthy that it would have stood up by itself and the bedding so terrible that it almost made me sick.

The next morning they insisted I eat breakfast but I told them I never ate any breakfast but did have a cup of black coffee. By lunch time I was starving and stopped at a sheep ranch where I was well fed. Most places wouldn't take any money but the sheep rancher's wife charged me a quarter, probably because I ate so much. Also, food was sometimes scarce.

That night I arrived at the Corb Morse ranch six miles east of Rapid City. It was Saturday night and Mr. Morse invited me to spend Sunday there and let the horses rest. There wasn't much grass for them to eat but they had the run of the whole pasture since he had sold all of his cattle and horses due to feed shortage.

Sunday Mr. Morse took advantage of my presence to help cut down a big cottonwood tree beside the house — another victim of the drought. Mr. Morse was quite elderly; he had come up from Texas after it had been opened to homesteaders in the 1890s. Like many others he liked western Dakota and eastern Montana's open range. Anyway because of Mr. Morse's advanced age, the hired man and I did most of the work removing the old tree. One large branch extended over the house and had to be cut off before we could fell the tree. We finally got it down, using human power, since there were no chain saws in those days.

About twenty-five years ago I was stationed at the Rapid City airport in my job with the Federal Aviation Administration. Mr. Morse was no longer around but I saw many items he had donated to the museum in Rapid City, and then remembered a couple of hours we had spent discussing his antiques years previously, on that Sunday.

Tuesday night I stayed at a ranch about twenty-five miles on towards the reservation and Wednesday night I arrived at the Cheyenne river where it borders the Pine Ridge Indian reservation. I met a young couple there who lived in an old abandoned home. The next morning the horses and I forded the river and were finally on the reservation. There I met the only Indian I ever saw on this reservation; he directed me to the camp where my cousin had taken up residence.

I stayed there for about four weeks, herding Maurice's sheep till it was time to ship the lambs. Although the grass was good, the only water was one pond formed by a dam. In order to take advantage of all the grass, we decided to water the sheep only every other day. On the day I took them to water, they were so thirsty that they crowded each other so far into the water that many got stuck in the mud. I spent half the night pulling them out with my lariat. That water was very valuable to us in the middle of a drought.

He sold the lambs to a man named Firm Clarkson who had a feed lot near Belle Fourche. We loaded the lambs on the train at Smithwick and I rode the caboose to Belle Fourche. At Whitewood they put the cars on a siding and left them there for a day and a night. The lambs got so hungry that they were eating the wool off each other's backs. I got a good scolding from Firm when we finally arrived in Belle, saying I should have insisted that they take them off the train and feed them while in Whitewood. Anyway, I got rid of them there and went back to herding sheep for Uncle Dave.

I remember that nobody in my part of the country ever had any goats, so I knew very little about the animal. It was too early to turn the bucks in with the ewes, but many of the ewes were already in heat and I noticed that there was a billy goat in his herd that was really having a ball, mating with all the ewes that were in heat. The Indian advised me that sheep and goats are close enough related to mate but would not produce any offspring. However, years later when I was living in Rochester, Minnesota, working for the F.A.A. there was a picture in the paper of a farmer's ewe which had given birth to twins, one being a lamb and the other a half goat.

Anyway, that's my story of travelling by horse across South Dakota in the heat of the drought in 1936.

M. Earl Patterson   '
Burnsville, Minnesota

UNCLE HAD ELECTRICITY AND A KEROSENE REFRIGERATOR

In January, 1936 I was living on a small farm with my parents south of Des Moines, Iowa. I had graduated from high school two years before and had gone to Simpson college in Indianola for a year. Then I worked as a farm hand and also helped my dad on the farm while he worked as a coal miner.

Because the work in the mines was mostly in winter, my dad worked until January and then lost his job. This happened because he refused to pay his union dues for the summer months when he wouldn't be working anyhow. As long as he wasn't working, he didn't need me at home so I grabbed a chance to go to Pocahontas county, Iowa, near Rolfe to work on a farm for an uncle.

I arrived there about January 15, having hitch-hiked and walked from Des Moines. I was to receive $15 a month plus board and room until the first of April when the wages would increase to $30. There was already quite a bit of snow on the ground and it started to snow more nearly every day.

My uncle was a county supervisor so he wasn't home very much. He had a son a little older than I so we did the chores. There were chickens, hogs, a few milk cows and six horses. The first few days we hauled hay from the stacks and did other odd jobs but then the snow started getting deeper and it got colder and colder. Then we couldn't do much except the basic chores and sit in the house and play cards.

Every day it got worse and my uncle couldn't get to the county seat to his job. The mail couldn't get through but we knew that every two weeks the snowplow was going to get through some way because my uncle had to sign the county checks. Snow removal equipment didn't amount to much back then. The county had one rotary plow and small maintenance; I remember that when it was time to open the road that the neighbors would break the snow ahead of the plow with shovels because it was so hard and deep. I remember being able to hang our jackets on the telephone lines some days when it would warm up a little. When the snowplow finally made it through, all the neighbors would get in a car or usually a bobsled with a team and head for Rolfe, six miles away. They had eggs and cream to take to town and groceries and coal to bring home. The road never stayed open overnight because the wind blew all the time.

The telephone rang at my uncles all the time. Women were having babies. People were sick. Some died. Others were out of fuel. My uncle did what he could to get the roads open and doctors to the sick. The schools were closed for six weeks.

Towards the end of winter the coal supply in town was gone because the trains couldn't get through so we cut down trees in the grove and picked corncobs out of the pigpen for fuel. Most days the snow blew so much we couldn't see from the house to the barn.

My uncle had a Delco light plant in his house so we had conveniences that most farms didn't have — like running water, radio and indoor plumbing.

Finally, about the middle of March the weather warmed up and there was water everywhere. The roads then got very bad.

We got the crops in and it started to get hot. As early as June things were already hot and dry.

I remember after the fourth of July we were ready to harvest oats and a bum came one night saying he would work for his meal and a bed. He was clean so my aunt put him up. He ran the binder during harvest. His name was John Asher and he had been on the road since he was a young man. He must have stayed a couple of weeks because he was a cement man and built a lily pool for my aunt. When he left he put his belongings in a shirt, tied it to a stick, and down the road he went. He returned several times after that.

It was so hot we would usually go to a gravel pit in the evening after chores and take a swim. Our clothes would get stiff from the salt and sweat and our shoes would be white in the morning. On Saturday nights we would get the eggs and cream to town and bring home groceries but they had a nickel movie in Rolfe and nearly everyone went. After the movie we would go to the pool hall, shoot some pool, have a few beers and by one o'clock the town was pretty well buttoned up.

When it got unbearably hot my uncle sent to Montgomery Wards for a kerosene refrigerator. It was huge but it worked very well.

Also, my aunt made home brew. She would make it in a fifteen-gallon crock and set it by the furnace. My uncle had a tin cup beside the crock and he would get up early and sip on the brew. Sometimes I'd get up about five and would see my uncle outside struggling toward the barn. Sometimes my cousin and I would have to go bring him and put him back to bed. The pressure of his job got to him, I guess, because there were many problems with the poor people. Anyway, my aunt always managed to get some of the home brew bottled and it was good that hot summer.

I worked there until the middle of August and it finally started to rain a little. The crops didn't amount to much anyhow. I went back home and helped my dad the rest of the summer.

After I served in the Navy during World War II I farmed in Pocahontas county for seven years. I was married in 1948 and in 1954 bought a farm in Crow Wing county, Minnesota. We raised three boys and two girls. I'm retired now and my boys are all on the farm. They have 900 acres and also an agriculture service business on the farm. Our girls—one lives in Plymouth and teaches in Hopkins. The youngest is a senior at St. Cloud State.

Herb Barrett
Brainerd, Minnesota

SHATTERED DREAMS

The years of the dust and cold, northwest winds was what it was all about in the thirties. I cannot say for certain when it came but I'll never forget those years because I was in my teens. It wasn't much of a problem to me like it was for farmers. The district schools were still there for us kids to get our education and the joys of being kids kept us distracted. We could take it but we knew it was very bad in many ways. There was always plenty to eat and a bed in which to sleep because our elders made it so. On the farm, life went on with me about the same as it always did.

The soil was up there, being moved across the land in a nasty way because of that stormy wind coming in from the northwest or, later on in the summer, from the southeast. It was always there during the day and sometimes at eve. At times it became so still it was like some monster that we knew would be there again the next day. I remember that very well because there was a cottonwood tree in the farmyard and always the song of a thrush sitting on a branch chirping away. I remember in the field I used to hear the meadowlark perched on a fence post, giving out his mournful song. I could hear that meadowlark and another on a distant fencepost, as if they were put there for some special reason. Now the fence posts are gone, so is the meadow lark which was an important,good part of the prairie. Thanks to man-made chemicals the things that nature put there for good reasons are gone. The horse was the means by which we farmed in those days and I could hear things that I couldn't hear today, even if they were there.

One fall four of us guys went to North Dakota to work in the harvest fields, my cousin having been there before. It was great because we got into a threshing run that lasted about five weeks. We planned to go back the next year but nature changed all of that with no rain and no crop. The drought had moved down on us and we had nothing but that dry dirt day after day. No rain, not even a drop; no snow, just that bitter cold wind which was there summer and winter.

Most of the old feed boxes are gone now. They were important. I knew how much oats to put in them to satisfy each horse; some needed just a handful while others needed a bucketful. It was important they be fed just the right amount. The hay from the lakeshore was useful when we had horses, but it had to be stacked in the summer and hauled home in the winter. Now both the horses and that hay meadow are gone.

When I look at that horse barn now I remember many things dear to me — things that had taken place there — but some I'd rather forget. To have a horse die there on a cold winter night was not pleasant; there were other animals I took as pets and had them get sick and die; that was not a pleasant part of farming but the farmer had to put up with it.

In winter time when it was below zero the hogs would go into the hog house and pile up to get warm. When I'd open the door one would grunt and they'd all try to get outside at once through a small door meant for a pig to enter; it was a dirty shame to see them piling up. I tried to let them know I was coming before I got there but that grunt from one hog really got them awake in a hurry. No damned sense to it. In those days the hogs had it nice. We cut corn stalks and put them in bundles with a corn binder pulled by three horses. Then I had to shock those corn bundles, which was one of the worst jobs on the farm. When it was hot and windy the dust would blow around, the leaves would cut my hands or face and it seemed as if I stumbled over every corn stalk in the field.

Then we had to haul the corn bundles home and stack them along the cattle yard fence. We'd throw about twenty-five bundles into the hogs and let them eat the corn on the ears; later we turned in the cattle to eat what the hogs had left. We tried to take care of all living things in a satisfactory way, wanting them to be comfortable. The chickens, too. Every night they would sneak into the coop, climb onto a roost quietly and spend the night in comfort. In wintertime they stayed inside but in spring, as the days got warmer, we would let them out; they seemed so happy about it. The old rooster would tell the world about it because he was so happy. Yes, it's all gone now.

Fences were a lot of work. I got in on that too. Carry the staple pail and pound in some of the staples. The fence was woven wire with two strands of barbed wire on top. Thistles would roll across the field, coming to rest on a fence; then dirt would fill up next to that fence and thistles and in some places you could walk over the fence. Sometimes the horses would do that too. You needed no gate. It was like a solid snowdrift. Now the fence, dirt and thistle are gone. Nature in its own way took care of that in later years.

I recall one farmer who was plowing with a gang plow and also a tractor plow. He could hear the tractor but the dust was so bad he couldn't see it; the lead horses stopped because they couldn't see where they were going; it turned out the hired man on the tractor was in the same farrow and had to be stopped before he ran over the farmer. Sometimes a horse would pass out because it had so much dirt in its lungs; they had to be watched carefully.

There wasn't much feed for cattle. West of Clinton the thistles kept them alive but to the east there wasn't even thistle. Some cattle were so poor the government bought them for $21 each, most of them being so bad they were about to die. We herded them into Clinton where they were put in boxcars and sent to St. Paul. Sows had small pigs and the farmers had to kill them — no feed.

Another boy and I went to New Ulm to help in the harvest fields. Their crop was pretty good there and they couldn't believe things were so bad up our way. While there I got word that my Daddy had passed away so I drove home. About twelve miles from Ortonville I stopped on a high spot on the highway and ahead of me there was nothing green. The trees were dead, there was no grass, not a thing was growing. It made me somewhat sick. I got home and there was my brother loafing around, something I had never known him to do. I stayed home because they only paid $25 a month down there with the depression on; it was a bad time for everyone.

At that time I didn't realize how much my parents suffered. Their hopes and dreams must have been shattered in many ways. Some of them passed away during those terrible years. My parents had spent a lot of work and money building up the farm. The line fence alone must have been like a dream come true, only to have that wind and dry years destroy it. My Dad and mother never did see it get better like it is today for me. I never gave it much thought at the time but now I realize that the trees and plants were planned not in a week but over several years. I try to think of how that land must have looked when they first saw it and decided to homestead right where they were standing — with the prairie grass, the slope of the land where they planted trees and built a house, the ash trees that grew slowly but were ones that the dry years didn't kill.

There were houses in those days that you could hardly see because they were surrounded by trees which the farmer had planted. There were many families, kids making the land alive with their laughter and songs. Those trees were soon all gone and those houses were just sitting there atop a hill. There were no wars at that time and I now realize how many sacrificed their lives in war and on the farms so I could have it nice today.

I never knew when the first raindrops came. It never worried me much. I got myself a piano accordian and played that thing everywhere, all over the land. When they passed the hat and put in it what change they had, it kept me always with a pocketful of coins. I kept it in a cigar box on my dresser and when I had a date or going out for some fun I would grab a handful of coins; it didn't take much in those days. There was a watch pocket in my dress suit and there was always a dollar bill there in case I needed it. I never did.

The farm was good to me, like the way my parents wanted it to be. The land gave us plenty to eat and we lived off it. I always felt my parents had faith in the land but were wise enough to know that they must correct some mistakes they made with the land. Maybe those dirt storms came for a purpose.

Wilmer Sandberg
Ortonville, Minnesota

WHEN ONE DIED A THOUSAND CAME TO HIS FUNERAL

Before the dust bowl days we had two years during which the grasshoppers ate all the crops. We, my husband, three small sons, and I lived on a farm about seventeen miles northeast of Gregory, South Dakota. Grasshoppers ate all the small grain and all the corn in the fields except for a 1 ½ to 2 foot stub of stalk.

We knew the sun was shining but couldn't see it because of grashoppers in the air. They covered the fence posts until we couldn't see the wood and got into the house and ate holes in my window curtains. We dug small trenches around the fields and got up early in the mornings to spread poisoned bran in the ditches, trying to stop those grasshoppers. We used to say that "When one died, a thousand came to its funeral." After the hoppers ate the oats in the field, Russian thistles grew in the stubble and we mowed it, stacking it for hay.

Rather than see our cattle starve we hired a truck and took fourteen head to Bassett, Nebraska; when the trucker was paid we had $92 left for the fourteen head. And since they were mortgaged we had to give that to the bank.

My husband had to work for the Works Progress Administration (W.P.A.) driving four head of horses twelve to fifteen miles a day working on a road. He left before daylight and got home long after dark. By working on the road we could buy grain and hay for the horses and some commodities for us. One week they didn't come in so we lived on bread and flour gravy made with water.

Then came the dust storms. Because of no crops there was nothing to hold the soil so away it went.

We had no car so used a lumber wagon when we went anywhere. My sister and her little boy were visiting us from Sioux City, Iowa, and we went to town one day. Before we got home a bad dust storm struck us. Our house was almost a quarter mile off the road with just a lane through the field leading to it. When we got to the lane we gave the horses their own way, thinking they could take us to the house. The first thing we knew they bumped up against one of the thistle stacks and stopped. We couldn't see a thing but finally heard the squeaking of the windmill near the house so knew where we were and made it home.

My sister's boy, Lyle, said he wanted to go back to Sioux City since he didn't like those dust storms.

One time when I was out in the yard I saw a thunderhead coming up over a hill about a half mile west of our house. It came rolling and tumbling and I finally knew what it was. At the same time my husband, who was out in the field working. saw the cloud, quickly unhitched the disk, jumped on one of the horses and tried to make it to the house.

He made it only to the barn where he had to wait until it let up a bit. It got as dark as at night. I took the boys into the house and lit the kerosene lamps, but we could barely see the light for the dust in the room.

The next year we left that rented house and moved to another farm where the dirt had almost covered the hoghouse. We had to use four horses on a Fresno to scrape away the dirt. It was a mess.

I am eighty-seven years old.

Hazel D. Horner
S. Sioux City, Nebraska

BARN WAS A BETTER BUILDING THAN OUR HOUSE

In August 1936 I was nine years old. Summers were horrible during those years. My mother kept the butter in a crock within a crock in a cool cistern water in the basement. Even then it melted. We had a new but inexpensive house but our beautiful big barn was a much better building. Fine dust constantly sifted over the floors and furniture.

My favorite horses, which my father had let me name, became ill with sleeping sickness and at least one of the mares died. We had an orphan colt to bottle feed.

The oats and barley did not mature properly and my father put up both for hay. I know now we were poor, although my parents kept the fact from me. The only thing I ever heard Mother snarl at Dad about was debt. Their Federal Land Bank loan, taken out in the optimism of the late nineteen twenties, had to be rewritten. Not only could they not pay the principal, they couldn't pay the interest. I realize now they were quietly desperate. As Thoreau said "Men live lives of quiet desperation."

It was no wonder that my mother sent me by bus to visit my grandmother in southeastern Minnesota. I was an only grandchild and at Preston there were both a bachelor uncle and a grandparent to spoil me and shield me from the harsh reality of the times. Nevertheless, life went on in southwest rural Minnesota. My older cousins got married and had children who don't even remember the depression.

The northern lights were beautiful that winter. I remember everyone being awed when we took a hayrack on sled runners to a cousin's place to play cards. My uncle's herdsman for his purebred shorthorns was from Alabama and, of course, he had to be awakened to see the display.

There were still quail (Bob Whites) here in those days. All gone now. There were lovely pastures with grazing animals, not such intensive farming and confinement feeding as today. Perhaps I'm just a sentimental old fool, but I think those years of drought steeled me for life a little, and for that I am grateful.

Helen Murphy Nordstrom
Lakefield, Minnesota

THOSE SAND HILLS WINDS

I came from the Los Angeles city school system in July 1929 to the beautiful sand hills of Nebraska to be married. It was just four months before the big crash of 1929. My husband and I had nothing except my $50 war bond from World War I but that was when a dollar was worth something and not affected by inflation.

We used our limited money to buy necessities and groceries from Sears Roebuck, things like raisins, oatmeal and dried apricots in 25 pound boxes—for our family of three in 1931.

We lived in a former KinKaid 1½ story house built by a carpenter of sorts. We had no insulation, one small closet under the steep stairway, no inside plumbing, no telephone, no ice box, no electricity, and no car. We did have a pitcher pump in the kitchen, which was only eighteen feet above the water level.

When it became sufficiently cold we would butcher a beef and hang it on the north side of the house, covering it with a sheet to keep off dust and flies. When we needed meat, we would saw off a frozen piece for cooking.

The sand hills are noted for winds, which are needed to turn the many windmills which supply water for the cattle. We had a barrel sunk in the ground near a windmill which caught the overflow from the corral tank. That's where we hung our butter jar. We also hardened Jello in this barrel and had lots of cold milk and good sweet water there.

I raised a huge garden which I watered from the overflow and had ditches running between the rows. I canned many jars of vegetables and jellies. We protected the canned produce from wintry blasts in a cave under part of the house; we reached the cave through a trap door on the outside of the kitchen.

We sometimes burned Heifer City coal in the front room stove but it was a hot fire requiring lots of carrying in and carrying out; we saved on other things so we could afford the coal.

When I was married my paternal grandparents in Massachusetts gave me $200 to buy a gasoline-engine powered washing machine. Thus I didn't have to use a wash board but did need to heat water in a wash boiler on our Skelgas stove. Then I had to carry it in buckets to the washing machine.

Those were the dry years and little rain fell. The sky would cloud up, lightning would start many fires. One night I counted eight glows in the sky from fires. My husband had gone with his dad to fight a fire which looked to be just over the next sand hill; they never did get to it since it was further away than it looked. Imagine how terror struck me with two small sons, no car, no telephone and being alone with fires apparently all around me. I collected a broom, a shovel, a wash tub of water, some gunny sacks and prayed that none of the fires would come our way. They didn't.

Coming from California, a state with many mountains, I felt secure from tornadoes and cyclones in Nebraska but, boy, did I get a surprise. Sometimes in 1936 our older son rode a safe old horse to school, Old Tony, and sometimes he walked a path strewn with cactus, a scampering bunny or maybe a desert tortoise laboriously moving along. One day when he walked, a storm came up. By midday the wind howled, the sky darkened and the teacher let school out early. A kind neighbor, picking up his three children, saw my son afoot and started to bring him home too. It became so stormy the neighbor decided to wait out the storm in front of a large sand hill and faced his car east. Eventually they made it safely to our home.

In the meantime our house had been rocking back and forth on its poorly constructed foundation and our corral fence had moved half way to the house — all by the wind. My husband had been on horseback in this storm and just gave his horse his reins and the animal brought him safely home just as the storm was abating.

Sometimes conflicting air currents would meet in our meadow, even those of different colors. After one such storm I had red mud from Oklahoma plastered all over my newly washed windows.

Dorothy P. Merrihew
Ashby, Nebraska

OUR PUREBRED HOLSTEIN BULL CALF

In 1936 we bought what was known as the John Agnew farm only one mile southwest of Mahnomen, Minnesota. We moved here March 17 from a farm near Winger. There was a lot of snow and we had a terrible time getting our cattle through that snow. They waded belly deep through it for almost a half a mile. Of course there was no snowplow in sight then. We used horses for almost all power. But, with the help of neighbors, we got the cattle through the drifts. That winter I was told was the coldest winter on record.

That spring we bought a purebred Holstein bull calf for $65. It weighed a ton. I also remember that we kept it for a few years and sold it for the same sum — $65. Also that $65 was exactly what we needed to buy my husband a much needed winter coat.

There were only twenty-two acres open for field that year and most of it was seeded in wheat. It was a very hot and dry summer. The wheat looked good from a distance but up close it was nothing since it was shrivelled.

It was too hot that summer for horses to pull the binder in the middle of the day. They rested in the barn and the men sat in the shade until it cooled a bit towards evening; then they would work as long as they could see.

We pulled through that year, and fifty more. Part of the city limits is next to the farm now but it's still known as the Larson farm.

Emily Larson
Mahnomen, Minnesota

BROTHER'S FUNERAL SERVICE IN FRONT YARD

I was eleven at the time and can well remember many happenings.

We lived on a farm and had running water in the house but had to use the outhouse because we had no stool. I had to take a bath in a wash tub by the kitchen wood-burning cook stove. We had electricity—32 volts—provided by a Delco engine. This was before the Rural Electrification Act.

I tell you these things to let you know we weren't destitute. However, we lived on receipts of our produce, cream and egg checks.

It was very hot and dry in 1936. One bad thing about it was that it never cooled off even at nights. I think the temperature stayed in the eighties at night and 100 plus was common for daytime. We had no fans and air conditioning was not heard of then. It was so hot at night that I would ring out a dish towel in cool water and spread it on my bed to lie on—the only source of comforting cool.

Besides having crops dry up we were plagued with grasshoppers. We spread a mixture of sawdust and poison around our fields, trying to kill the hoppers before they got into the fields.

Times were so hard that my dad had to go to the bank to borrow money to go to the state capitol, Lincoln, for a loan. It was 115 miles from Fullerton, Nebraska, where we lived. Fullerton is 45 miles northeast of Grand Island, the third largest Nebraska city.

My little brother Bobbie was four years old. He was stricken in 1936 with scarlet fever that summer and he died. My folks were a long time paying for that funeral. The service was held outdoors because we were quarantined. Bobbie's casket was on the porch and the funeral attendants sat on chairs out on the lawn—but I should say in the yard because I'm pretty sure we had no grass then. So hardship was piled on top of hardship.

Being farmers, we went to town on Saturday night. I can remember sitting in our Chevy in town. Mom and Daddy were sitting in the front seat and I was in the back. Mom was crying because they had no money for groceries. I told them they could have my $18 I had in the bank. I got that from selling my one sheep.

Let me stress that there never was any respite from the heat. The hot nights were so repressive; as I said we had no fans. I had to stay in the bedroom with my sick brother while Mom did the housework.

I married and had four fine kids—two boys and two girls. They in their maturing years have done me proud. My husband was a carpenter's helper and then an auto mechanic so you can see we weren't plush with money. We didn't have much for clothes but since groceries had top priority we ate well. It took cooking expertise even then to make a little go a long way. On my one day a week for mending I patched overalls and jean knees, darned socks and did whatever else was necessary.

My husband and I were divorced in 1975 and I am living on welfare in a semi-nursing home. My health is good.

There might not be too many people living now who experienced the drought of the thirties. I'm getting up in years.

Mrs. Donna Weller
Genoa, Nebraska

THE LOST ART OF SOAPMAKING

To this day I hate a very thin remnant of bar soap. It must be a symbol of being poor to me.

"Don't throw that soap away yet—there's still some good in it."

"Don't be so wasteful. That costs money."

I'm surprised our elders never said "Save that soap. Think of the poor Chinese children who would be glad to have it—maybe to eat it." It was always the Chinese or the Indian children. Most of us could never figure out how badly off those poor people really were.

When a bar of soap gets so thin it's like a razor, perhaps we should try shaving with it in lieu of a new double-edged whatch-a-may-callit. It's just about as sharp and has the same qualities.

Of course some of us can remember when some one among our elders actually made soap. That's right! They made it in the back yard out of such esoteric things as hog fat, wood ashes and lye. They bought the lye in cans at the grocery store and put all the rest together in some mysterious manner and cooked the hell out of it. When completed, it was a laundry soap very similar in color to a soap called Fels-Naphtha. I suppose they also used it for bathing, lathering up a dirty mule and cleaning up the privy. It was strong. Very strong. But it was probably all they had except for something they had to buy at the store.

And in the early thirties people didn't buy anything they could do without. If you would like to try making your own soap, kill a hog, render the lard—or, better yet, go to the library and look for a book called "The Good Earth Manual" which I'll bet has such a recipe therein.

William H. Hull

NOTHING BUT HARD WORK
AND DO WITHOUT

We had seven years of depression. We lived on a poor sandy rented farm on the Platte river about six miles east of Bellwood, Nebraska.

It was bitterly cold until late spring in 1936 and the snow was very deep. Many days in January, February and even March it snowed every day and the temperature never got above zero. For several years past we had raised hardly any crops because of the grasshoppers and drought; then that year from mid-April until fall we had no rain. What the grasshoppers didn't eat or the drought didn't destroy, wasn't worth having.

We did have a little oats and wheat, the oats having to be saved for the few chickens and livestock we had around. We farmed with horses and lost several from sleeping sickness due to grasshopper poison. Before that the government made everyone kill their hogs, due to over production, so there was no meat. What few livestock we had, needed to be saved because there was no money to buy more. We had a few chickens to eat but they had been living off grasshoppers and their meat was greasy and not fit to eat. We did try to eat one and we were all sick. Mom soaked some wheat overnight and cooked it for cereal for breakfast; the rest was mixed in the dough for bread.

Many days and months all we had to eat was cornmeal mush or cornbread and plain boiled navy beans, dry bread and plain boiled potatoes or pancakes. We couldn't have a garden due to the drought and grasshoppers. The grocer would give us a little credit and with luck in the fall harvest we could pay him off and get a little sugar. With more luck we could pick plums along the river bank and eat them as sauce or jelly, wild grapes if someone didn't steal them for wine, or for pudding, even a few gooseberries if we could avoid the snakes in the bushes. There were also choke cherries or, when we could cross the river to get to an island, we could get buffalo berries for jelly—unless the worms had beaten us to them.

But first, after the harvest, we would cross to the island, cut logs and haul them home on the running gear of the lumber wagon; then every chance we had someone would cut the logs by hand, split them with an axe to fit in the stove, and lay aside the bark to dry for quick starting the fire.

All the water you needed for yourself and the livestock had to be pumped by hand. Do you have any idea how hard we had to work in burning hot summer heat and bitter cold winter? We didn't have the warm clothes available today, let alone money to buy them had they been available. We three girls wore made-over clothes from an aunt who was a teacher and a cousin who was an only child.

Our dish towels, underwear, sheets, pillow cases, curtains, bedspreads, dresses, shirts and quilts were made from flour or feed sacks if we were lucky enough to get enough of the same pattern.

Kerosene was ten cents a gallon but we didn't have the ten cents, so had to go to bed as soon as it got dark. If we were late for supper, we opened the fire door of the cookstove in order to see to eat, and wash dishes.

The bathroom was an old two-holer behind the house and what kerosene was in the lamp needed to be saved in case some one got sick in the night.

We had to go a mile and a half to the country school; many times we walked in the ditch trying to keep warm. My sister and I, a couple of neighbor girls and a teacher friend went to high school in Octavia which was 5 ½ miles away. When the weather was bad we had to stay in town and give the dear lady where we stayed whatever we could spare for room and board. Several times when the roads were blocked we couldn't go home nor could anyone come to bring us food, the lady had to borrow a dollar so we could eat. Remember—there were no food stamps in those days.

That lady's brother-in-law brought her cobs and wood so we had to count the cobs and wood used to cook our food until we could get into town with the wagon to repay her.

If a girl were lucky she might get a job baby sitting for a bunch of kids whose parents had ten cents extra and the gas to go to a dance or a neighborhood party. We got 25 cents until midnight regardless of the number of kids and 50 cents after midnight. Or you might get a job as a hired girl for three dollars a week. Believe me, you earned it. Hard work from early morning to night; most of the time you had to milk cows, take care of the chickens and maybe a big garden, and a big washing where you again pumped the water and carried it in and again out when through. Sometimes you had to split wood if the menfolks or maybe the hired man didn't have time or was just too lazy.

My husband worked as a hired man for three years during the depression for $20 a month, room and board. He was lucky because he had good people to work for. Many men tried to get harvest jobs and were paid a dollar a day and meals. Sometimes they had to sleep in the barn or a haystack and, if they smoked, you had to be concerned that they didn't burn you out. Those were tough times.

By the time I was fourteen I had finally saved enough money to buy a new coat, my very first "boughten" one; I wore it until I was twenty-one.

For birthdays we might be lucky enough to have a cake. For Christmas we got a 29 cent pair of cotton socks and Mom made a little candy. All winter the cows gave very little milk and the chickens laid few eggs. There wasn't enough feed for them and the barn and chicken house were so cold and so old that they were ready to fall down.

I pray my children and grandchildren never have to go through all the hard times that we did. In this day too many people don't know how to save — or don't want to know — and are so wasteful. We had to learn.

The good old days. You can have them. Nothing but hard work and do without.

Mrs. George Borchers
Columbus, Nebraska

SIX BUCKS FOR HUNDRED POUND HOG

1936 was not a good year. I have some pretty vivid memories of it. Most farmers were still trying to recover from the depression years and 10 cent a bushel corn. We got 18½ inches of rain in 1934 here in Nebraska and a corn yield of 10 bushels per acre. 1935 was better but the year ended with no subsoil moisture and deep cracks in the ground.

There were many sheriff's sales and 600 people in the county were getting some kind of public assistance. Many farm hands worked all winter with no pay other than having a place to sleep, a roof over their heads and a chance to put their feet under a table when mealtime came.

There were homeless and jobless men riding the freight cars, eating in soup kitchens and sleeping on cold nights in the county jail. They could be seen picking up cigaret butts as they walked down the street headed for the local hobo jungle. Sometimes there was an old shack just outside the city limits. A few got day-old bread or rolls from bakeries, eatshops or anywhere they could get something to add to the pot of mulligan stew often cooked in a gallon can picked up along the way.

These drifters would chop wood, sharpen scissors or unload a car of coal even if the pay were only 10 or 15 cents an hour. They were not dangerous men; life had dealt them a hard blow and they would be desperately poor until a wartime economy made work for them or they went into the service, which paid $21 a month. Often their only cover at night was a sheet of the building paper used to line freight cars when hauling grain. Under those conditions cleanliness was next to impossible for long.

By mid-January there was 13½ inches of snow on the ground. The last 14 days of January the temperature never got above zero. The wind blew the road cuts full of snow so hard it was impossible to stick a shovel into it. Dana college was burning five tons of coal a day and the Blair schools were burning three tons.

Highways were blocked by drifts even though the county had 100 men scooping snow. The county roads remained closed although the C.C.C. boys were trying to keep them open. Farmers worked together at the nearest deep drifts, often with three men each throwing snow to the next on three different levels, trying to keep a narrow track open at the bottom of the cut.

We sat it out for 19 days with no mail, no groceries from the store and no way to get the cream and eggs to the produce buyers. At last the county got a strong blade mounted on a Caterpillar tractor and cleared a track wide enough for a car or a team and wagon. Everyone rushed into town to buy basic foods and a can of kerosene for the lamps. We barely got home again before the cuts drifted full and we were snowbound for another 14 days. At some places we cut fences and drove in a field to get around the deep drifts on the road. There were folks the mail carrier didn't reach for six weeks, unless by mutual agreement he left their mail in someone else's box.

A train took 9½ hours to go from Arlington to Omaha—a distance of 25 miles. When the weather finally began to moderate there had been 27 days when the temperature fell to zero some time during the night.

The Citizens Savings bank had gone belly-up on January 19, 1933, which left Blair without a bank. I had $50 in that bank but eventually got back a bit over $8. It was little consolation that prices were low; we just didn't have any money.

A 48 pound sack of flour cost $1.49 but a sack of Leader flour could be had for $1.27. A quart of peanut butter cost 27 cents, 10 pounds of prunes cost 59 cents, bread was 7½ a loaf or three loaves for a dime on special days. Publix brand coffee was 18 cents a pound, Peaberry cost a penny more. Milk sold for 8 cents a quart, cream 35 cents. Log Cabin syrup in the tin log cabins cost 22 cents, sometimes with a pound of pancake mix thrown in free. Hamburger or roast beef was 15 cents a pound. Postage dropped from 3 cents to 2 cents for about a year and the local weekly newspaper cost 75 cents a year.

By March 5 some of the rivers were beginning to go out of their banks though some road cuts were still blocked with snow.

The fire in the heating stove might go out at night and then the dipper would be frozen tightly in the water pail. There were no water pipes to freeze. It took a lot of firewood and we also burned all the corncobs from the corn acres, even those dirty ones picked up in the hog yard after the hogs had eaten off the corn.Being dirty they held a fire longer than the clean dry ones. Soft coal was 7 or 8 dollars a ton and hard coal for a base burner was $23—but who had money? It was fortunate that most country folks still had a feather tick for each bed and many heavy, homemade quilts.

For a week or two Ethel's grandfather and the hired man carried logs into the kitchen to saw them into blocks when it was too bitterly cold to stay outdoors. When the kerosene can ran empty, they twisted a strip of rag, laid one end to a saucer of hog lard, and lit the other end. It smoked some but so did the kerosene lamps when the wick wasn't properly trimmed.

Our wintertime meals were short on greens, as those were seasonal, but we always had plenty of homemade butter and thick cream, and the platter of meat we put on the table was a size now seen only on holidays or family gatherings. When I look at the $1.80 size jars of jam at the store I realize I ate that much at one meal on pancakes or toast. Lemonade was always made from fresh lemons. We overate when we had fresh fruits and berries as it seemed a shame to let them go to waste. Even in 1936 we had jars of such things in the cellar because we never planned to run out from year to year. In a normal year we always bought a hundred pounds of sugar just before canning time.

Chicken stealing was not unusual. Ordinarily it would just be a gunnysack of four or five hens, but at times as many as 150 were taken. There was a share-cropper living near us who always took a few fat hens to town to pay for his groceries. One neighbor got the drop on him one night and extracted $50 from him to keep his mouth shut but news has a way of getting out. Once when the threshing crew was at our place he said he thought someone had stolen a few of his chickens. Someone replied "Maybe they just went home to roost." A hint was passed to his landlord and the next moving day he left the area. Many years later I read his death notice in the paper. The old man was 94 years old, so the chickens or the excitement must have been good for him, or as they say, "The good die young."

Most of the country schools stayed open if only for those kids who lived near the school. The large potbellied stove in the center of the room didn't keep the whole room warm and we were allowed to bunch up in the seats nearest the stove. I have seen two teachers burn a hole in the back of their dress when they backed up to the stove to get warm.

One lesson we did learn from those dirty thirties was to do without things we really didn't need. Playing Euchre, pitch or pinochle with the neighbors cost nothing except a few spoonsful of lard and some popcorn, all of which we grew in abundance.

Almost everyone did their own butchering and curing meat, though there was Butch Nelson who lived in a boarding house in Blair who would kill and dress a hog for a dollar plus the liver—or two dollars if you wanted to keep the liver. He had no transportation so you went into town to get him and took him home again.

Once Ethel's grandparents had a cow break her leg when another cow pushed her off a narrow bridge. Since it was mid-summer the meat had to be canned the hot water bath way. A woman came from town to help with it for a share of the meat. Besides the big washboiler on the stove they also had a large canner in the oven going at the same time. Don't ask if the kitchen was air conditioned!

By mid June it was obvious that hoppers were going to be a problem and we had chinch bugs which we had never known before. The government furnished poisoned bran for 25 cents a bag but it did little if any good. Our chickens had to eat hoppers until they loathed them, but it was hoppers or nothing. Each day they ranged farther out into the fields. The tops of the trees died for want of moisture.

The first and only short cutting of alfalfa had been mowed and put up when the pastures burned up and we had to start feeding hay or damaged corn stalks.

Some of the seed corn laid there in the ground too dry to sprout; what did come up only needed one cultivating because the weed seeds didn't sprout either. Some garden seed laid in the ground until August 27 when we got very strong winds and as much as five inches of rain. Grass, which the pioneers called "poverty grass" then came up between the rows of corn and grew to six inches or so before frost came.

The oats crop had been a failure; I got three hayrack loads of a mixture of stunted oats and last year's corn stalks—because oats was always planted in last year's stalk fields.

The Blair canning company was contracting with farmers to grow sweet corn for them at six and seven dollars a ton for snapped corn ears. This also was a lost cause. I grew one quart of shelled corn from 45 acres that year.

Some gumbo lands on the river bottom got a little corn but every farmer had cattle or hogs and there was no corn to sell. Our neighbor had some pigs he wanted to feed and had to go 60 miles over into Iowa to get two truckloads of shelled corn. The rest of us sold our underfed 100 pound hogs when we ran out of feed. We got six cents a pound or six bucks a hog.

The shallow wells around the county began to go dry or not put out enough water. I dug a seven foot hole in the bottom of the creek and dipped up enough for the horses with a rope and a bucket.

On July 10 I drilled some corn into five or six acres of fallow land which managed to shoot silks before frost. I cut it with a corn knife, shocked it and that was the best feed I had. Most of the corn that fall was cut with what was known as a Richmond corn harvester. It was a sled drawn between the rows by one horse. Some had a knife on one side only, to cut the stalks which a man seated on the sled caught in his arms and dropped off when he had an armload. The sleds that had a knife on each side needed two men to catch the stalks and a man to drive the horse.

On July 23 there was a severe dust storm that blew down trees on the phone lines. Dust storms of more or less intensity had been a way of life since mid-May. Dust, often a red dust from as far away as Oklahoma, blew into the homes and had to be swept out each day. The sun rose late and set early.

On July 25 the temperature reached 116 degrees and the next day it was 114. It was always too warm at night to sleep well; there was no dew at night and it even got too hot for flies and mosquitoes. There were 26 clear days in July and four partly cloudy ones, with less than ¼ inch of rain. August also set new records.

On September 10 there was a free watermelon feed in Blair of shipped-in melons; there were free tickets to ride the merry-go-round and the ferris wheel and free dancing on the street when night came.

Dry as it was here, it was worse in Kansas and everywhere west. Jackrabbits, magpies, and prairie horned larks showed up in numbers. Each morning I could look up the hill and see where the rabbits had eaten more of the damaged corn to get the moist centers of the corn stalks. The magpies and larks disappeared within the next couple of years. We ate the rabbits.

I had plenty of cracked walnuts and beef suet for the chickadees, cardinals, woodpeckers and nuthatches, but only a mixture of foxtail seed, dust, crushed hay leaves and maybe some sweet clover seed which had accumulated over the years on the hayloft floor for the seed eaters. They seemed happy with it and came in flocks. Pheasants had been introduced earlier but there was no hunting season in 1936.

I remember that a new V-8 Ford cost $480 but I doubt if many were sold for cash. Car salesmen scoured the country trying to sell cars on a commission basis.

By fall farmers could get on Works Progress Administration (WPA). Farmers went to town and bought what came to be known as the long handled WPA shovel and they went to work cutting the tops off the steeper hills on the roads for $35 a month. Men who had their own team and a wagon running gear with loose plank bottom and sides hauled the dirt down the hill and got $45. To these old farmers it was back to carrying a lunch pail which they hadn't done since school days.

On December 10 a rain that froze as it fell and then was covered with seven inches of snow kept most folks off the roads for a while.

Before I had the corn planted in the spring of 1937 I ran completely out of feed for the work horses. A neighbor gave me a stack of old wheat straw, two years old. I got a hayrack load of straw which, along with a handful of soybean meal three times a day, helped keep the horses in good shape. I also stopped at each end of the row to let the horses eat the weeds coming up in the fence rows. I had let stand two acres of second year sweet clover, from which I cut hay with a scythe each day when the clover began to bloom. The patch was near the barn so I could carry enough dry hay each day with a fork to fill the mangers.

In closing I will just quote two lines from the old song "Nebraska Land": "We do not live, we only stay. We are too poor to get away."

Neils Miller
Herman, Nebraska

WHO IS THAT WOMAN WITH THE GRAY HAIR AND WRINKLES?

The self-demeaning expression, "Oh, I am just a housewife" didn't count in the days of the thirties. Homemakers had to be a combination of many occupations. Only one with the mentality of an Einstein could cope today under conditions which were prevalent at that time.

We lived on a poor clay farm on a high ridge of hills that crossed the bootheel of southeast Missouri. Fire destroyed the old Victorian house and priceless antique furnishings that had been home to my husband's family since post Civil war days. Without insurance, it was necessary to erect a smaller house.

Large families were normal in those days. My husband was the fifteenth of sixteen children in his family; I was the second of four. Each new addition to the family was embraced with a special love and understanding. As with unexpected company, each new family member forced the homemaker to add another cup of water to the soup.

The summer of '36 was unbearably hot. It seemed as if the windows of heaven were closed and refreshing rains were not forthcoming. The drought caused little demand for chopping field hands for crops such as cotton, corn and potatoes. That work would have supplemented the incomes of rural people.

Lots of calamities came about. I remember the defeated expression on my husband's face when he explained that the horrible stench coming from the spring woodlot pasture was caused by the death from swine plague of several fine brood sows and their babies. I remember how the bitterweeds survived and caused the cows' milk to be unfit for human consumption. Soon the water stored from winter rains in underground cisterns was gone and trips to the spring became an increasing burden. We had to hire huge tank trucks to haul artesian water, purchased from the nearest town. The freshly cleaned cisterns and the good water were so welcome, as were the palm leaf fans the local funeral home gave us.

Some of our neighbors were from Kentucky and had a family "string band"; they urged us to work in the cool of the morning, then relax and try to survive the other hours of the day. At the drop of a hat they became hosts to neighbors at a spring area on their farm. A goat, calf or pig which they had received as payment for playing at some special occasion would be barbecued and lemonade made from the spring water.

That string band, accompanied by our oldest daughter at the piano, practiced their music at our house. Deep into that summer, my usually quiet husband practically shouted for me to count noses, vowing he was going to the local butcher shop and buy that many fresh pork chops. He remarked that he was very tired of makingdo with whatever food was on hand.

Our family and guests, large and small, started to dance and celebrate the occasion; then it struck me that pork chops were about twenty cents a pound and away went our strict budget. Everyone present assisted me in preparing a delicious meal which I am sure was remembered for a very long time.

The forty-hour work week had not come to the rural area yet and our hired hands put in long hours of extra hard labor for the paltry sum of a dollar a day. We were severely criticized because we threw in their noon meal and were accused of ruining the economy in the community.

Our large garden was so parched by the drought that it lent little to our food supply. It was difficult to feed a family and also hired men. I still thank the good Lord for beans. A large white bowl found its way each day at noon to the center of our dining table. It would be filled with beans and strips of sugar cured, smoked pork jowls. The men would stab at those pieces of meat, often declaring "Wow! Another thousandleg* in the beans. Now bring on the onions and cornbread!" I recall making hundreds of pies and fruit cobblers that year. We were thankful for the ample supply of flour, salt, lard and sugaar we had stored for wintertime and the ensuing crop year.

Foods subject to spoiling were kept in huge buckets attached to long ropes let down in an old cistern. When Saturdays came, which were going-to-town days in our area, I was reluctant to hand the grocery list to my husband, because I knew money was in such short supply.

It was for that reason a Sears Roebuck special barber set was ordered because town haircuts had gone up to twenty-five cents each. My inexperienced barber husband cut our little three-year old son's hair but when the child looked in the mirror he was bewildered and decided to finish the job himself. When I found him his beautiful black hair was clipped completely to his skull on the right side. He was so pleased with himself that we didn't have the heart to punish him. However, the barber set was sold the next week just to get it off the farm.

August brought blessed and abundant rains in time to plant and harvest late gardens and truck patches. I recall so vividly the twenty-second day of that August; we had turned the last of the home vineyard grapes into juice and jelly. That was a special day in our lives because our little son was born at home at five that afternoon. This event was followed by a beautiful fall on our Crowley's Ridge where the heavily wooded area put on its finest display of many years.

We had canned hundreds of jars of foods and managed to dry several varieties of beans and peas, as well as the little fruit the drought had left us. Somehow, our forty acres of sweet potatoes had matured and were curing in the huge sawdust-insulated storage barns. We were thankful for the crop but sad that there was no market for them.

Time passed and we realized the Christmas season was near and money was still scarce. We knew our small daughter would receive another member of her doll family, the oldest girl would be glad to receive something in girl-type gifts, but the smaller boys required some thought and preparation. Our problem was partially solved when they dragged home from the community dump some wheels to a discarded little red wagon. We borrowed those wheels for a special project and the boys were so pleased on Christmas morning to find a little green wooden wheelbarrow with a red wheel for each of them.

We were fortunate to have a new truck with a long wheelbase and a stake bed. It was the community's means of transportation. It hauled people, like cattle, everywhere. To church, to town on Saturdays, to Christmas events and Fourth of July celebrations. People waited anxiously at nearly every house and mailbox along the five mile route to town. Many of them were loaded down with eggs in egg crates, cans of cream, gunny sacks of assorted chickens, even butter molded with the usual oak leaf decoration. They were trying to buy a few staples for their family larder. God blessed all of us because we never had a wreck; with that assortment of livestock and humans in such close quarters, a wreck could have been disastrous.

Now, with humble thanks, I look back at those days and my heart quickens when I recall what a heap of living we did under primitive conditions. Many lovely memories and some heartaches are buried deeply in my being. My husband, still slim and trim, is looking forward to his eighty-sixth birthday. That woman with the gray hair and the wrinkles who stares back at me from my mirror—who could she possibly be? It is then I realize that she is the keeper of the secrets of my life. She sighs and remarks "Those were the days."

Virginia Hopkins Stewart
Campbell, Missouri

*In the bootheel of our state, there is a small elongated creature we call a "thousandleg". When unearthed, such as under a decaying plank, it draws its ends together to form a circle. This creature has many, many legs. When the sugar cured pork pieces were cooked, the skin shrunk, causing ends to meet forming a circle. Thus, it was called a "thousandleg" often in our area.

OIL TRASH CAME IN. WE LOCKED OUR DOORS

In May my brother and I were graduated from high school in Baker, Montana and I became engaged to be married.

That winter we had lots of snow so the crops got their first shot of water. From then on it was a matter of carrying water to the garden, the chickens and pumping water for the cattle. Electricity didn't come along for another fifteen years.

Hordes of grasshoppers came too. Anything outside had nips in it, even the clothes on the clothesline. Chickens even got tired of eating the grasshoppers. These were still depression years. Mother and I canned or dried any fruit, vegetables or meat we could get our hands on. Paotatoes and winter vegetables were put in the root cellar. Dad and my brother took a job away from home measuring fields and grain bins for the soil conservation society.

We were a close family, all working on farm projects. Twelve cents a dozen for eggs and a dollar a hundred for potatoes, traded in town, gave us some groceries. Mother and I had many sewing projects, including our own dresses and aprons and things for my hope chest. Marriage was a year and a half away.

Social life in the community consisted of things like dances, where a dollar paid for the music and a lunch for two, card parties in the homes and community hall; young folks pooled cars and went to rodeos, baseball games and picnics at Medicine Rocks, which is now a state park. We had barn dances, fireworks and neighbors visiting neighbors. And we did have fun.

That fall my brother did go to college at Bozeman to study agriculture. My dream was to be a teacher. That fall I worked three days during the Fallon county fair as a waitress and for eight hours work received five dollars. Later I worked at a home in town for three dollars a week and room and board. The lady of the house was away taking care of an ill mother. During this same time my future husband was working for fifty dollars a month and living with his folks.

This was the year that oil drilling equipment came into our area to make the very deep wells. The population of Baker grew rapidly and these people were called "oil trash". Pipe lines went in and people began to lock their doors.

Our Fallon county fair was the last week in August which brought the rural folk to show their produce and hand made articles. My folks were in charge of "Departments". This was the fair where George Guch displayed his steer Montana which weighed 3,980 pounds. It stood six feet high to the middle of its back and is now in Baker's O'Fallon museum. Ekalaka, to the south, is known for having the most mammoth, dinosaur and mastodon in the United States.

So Harry and I were married on October 16, 1937. In 1982 we celebrated our 45th wedding anniversary and shortly after that my husband passed away. This year I was selected senior citizen of the year.

Marion Fost Hanson
Baker, Montana

THE OL' SWIMMIN' HOLE

Once when swimming in the old swimming hole I had old Rover with me. He sat on the bank and watched. Once, in fun, to see what Rover would do, I acted as if I were in trouble and drowning and old Rover jumped in and swam out to me. I grabbed the fur on his shoulder and he turned and swam back to the bank, pulling me with him. I praised him and made a real fuss over him. He wiggled happily and licked my face. He really thought that he had saved me. And I never pulled that trick again. I didn't want him to be fooled.

After that, when we were swimming, no matter how many boys were there, old Rover would always have his eyes on me.

Then when Rover was about ten or twelve years old, a neighbor accused him of killing his sheep. I was sure he was wrong. In fact, he never had any wool in his teeth and whenever I had him out hunting and we came on sheep, he never chased them. But they told me I had to kill him or they would do it. Mom told me to avoid trouble and dispose of him.

I took an old rifle and Rover and I went out, like we were hunting. Rover treed a rabbit in a hole and I shot at the back of his head. But my eyes were so tear filled, I only wounded him. He turned and came running to me, his friend, for comfort. I panicked and, while bawling, fired again, just wounding him again. The poor old fellow cried, looked at me in disbelief and turned to run away from me. My third shot killed him and I sat and cried and cried for hours. I felt like a murderer—almost shot myself, I felt so bad.

Even now at 69 years of age, I have tears, remembering and writing this incident. It seems like only yesterday,

Wasn't that a cruel thing to do to my pal who rescued me from the swimming hole? I have never really forgiven myself for doing that. It was horrible.

Later on we found out that it was the neighbor's dog which was killing their sheep. They said Rover taught their dog to do this but this not true, because Rover and their dog hated each other and always fought when they met, so they sure wouldn't have chased sheep together. Such is life.

Ed Hahn
Oakville, Iowa

ALL HIS LIFE IN ONE COUNTY

I grew up in the dry, hard years, having been born on a farm in the southeast corner of Walker township in Platte county, Nebraska, on March 8, 1915. I was the youngest of six children and only a brother and I were left at home when the thirties rolled around.

When I was a little boy I raised chickens and would sell them in the fall and took out a thousand dollar life insurance policy. It cost me $26.13 a year; I had it about half paid off and the company went broke and I got back $26. That was a disappointing experience for a little boy who had saved his chicken money to pay that premium every year. One year I took my pullets to town and sold them, getting $1.25 each; I thought I was a millionaire that day.

The Lindsay bank went broke and sold Dad out, leaving us with four horses, four cows and our chickens. That's all we had to live on plus the cream and egg money we received weekly.

My folks lived for thirty-two years on the quarter where I was born, but after the dry years turned it back to the Federal Land Bank; when the old place was sold, my folks moved in to St. Edward and my brother and I bought farms, my brother 120 acres and me only 80. If I remember correctly, our home quarter brought $42.50 per acre and the reason my brother didn't buy it was that it required less down payment to buy the 120 acre farm.

I'll never forget those days when the wind would come up and black clouds of dust would fill the air. Sometimes my mother would have to light the old kerosene lamp in the middle of the day.

I think the job I hated the most was having to help Dad burn thistles. The stubble fields would be covered with thistles in those dry years. They would blow into fence lines and those that didn't blow off the fields had to be harrowed to roll them together. Then we'd work with pitchforks getting them into piles to burn; they had to be destroyed before we could plow.

It seemed that year after year the corn would come up and look pretty good until about the fourth of July when the hot winds would arise. In one day the entire corn crop would be shot for another year. I remember one year we cut corn with a grain binder and don't know how we could be so stupid but instead of shocking it and giving it time to dry, we hauled it home and put it in our cow barn; in a few days it was so hot we had to carry it outside because it was smelling like silage. It's a wonder we didn't burn down the barn. Although the stalks looked brown and dry there was still moisture in them and we should have known better—but one lives and learns.

After seeing my folks go through all of those hard years I still grew up wanting to be nothing but a farmer. I married a home girl who grew up just a few miles away and we have lived on the same farm for almost forty-two years, just two miles from where I was born. The farm has been good to us and at seventy-two I still have a few hogs around and just bought six brown Swiss steers to make into pets. When they're fat I'll have one butchered and share with our children.

My advice to young folks is if you love the farm, try your best to be a farmer. It wasn't easy back then and isn't easy now, but can still be done. I see many young couples making it today in spite of all the negative things you read.

I have happy memories of walking to and from school with my schoolmates. I went to a one-room country school and one year remember there were forty-two of us and one teacher taught all eight grades—and we never missed a class. I have this old school on my place now and walk in there to look at those walls and think of all the happy times I had there. A little boy standing up in front saying his first recitation and the happy community club meetings we used to have monthly. I went all my twelve years together with just one neighbor girl, to this Palestine country school through the eighth grade, then to Looking Glass country school through ninth and tenth and then we graduated together at St. Edward high school. Not many country kids can say they went all twelve years together. We had a good visit at an open house birthday party of her sister and husband's eightieth and ninetieth birthdays very recently. There were a lot of good years in there.

Donald Benson
St. Edward, Nebraska

I SAW A GROWN MAN CRY

B. J. was the neighbor man who farmed Mom's little farm and was practically an adopted Dad to me. I followed him everywhere and learned a lot of wisdom from him.

He broke all of his own colts to harness and they always turned out to be good, dependable, sensible horses. One day when I was around eleven years old, I tagged along to a timber stand he owned where he was going to load some saw logs he had previously cut. This was in the winter time and he was using the bobsled running gears with stakes in the bolster pockets to hold the logs in place.

To load these logs he cut two poles, ten to twelve feet long and six to eight inches in diameter and laid them up to the bolsters of the sled; the logs were to roll up this makeshift ramp. He tied one end of a log chain to the front of the sled coupling pole and one end to the back of the coupling pole. Then he rigged up a series of chains in a manner too complicated to try to explain here; then he took Old Belle, a big black mare, and hooked her to the chains.

My job was to lead Old Belle and she would pull and roll these logs up the pole ramp onto the sled. The Y effect kept the logs running straight so one end did not get ahead of the other.

All went well until we got to the last log. By then the ramp was steeper, because he had to raise the ends to the top of the loaded logs. The pile was simply getting higher.

This log was a large one, plus it had a bad knot where a limb had not been trimmed close to the log. Almost at the top, the log caught on the knot, which threw Old Belle off balance; her front feet slipped from under her and she went down on her knees.

B.J. was using a cant hook trying to help get the log to roll but when Belle fell the log came back and caught his leg. It had him pinned between the log and one of the ramp poles.

He was in terrible pain as it was almost breaking his leg. I will never forget how he screamed at Belle, saying 'Belle, come on, get-get-get.' I think Belle sensed the frantic urgency in her master's voice because she regained her footing and then with supreme all-out lunges she jerked the log off his leg and it rolled into place atop the load.

I believe that Old Belle knew more about what she was supposed to do than I did. She completely ignored me, standing to one side, hanging to the lead strap, and acted solely to the command of her master.

When the log was safely in place and B.J. could hobble on his leg again, the first thing he did, was walk over to where Old Belle stood, put his arms around her neck and buried his face in her mane, talking praising, soothing words to her. She stood there, arching her head, with her ears forward, seemingly accepting his thanks.

The point is to emphasize the comradeship that existed between a man and his animals, providing of course that the animals had been treated with love and kindness all their lives, which these had. Sometimes a man's very life depended on the obedience and faithfulness of his horses.

The following summer this same B.J. was in the timber dragging some logs upwards from a steep hillside. He was using a team called Dan and Dick. Dan was a big sorrel horse he had bought to replace one which had died. He was inclined to be a very nervous animal and when he pulled on these logs he would go all out.

We had just hooked the chain to this big log and Dan had been dancing and prancing, raring to go. When B.J. said 'Get up' Dan grabbed the bit in his teeth and charged up the hill dragging the log and his team-mate along. In fact Dick could hardly keep up and B.J. couldn't even guide them. Suddenly about at the top of the hill, Old Dan slumped down on his knees. B.J. went up to see what was wrong and Dan gave a couple of gasps and was dead.

B.J. sat down and stroked Dan's head and cried. Dan had died from a heart attack.

B.J. then told me to run back home and get old Bud out of the barn. I was only a about eleven years old but was I thrilled that B.J. needed me to do a job. He told me, just put Bud's collar and bridle on him and he'd use Dan's harness. So I hurried to his place, about a mile away. I put Bud's collar on him. It was a job because he was a big bay horse and I was just a kid. But Bud was a gentle animal and even put his head down for me to put the bridle on him. Then I led him to the trough, let him have a drink of water, led him to a gate, which I climbed up and slid onto his back. We then rode the mile back to the timber.

B.J. had succeeded in getting the harness off and from under Dan but when Bud saw Dan laying there, he snorted and didn't want to go closer. He sensed death and it bothered him. But B.J. calmed him and put Dan's harness on him, adjusted it and then hitched Bud and Dick together; they dragged Dan up to level ground where the rendering company truck could load him and haul him away.

I could remember Mom always used to tell me, whenever I would hurt myself and cry 'Now, don't cry; be a man. Men don't cry'. But I saw a tough, hardened big man cry that day when Dan died. If anything, I had more respect for B. J. than than I did before. He showed he was human and had a deep love for his animals.

There was an old saying around our area; it was that a man who beats his animals will probably be a wife beater too.

I'm glad I had a chance to know B.J.

Ed Hahn
Oakville, Iowa

ONE END ALWAYS FELL SHORT

We had many experiences during the dirty thirties. For seven years we didn't raise a grain of any kind. Well, we did raise some fodder that made feed of a very poor grade for the cattle but we had to buy shipped in hay and grain. We had to sell most of our cattle; steers only brought six dollars a head.

My sister and I hauled twenty milk cows, a young bull and our saddle horse to Wakita, Oklahoma (just south of the Kansas border) where there was wonderful wheat pasture.We stayed from December to the next September; we milked those cows and sold the cream to pay for our pasture bill and living expenses. Our father was bedfast and asked us to return home because he was not improving, so we returned, hiring someone to haul our twenty cows back home. Father passed away soon, on September 9.

We had a rough time trying to make ends meet. It seemed like one end always fell short.

The rains came, the weeds grew, and we lost several cattle from weed poisoning. Then the grass grew and things were better for a while.

The fences had blown full of weeds and then the blown dirt drifted in to cover the posts and wire. Cattle could walk over the fences and go any place they wanted, looking for food. We had made a let-down in our fence so they could go through to 160 acres of grassland which no one farmed.

One beautiful day our twelve-year old boy mounted his pony and went to round up the cattle for the evening. He had only been gone a short time when

I noticed the sky becoming very dark. In just a few moments the dust had blocked out the sun and I could see only a few rods distance.

It was perfectly calm but very dark. I lighted the lantern and went to the road, where I called the cattle. Soon I could hear them bawling. The boy had rounded up the cattle but had lost his way to the let-down, and was trying to drive them in the wrong direction. They just milled around until they could hear me calling; then they headed for the let-down and the boy followed along behind. Those cattle weren't so dumb.

Fern Pounds
Elmwood, Oklahoma

I WENT THROUGH THE THIRTIES WITH NOTHING AND STILL HAVE MOST OF IT LEFT

One of my goals in the early thirties was to ride in a car that travelled a mile a minute. My first such ride was in 1935 in a new DeSoto owned by a railroad man. Farmers couldn't afford such a vehicle. He also had one of those things with two large steel balls that in some way kept food cool without ice.

We had a Sinclair oil pump station at Ponemah. The man who ran the station could put two pieces of iron together with a bright light.

The teacher kept telling us we should fear the Russians. I wonder today if that was a planted story to protect this country from going communist during the depression.

I always looked forward to the threshing season and the fifty cents a day I received for hauling water for the men to drink. I had a pony and cart. It was through this experience that I learned all water doesn't taste like the water at home.

We had an old threshing machine and when they went from steam power to motor power the old machine kept breaking down, prolonging the harvest. I put my jugs, cart and pony in a labor day parade wih a sign 'Ponemah Threshing Company — Only Part That Runs'. I won first prize, a weeks wages of three dollars. Cloud nine, move over.

When the Country Gentleman magazine subscription came due the folks didn't have money but we did have chickens. They were running a special — three hens for a year's subscription. Dad, being knowledgeable about laying hens, gave the man three sitting hens. The next day the man was back. They couldn't take barebacks which was a sign the hens wouldn't lay any eggs for quite a while.

We country kids alway wore bib overalls. I can't remember seeing blue jeans until the late thirties. My bib pocket always had a few sticks of chewing gum in there. In the thirties a trip to the country grocery store meant the clerk would go to the brown sugar barrel and hand us a lump of hard brown sugar. Oh, how good it was. But it didn't give us the security that a bib pocket of gum provided.

It was a mile and a half of mud road to the store at Ponemah, Illinois (which lives today only in memories). My dad lost a tire chain in the mud track. We took three pitchforks and walked that road for two days; it was the second day before we found that chain. It never occurred to us that someone might have found it without telling us.

In those days you didn't say you have to go to the restroom. You said 'I have to empty my ash pan'.

Kids would come to school with the strangest odors. One family of transients lived in a tent in a willow swamp. They made willow furniture that they peddled. They skipped many Saturday night baths. One of their girls, named Billie, was in my class. Several years ago there was a fist person story in Reader's Digest telling of a person's life travelling from one willow swamp to another making willow furniture with her family — and her name was Billie. I still wonder if it was the same girl.

We were close to the main east-west line of the Santa Fe railroad. Barnstormers used it for navigation. You could hear those planes coming and going for a long time. I remember seeing pilots sitting out in the open in planes with no fuselage.

Several times a year gypsies came through with their wagon trains. They camped several days in our neighborhood, right on the roadbank. We kids were kept inside like all the rest of the farm animals.

There wasn't a week went past without several tramps stopping for a handout or permission to sleep in the barn. Some pushed all their earthly belongings in a wheelbarrow with a steel wheel. My mother made a nice ham sandwich for a tramp one day but then saw him go behind a shed. After he left they found he had trimmed all the fat from his ham. Dad didn't think he was hungry for wasteing that good fat because Dad ate that kind of stuff all his 86 years of life.

We always went to town on Saturday night with our radio wet battery and brought home a recharged one. Also when we went to town we took the chickens or little pigs that had died and threw them off at a timbered area for the wolves. The Model T had a space between fender and hood that would hold a gunny sack with the dead offerings. One time I remember Dad forgot to discard the sack on the way to town and people turned their heads as we drove down Main street, wondering the source of that smell.

Yes, I went through the thirties with nothing and still have most of it left.

Bill Gullberg
Stronghurst, Illinois

MOVING OUT OF NEBRASKA

On a farm about four miles northwest of St. Paul, Nebraska, the summer of 1936, for example, was a memorable one. The soil on our farm was sandy so when the dust storms blew in sand would really fly. It would get into one's food no matter how well it was covered.

Temperatures were usually in the hundreds. It was so hot that chickens would squawk when walking across the hot sandy yard, as their feet were burned. When we fed the dog he would move his bowl into the shade.

Most farming was done with horses in those days but they had to be worked with caution in order not to overheat them. They would grain shock after sundown because it was impossible to work in the hot sun.

There was no electricity on the farms at that time, which meant no refrigerators, no cooling systems. Food had to be kept in caves. At night people slept outdoors whenever possible. Many slept with wet sheets over their sleeping area in order to put moisture in the air, for better breathing.

Some days there was no breeze at all so the windmill didn't pump the well to fill the cattle tank. Hence the herd of about thirty cattle on our farm had to be watered by hand-pumping the tank full. At times the thirsty cattle would fight to get a drink. That year the government offered to pay $30 a head for cattle and ship them to some southern states.

After years of drought, along with the depression, many of our neighbors moved to other states. My family moved to Arkansas, abandoning 240 good acres. Others we knew moved to California, New York, Missouri and Iowa. They moved as portrayed in the movie 'The Grapes of Wrath' which was just the way it was.

Rose Aschenbrenner
Mukwonago, Wisconsin

BLACK SUNDAY'S WIND BROKE WIND GUAGES

I remember that Black Sunday, April 14, 1935.

I was celebrating my birthday with a group of young people and parents who had come home with us from church. I was spending the weekend with my parents at home five miles southeast of May, Oklahoma.

After dinner two carloads of us drove in to town to attend graduation services at the high school. The wind had gone down and it became very still — stifling, hot and sultry. In those days, before airconditioning, all the windows were open, but no air circulated. The speaker didn't arrive on time and everyone was restless and milling around outside watching the sky. There was an anticipation of disaster in the air and everyone was nervous. Some even went home.

The speaker was late, having been lost on unmarked highways. The ceremony was over about four o'clock and it was still hot and threatening. No one had been able to keep his mind on the speaker. We were hoping for rain but afraid at the same that we would get a devastating hailstorm. One extreme usually followed another when it had been so very dry.

When I arrived home I stopped the car by the back door. My folks had just arrived from a funeral. The wind had turned to the north and we could see it rolling tward us at a terrific speed, like a prairie fire — except there was no fire. Then it became still and black; it was rolling and boiling and the air was full of static electricity. And, since we lived on a high hill, we could see it coming three miles away.

My father was changing clothes to do chores before the storm reached us. I remember telling Dad it was coming fast and asked if I should put the car away. He said he would do it as soon as he could get his shoes on.

I looked again and said 'You don't have time. It's here right now!' And it was upon us.

The wind was so strong that we heard later it had broken the wind guages. Birds had flown in front of it, rabbits scurried to get out of its path. We could hear their frightened calls. It was terrifying. When it hit, everything became very still and we were enveloped in this terrible blackness. We couldn't see our hand in front of our face. Some people thought they had been struck blind. Of course we were all frightened but there was nothing we could do. My girl friend and I were watching from the north window; we grabbed each other and put our heads down. I felt my time had come and expected to be blown away. It was an erie feeling. It was so pitch dark that I couldn't even see the outline of my grandmother who was sitting by an east window.

I wanted to light a lamp but my father said 'No, better not even strike a match'.

I have no idea how long the blackness lasted, but it seemed an eternity. Some say about an hour before the worst was over. As the eye passed over us the wind remained in the north behind it. It was morning before it finally cleared. Everything was covered with dirt and dust.

We decided we were all right and began to check with our neighbors. The ones that were caught in their cars were quite shook up, saying the car lights couldn't penetrate that darkness. They had to stop and sit it out beside the road.

I doubt that anyone living will ever forget that black Sunday. I'm in my eighties and I can still see that black cloud rolling in.

That is just one part of what I remember about the dirty thirties, following the Great Depression with the stock market crash of 1929. Going back in time, I was a young school teacher at the time of the crash and getting $100 a month and sending myself to summer school to keep my two-year certificate renewed and working toward a lifetime certificate. I was teaching at Kokomo, a rural school near Beaver, Oklahoma.

In the fall of 1929 I had obtained the first and second grade at my home town of May with wages of $90 a month. Although I was only five miles from home, we were required to board in the district and to take part in community affairs. Our board and room took one third of our wages.

Teachers were a dime a dozen at that time and rules were very rigid. If you wanted to keep your job you had to be an example for children to follow. No smoking, drinking, dancing or card playing- and church attendance was a must. No going with high school students either. These rules were written in your contract.

Children were taught to respect their parents and teachers. There were no discipline problems.

By the school year of 1930–1931 the drought and depression were beginning to be felt, so teachers wages were cut to $85; then by 1932–1933 we were hired for $75 and before spring we were cut to $60 — and there wasn't even money to pay that amount. That was before state aid. We were given warrants in five and ten dollar units. We traded them for our needs if we could find someone willing to do so. They weren't redeemed for five years.

By that time President Roosevelt had started the WPA and all the men were trying to get jobs on the roads; those with good teams of horses had the best chances. They were willing to do anything to feed their families. The drought was getting very bad by 1933.

I had taught at May for four years and needed a change. I tried to get into a nursing school, a life-long dream, but it was full for the year so I moved to the Luther Hill community and taught the primary grades there. I boarded with a young couple named Turner and Margaret Barret. They lived a mile north of the school house and I walked to and fro school.

The wind blew in hurricane force many days. One day it blew from the south and the next from the north. It was so strong some days I could hardly stand up. The dust blew and blew. By the time I reached school I needed a bath. My eyes were full and my teeth gritty. It blew sand in the fence rows and many were completely buried. Wherever there was a thistle or a piece of machinery, it was soon covered. I remember we had to scoop the sand and dust out of our attic at home. It got so full it was causing the plaster to fall. Nothing was tight enough to keep it out. There was no moisture that winter that I can recall now.

The Barrets house was old with windows and doors that didn't fit very tightly; after the frost that year, there wasn't much to stop the wind. The sand and dust blew in until there was sand in the water bucket, a coating of dust on the water. There was no such thing as running water, indoor plumbing or electricity. So before each meal someone had to get fresh water from the well.

We stuffed rags in the windows to help keep out the dirt. Some times gunny sacks were opened and either dipped in old tractor oil or wet with water, and tacked over the windows to keep out as much dirt as possible.

The beds and furniture were covered with sheets and we had to shake the sheets before we could go to bed on bad days. Some times it was necessary to wet a washcloth and lay over our nose to breathe.

As spring came it got worse. We cooked and had to wait to clean the table until the last minute. Then we hurriedly set it and ate before the food got gritty. I sincerely hope we never see another drought like that one. It was if we had moved to the desert.

There was a field just west of the school house where the wind blew very powerfully. The owner tried to keep it from blowing by using a lister. The next morning the ridges were level and he'd try it again with the lister. Soon he gave it up entirely. (Ed.: A lister is 'a double-moldboard plow often equipped with a subsoil attachment and used mainly where subsoil is limited.' (Webster))

Dust clouds would sometimes make it so dark that the buses would come by noon to pick up the children in order to get them home before the early dark. Sometimes the wind would go down with the sun, for which we were thankful. The roads would drift like snow with sand and it was a trial at times for the buses to get through.

I remember one occasion when the wind shook open a north window in the school. A pint jar on the window sill was half full of sand the next morning. Our school books would be so covered with dust that we had to brush them repeatedly.

Food became short for people and livestock. The government shipped in hay by carloads and the men lined up for their quotas. Then the government started giving out commodities which gave people something to eat. Schools began receiving canned meat and children would bring a few vegetables, mostly potatoes, and the hot lunches were born. We got an old coal oil stove and someone brought a washboiler in which we cooked our stew.

The government sent crews to kill the cattle and hogs because there was no feed for them. They paid a small fee for each one killed. People followed the crews and butchered the better cattle, taking the meat home to can. It wasn't prime beef by any means but we were grateful to have it. That was about the time of the great exodus from western Oklahoma, the times John Steinbeck describes in 'The Grapes of Wrath'. Some went to California. Others to Washington, Oregon and Arkansas.

Through it all, however, there was a closeness and companionship in the community that does not exist today. There was no money to go to shows, so we had parties, programs and the church held every one together. There was faith in God and your neighbors and faith that the rains would come. There was no money so we were all equal. We enjoyed what we had and life was good. We shared what we had.

Those that stayed and hung onto their land were far better off than those who gave up. It wasn't easy trying to pay mortgages and interest. My folks were among the stayers and saved their land — and passed it down to me. They worked like slaves to do it and I have worked too. We didn't hire our work done but did it with old machinery and every penny saved went for interest.

The rains finally came. It took several years to get the land back into production. In recent years we have had abundant rain and we Oklahomans produce top quality wheat, cattle and feed. People have been planting grasses and fertilizing and we can grow almost anything as long as we have rain because our soil is good. There are many things to tell and a lot we don't want to remember.

Thelma Bemount Campbell
Woodward, Oklahoma

CAN'T REMEMBER ANY GREEN GRASS

These are the memoirs of a young girl born in 1927 in northwest Oklahoma, and I still live there. In 1934–1936 I was seven to nine years old.

Although we lived in town we had about a mile to walk to school. We'd start for school, the sky would be red and Mama would say 'The dirt is here but not the wind — but it's coming.' She would bundle us up, tie our heads on, and a handkerchief around our mouths and noses. She was right; the wind would be there before we reached school.

Many times it blew for days and never stopped. We had to brace ourselves against the wind. Oh, how the sand stung our legs, hands and whatever part of our face that showed. Sometimes we almost had to guess where were were walking. We would run into each other. It's a good thing that those were the days with little traffic or we would have been run down. Lots of times we walked backwards to school.

When we reached school and took off our wraps, including the handkerchiefs from our faces, we were a sight. The bottom part of our faces were white and the upper part red with dirt.I don't think I was ever clean, even though we tried. The teacher would come to our desks with a big blue lard can and we would scoop the sand off our desks with our hands, into the can. Our shoes crunched in the sand on the floor.

I don't remember green grass or flowers during that entire period. You did not see much grow except for trees. I remember Chinese elms with not many leaves because the sand would cut them off.

Car windshields were pitted badly by the sand. I remember going to Grandma's house in the country and sometimes the sand would be drifted across the road so badly we would be forced to turn around and go back home. That sand drifted over fences and farm machinery.

The poor animals I remember seeing standing in the protection of a shed, or a tree, their backs to the wind, their ribs showing. I wonder now where they ever got any food. What did they eat? I can't remember a single field with even weeds in it.

I don't know how people survived — but they did — and they stayed.

No home was immune to the sand. I remember sand in my bed. It got in no matter what was done. My mother tried to be a good house keeper; I remember her putting sheets over the windows and I can still see the red sheets over the windows and the red dirt in the bathtub. Every day it was there. On the floor — on the tables — on the cabinets — everywhere.

I remember what we called and still remember as 'Black Sunday'. All across the north horizon as far as we could see was this horrible black cloud, rolling and rolling as it came toward us. People saw it and were horrified. The wind was behind it and I remember I was scared to death, as my Daddy said 'I think it's dirt'. I thought the world was coming to an end as it got as dark as at night. The chickens went to bed. It truly was nothing but dirt with the wind behind it and the birds flying in front of it.

As I look back and remember the sand in my eyes, the dread of walking to school, the sting of it all, I guess I would not have lived anywhere else but here. I still love the hills, the canyons, the red dirt that I call paprika. It's all beautiful and I remember that home is where the heart is. We still have the wind but with good ground cover we don't have the sand.

In addition, today we have beautiful wheat fields and cattle and oil and gas wells — on those same old sand hills. And we have the friendliest people in the whole word — right here in Oklahoma.

Bonnie Reid
Woodward, Oklahoma

THE DIRTY THIRTIES IN HAPPY, T

On April 14, 1935, a Sunday afternoon, we had invited friends
with us on the farm. They were leaving about three o'clock to return to ⌐_
As we looked toward the west we could see a terrible dust storm coming. Although we were used to the 'bluster' as we called them, this one was different
and even I, a twelve year old, knew that the world was coming to an end.

A photoraph of that terrible cloud is attached to this story.

The friends left for home and my daddy ran to the barn to put the cows inside,
because they were our living. Mother, sister and I went to our concrete cellar.
There was a rope on the door to hold it down when the wind was so strong and
it was all we could do to keep it closed. We kept listening for my daddy to knock
so he could get in. It seemed like an eternity. I knew that I'd never see him alive
again — and prayed harder than I had ever prayed before.

As the storm came closer, it became dark as it is at night. I can't remember
how long the storm lasted but it is something that has stayed with me all of these
years. I am thankful I have never experienced anything like it since.

We lived three miles northeast of Happy, Texas, and I remember the big
snows that usually blocked all of the east-west roads. There was very little
equipment to open the roads. My father had one big John Deere tractor on lugs
instead of tires; it also had a flywheel that had to be turned fast enough to start
the motor. Since my memory fails me 57 years later, I am guessing that shovels
were used to open the roads.

There were no school buses. My father thought it very necessary that we not
miss any classes. Also we had to get to Happy daily because we sold bottled fresh
milk to houses and cafes. The milk had to be delivered daily because there was
no refrigeration.

Every farm family planted gardens during the summer months and would
can fruits and vegetables for the winter months. Neighbors would share, so
there was always a good variety of fruits and vegetables.

During winter months neighbors would bring their hogs to one farm and kill
them. It was a whole day affair. The men started fires under washpots in the
yard; the women got the utensils ready in the kitchens to take care of insides
such as heart, liver and intestines in which to pack sausage.

After the hogs were killed and hung up, the boiling water was poured on the
carcasses. The men would then start removing the hair by scraping and cut the
parts of the body to make sausage. These were cut into pieces, seasoned and the
grinding began. Some families used intestines and others used cloth sacks. The
hams, shoulders and bacon sides were blocked; the spices rubbed on and the
pieces packed away until they were properly seasoned.

Calves were also slaughtered. Usually one or two families would share a beef
since no refrigeration was available. The hind-quarters were wrapped in old

⌐ and hung on the windmill towers high enough so animals couldn't reach
⌐n. The front-quarters were usually canned in large jars or crock pots.

The good memories were of the times in summer when we were older. The
girls would go home with us after church. Then town boys would ride their
horses on Sunday afternoon and mother would always have goodies ready and
waiting.

Our lives were centered around our church, the Methodist church South, for
our recreation. Our father was chairman of the stewards and was very active,
insisting we attend all church activities.

There were very few school parties except at Valentine Day and Christmas.
Valentines were home-made from purchased construction paper. Occasionally
some one had a white lace doily to use for special people.

In 1935 a community band was organized; as more students became interested, the adults quit. The parents were real boosters. They took us to practice
at night and helped buy capes and caps. Our band road on a special train to
attend the Texas Centennial in 1936 in Dallas and stayed in 'tent city' on the
fair grounds. I remember it rained a lot while we were there and, since the
grounds were not paved, our black riding boots were in a terrible condition.
We had Happy on our military caps and people would say 'We know you are
happy, but where are you from?'

Again, in 1939, our band was invited to attend the Cotton Bowl in Dallas.
By this time we had bought Uncle Sam uniforms and were pretty flashy. Since
money was scarce, if a family had two students in the band, the school would
buy the uniform for the second family member.

Our top hats were partly home-made. We took Panama-style straw hats and
made them higher by adding cardboard; then they were covered with white
cloth and a blue band with white stars sewn on the band.

Happy's Uncle Sam Band seemed to become the official band of Amarillo.
We led the parade down Polk street there when President Franklin D. Roosevelt
visited there. We were the official band when Eleanor Roosevelt was a special
guest in town Mother-in-Law day. I remember that it rained and out cardboard
hats were droopy. On another occasion our band ate breakfast with Postmaster
General James A. Farley when he came to town.

I sadly remember one Sunday morning in the spring of 1934 when we arrived
at church a little early after delivering the milk. The windows in the basement
were blackened and broken because of a fire. Because there were so few tele-
phones we had not heard of this sad event. It was a tragedy because the two story
building had been started in 1930 but, because of the depression, could not be
finished until late in 1931. Dedicated members were determined to have a
beautiful church. Although I am no longer a member of that church, to me it
is a memorial to my father who worked so hard to complete the building, and
then to rebuild it, as he continued to serve as chairman of the stewards.

Dust Storm approaching Happy, Texas, April 14, 1935. Photographer unknown. (*Photo courtesy Maurine Allison, Happy, Texas.*)

During those days people couldn't buy everything they needed and had to rely on their neighbors for help, which made the community really close. So money can be both a blessing or a curse.

In the later thirties times were better, farm prices were higher and we are better people today because of those terrible depression years.

Maurine Prewitt Allison

DRY-LAND FARMING

The question 'What were you doing in 1936?' surely brought back memories of the years I spent on the prairies of Colorado.

I was born near Hugo, Colorado, in 1915 on a small farm. There were three boys and three girls in our family. My father was a small farmer but when I was seven we moved to Denver for three years on a three acre orchard in Wheatridge.

But my Dad was really a dry-land farmer, so we moved to eastern Colorado on a farm of 160 acres. It was still prairie land. Everywhere there were ground squirrels, rabbits, hawks, coyotes, rattlesnakes and occasionally a herd of antelope travelled through the country. All the land was flat; we could see for miles and not see anything. Cactus bloomed in the spring and we learned to enjoy them when they bloomed. Sand was everywhere and, oh, the dust storms were terrible.

A lot of our fences would be covered with sand, so much so that we could walk over them as if they were drifted with snow.

Our dinner plates were always turned over on the table and then covered with a cloth. The men wore either red and white or blue and white farmer's handkerchiefs over their faces when working outside.

The bank gave my father loans to keep him going through the years.

I went to the town of Brush to have my first baby in 1936. While laying in the hospital I would need a wet cloth over my face to keep from breathing in the dust that sifted throughout the room. When they brought my meals into me I could taste the dust. There would be a fog of dust throughout the room. But we all survived those conditions.

In 1986 my youngest son took me on a tour through that country and I just couldn't believe all the history and how the brave and steadfast people worked those farms, and still have laughter and fun.

None of my children, nor grandchildren nor great grandchildren will really understand all the hard work and no money that all of us went through.

What an experience!

Mrs. Opal L. Checketts
Santaquin, Utah

THERE WERE CHISELERS THEN TOO

I am a transplant from western South Dakota to Wisconsin after World War II but was in Perkins county in 1936 after the stock crash in 1929; it was bad until after the war was over in 1945.

The grasshoppers were so thick here that they shut light out from the sky, ate paint off houses, clothing off clothes lines, would make a corn field look like a field of broom sticks in a single day. The wind would blow the Russian thistles all over until they were stopped at a fence line. Then the dust would cover them so solidly that you could walk right over the fence. They had to use road graders to get the dust off the highways where it would drift like snow. Also it was impossible to keep that dust out of a house; it would even come through the key hole in the door and it was a constant chore to keep a home clean.

War clouds were forming in Europe and I was lucky to work for $3 a week from 4 A.M. to 8 P.M. on a farm. I took whatever job I could get, most of them not lasting very long. A lot of people were working for their board and room, driving a truck, working on ranches or the railroad, until WPA came along. Soon the majority were on it. It was not easy going but somehow we survived. Then I got a break and got the job of commodity supervisor of Perkins county, giving out the food that the government sent through the state. My job was to bag and get it to the clients. There were several different kinds of commodities: dry milk, grapefruit, prunes, cabbage, butter, fish and in the winter of 1936 we received seven carloads of potatoes.

I had 500 clients among whom I was supposed to divide the food and it wasn't easy. There were many times when I bit my lip to keep from telling off some of them who were chiselers because there were chiselers then just as there are now.

The WPA did a lot of different kinds of work—building roads, the women making clothing, overalls for boys and dresses for women, and baby clothes. One woman got a layette and changed her baby right then in the office.

Railroads were loaded with people going from Milwaukee or Chicago to the west coast to pick hops and if you have ever talked with one of them you know how they existed. When the train stopped in a city the cops were right there to keep them on the train, sending them on to the next town. They would do anything for a meal, going from house to house to do some kind of work, like washing windows, chopping wood, beating rugs.

Among the memories I won't forget were our sources of entertainment— dances and sports.

Charles E. Connery
Menasha, Wisconsin

IN PRAISE OF MY FATHER

If he were still alive, my father, David L. Harmon, would no doubt smile at my limited recognition of the problems that followed the '29 crash, because he was involved in everything in our community, from projects to bring about improvements in farm to market roads, to rural telephone services, rural electrification, livestock improvement, sanitary milk production, the American Farm Bureau, church and school activities.

As a boy of fourteen, growing up on the ancestral homestead seven miles north of Chester, Illinois, I was fortunately permitted to accompany Dad on some of his travels and missions.

I was aware that money was short because I often heard Dad and his friends discussing the troubles people were having with paying mortgage notes and that the banks didn't have money to lend to people already in debt. Farm foreclosure sales became very common yet none of our immediate neighbors lost their farms. When school chums started losing their homes, I wondered about ours. When the banks began to close I asked Dad if we would lose our farm, since the bank had $33.15 of my own savings. He assured me that we would last through the situation.

Dad always seemed to have money to pay for the livestock and machinery he bought at these sales. Or for the buildings he wanted for salvage, or the land he needed in spite of depressed market prices. He later explained to me that his cash position was adequate at the time of the crash and, since he had no debts, the bank readily provided loan money for him to purchase grossly undervalued livestock, land, grain and machinery.

We had little need for cash because, like all other farm people, we raised everything except our clothing which was cheap anyway. We did need to buy a few staples, such as salt, coffee and sugar. Mother quickly created substitutes for cornflakes, oatmeal and white flour. Dad simply started up the hammermill and began processing cornmeal and red-dog flour, a mixture of flour and bran. Honey became a table substitute for sugar. We had poultry and eggs galore, berries and fruits in season and Mother canned a hundred quarts or more of each vegetable and fruit—and the smokehouse was filled with sugar-cured hams, bacon, sausages and quarters of beef. Plus there was always an abundance of pecans and black walnuts. Milk, cream and butter simply came with the dairy operation.

Everyone in the community ate well and I really doubt that anyone suffered from lack of food. Giving away a ham, a side of bacon, raw fruits and vegetables, a dozen fryers, even several quarts of canned fruits and vegetables was a routine as daily gossip between friends. It wasn't charity: it was just being neighborly.

Here are some prices I remember: eggs three cents a dozen; hogs weighing from 180 to 250 pounds sold for a nickle a pound; cattle brought about six cents a pound but the farmer paid 25 cents per cwt (hundredweight) to truck them to the St. Louis stockyards, plus a two cent per pound commission; wheat was 25 to 40 cents per bushel depending on quality; ear corn as little as 15 cents; raw milk went for 50 cents per cwt and 25 cents of that went for transportaion. Work overalls were 75 cents; a blue work shirt, 65 cents; a pair of good work shoes, a dollar; good dress shoes, $1.50 to $2.50—and we replaced soles with cowhide; a boy's dress suit $6 and a man's $12. Calico yard goods from three to eight cents a yard; thread two cents a spool; white sugar $2.00 per cwt; gasoline was seven cents without tax—we always collected the tax rebate because we had the only tractor in the community; 22 calibre cartridges were 15 cents a box of 50; shotgun shells were 75 cents a box of 25. Rabbits were worth five cents each so you could convert a 75 cent box of shotgun shells into $1.25 worth of rabbits for a cool profit of 50 cents.

As a night hunter and a trapper, I sold furs for spending money. Opossums bought as much as 80 cents, skunks from 25 cents to $3.00, raccoons from $4.50 to $7.00, mink pelts as much as $9.00 (but I never got one).

Dad also knew timber and made money buying, logging and selling it at a profit. He also bought and salvaged buildings sold at distressed prices and then erected other buildings. We even bought beef cattle at distressed prices, fed them on corn and hay bought at distressed prices and sold them at a profit eight to twelve months later. Being an old horse trader he even bought wild horses from Wyoming ranges by the carload at prices ranging from $22 to $40 each; we broke them to the saddle and harness and sold them six months later at prices ranging from $80 to $125. Despite the hard times, Dad managed to make money consistently.

Trading became the basis of exchange and everybody pitched in to help when problems arose. We traded labor and balanced up using a minimum of cash money but, as I said, we didn't need cash very often.

There was entertainment during those hard times too. Movies were five cents for kids and fifteen cents for adults; the Opry House plays cost a dime for kids and 25 to 50 cents for adults; admission to the county fair was 25 cents for adults and kids were free. Admission to the Saturday night dance (like a barn dance) was 25 cents. If one had money, and wanted to spend it, those were the places to go. For others, the country store was a nightly meeting place for men who wanted to do business, play cards, or just visit. Churches were evening meeting places for young people and adults, for summer revivals and socials.

I don't recall there being more than three radios in our community. Two were in the country store and the third in our home. The church and the country store were the regular focal points of social contact throughout the week and had no competition. Country folks rarely attended the movies or Opry in town and only the young adults went to Saturday night dances and then only selectively because a long hard day's work on the farm didn't leave much surplus energy for a night at the dance hall.

Nevertheless, we really believed we were living the good life even though we had very little money to spend. When we were given 25 or 50 cents to spend at the annual church picnic for ice cream, fish ponds, grab bags, we were completely happy, because that's about all any one received. Greased pig races, kid games, baseball games, basket dinners and musical entertainment made the day for all of us and the church always made money.

Yes, I know they were hard times, but plenty of good things happened too. Thanks to Dad and his supporters, Governor Henry Horner approved Dad's Shawneetown Trail road request which resulted in an all-weather (gravel) road through New Palestine to connect Illinois route 3 to route 150 which, for the first time in history, got us out of the mud. Another of Dad's projects, the R.E.A., was approved and brought electricity and good lighting into our community. Through his leadership and personal drive, the country telephone system was upgraded to provide long distance service. He was also able to establish a regular market for milk with the Sanitary Milk Producers which brought better milk prices to the farmers. And, yes, he did manage to make a little money throughout the worst of the depression. This was due to his entrepreneural skills and drive.

Although I'm sure there were times when he was puzzled about what was happening in government, I'm quite sure he never doubted for a moment that the U.S. government would find a way to restore the economy. As a result, he chose to bet everything he had on a successful outcome, and he strongly voiced that opinion to every one who sought his advice. A man of strong personal convictions at all times, the deterioration of conditions only served to strengthen his confidence in his own judgment concerning the eventual outcome.

Coal mining areas to the north and east of us did suffer noticeable unemployment. My little world came through the worst without serious hurt for which we were most thankful and grateful. East St. Louis, 60 miles to the north of us, and the large cities, experienced real suffering, especially during the bitter winters. Having seen their cardboard shantytowns and the endless soup kitchens, I have indelibly printed memories. The Dirty Thirties were indeed rough.

I am now 68 plus years old and retired from the active work force. According to friends I'm called a conservative. If their analysis is correct, I suspect that trait may trace back to my life on the farm in Randolph county during the early thirties when I was rapidly growing up under the watchful eye of the greatest teacher I ever had, my Dad. To him, problems were new opportunities to create successes, and he never let me forget that.

David H. Harmon
Springfield, Illinois 62704

NORTH CAROLINA REVISITED

Although I now live in Illinois, my story is set in Elizabeth City, a small town in North Carolina, where there were no large farms nor major industry. I was the daughter of a pipe fitter at the local iron works, having been born in December 1924.

Our town had a Coca Cola bottling plant which always donated to each child two book covers, a wooden twelve-inch ruler (both with their advertising thereon) and a metal pencil sharpener in the shape of a Coca Cola bottle. We received these at the beginning of each school year.

Tugboats came down Charles creek, pulling their cargo. Not at all like the massive ones we see today, these were quaint little boats; when they passed the lumber yard they would toot their whistles and a man appeared to open the bridge for them.

It was a wooden bridge which moved around horizontally, instead of moving upwards. The tender had a pipe of almost ten feet in length, something like a wrench which he fitted over a gear and, as he pushed with both hands and arms, moving in a circle, the bridge would gradually open. After the boat had passed through, he would reverse the process to close the bridge.

We children could always hear the boats toot for the bridge and would run to help the man open the bridge. He always waited for us, until the last one of us was on board, before the action started. He was very kind and always had a pocketful of pennies, to make sure each little barefoot urchin received his thanks for helping.

Down at the corner was a grocery store. Most groceries in those days carried truly fresh chickens, a necessity since there was no refrigeration. There was a chicken coop in front of the store, packed with chickens. The favorites in our area were Plymouth Rocks and Rhode Island Reds. They were a plump chicken bred mostly for meat. You picked out your live chicken which the grocer removed from the coop and tied its legs so it couldn't go far even if it got loose. Then he weighed the bird and priced it for you, after which he cut a hole in one corner of a paper bag, put the chicken in the bag with its head sticking out the hole and tied the bag around the chicken's legs.

Mama kept a close watch on her ten kids. We each had to do our share and we never were allowed to leave our yard without permission. She knew where we were and she told us when to be back. I thought she was too strict, so one day when she was peeling apples on the back porch I decided she wouldn't notice if I walked down the street to a neighbor's house. I got as far as the corner store which I was passing when a big dishpan full of iced water was hurled full force from the store to the street. I caught the full impact—the whole thing. I was drenched from the top of my head to my bare feet and I was startled at the unexpected shock. It was so cold because it came from the pop cooler—and I was embarrassed for having been caught away from my yard.

All I did was to run home as fast as possible, slipped in the front door, found my other dress on a nail on the back of the bedroom door, and put it on. Just as I was buttoning the dress I heard a man's voice saying 'Mrs. Corbett, I'm so sorry about your little girl.' Of course Mama didn't know what to think. Which little girl? What had happened? Finally the story came out, I was called downstairs to confirm it. Boy, was I scared. The man asked Mama not to punish me any more, because he thought I had been punished enough. (I could have kissed his feet!) So I was only lectured.

My dad worked at the iron works six days a week, fifty-two weeks a year, for twenty-two years. No vacation, no sick leave, no insurance, no overtime pay. I remember him getting hurt on the job once but we never heard him complain. Another time he suffered heat stroke on the job and my sister and I went to his bedroom and sang to him. It made him very happy. But when he later lost his

job, I saw my daddy cry for the first time in my life. I happened to go into the
kitchen as Mama was pouring some coffee for him and he pulled her close, with
tears running down his face. He said 'Mama, what are we going to do?' I didn't
await an answer but just slipped back out of the room.

We never worried whether our chewing gum would lose its flavor on the bed-
post overnight. We considered ourselves very lucky even to have a piece of gum
to put on that post. It lasted indefinitely, If we had a piece and a sister or friend
didn't have any, we would share. It didn't matter if it was ABC gum (Already
Been Chewed) because we were happy to receive. If there were absolutely no
gum we would get a twig and wipe it in the hot, softened tar along the edge
of the street to gather a nice wad of tar to chew in place of gum. This could
not be put on the bed post, however; it had to be replenished daily.

Today's children think they must have their own bed room. During the depression we not only had to share with other siblings but we waited anxiously
for Aunt Beth and her brood to come to visit. Of course they were welcome.
We had five to a bed and considered it fun. Three smaller ones slept at the
head of the bed and two taller ones slept across the foot; it actually was fun
sleeping at the foot with someone's feet in your face.

Not everyone in our town was poor, not even in the depression. There was
a shipyard where many yachts and large cruisers docked. It was a beautiful sight.
There were sections of town with lovely homes. The hospital had a beautiful
setting by water, with birds and ducks everywhere. I worked at this hospital
when I was sixteen (1940) and really enjoyed it.

Often, hoboes would ride the depression trains and many times would come
to our house for food. My mom would never turn them away. If all we had
was cold water biscuits she would still share with them. None of us ever felt
slighted either. Instead we felt good that we could share.

I remember Mama sending me to the store with a dime to buy supper for
the twelve of us. She said 'Get four cents of side meat and six cents worth of
navy beans.' Then she'd make bean soup and cornmeal dumplings to add to
the pot. It was delicious.

She made a lot of one-dish meals, particularly soups. There were vegetable
and potato soups, black-eyed peas, cornfield peas, collard greens, mustard or
turnip greens, or kale. The greens always had potatoes and ham hocks, and
cornbread or biscuits. We also ate a lot of corned herrings. Daddy kept a wooden
barrel half-buried in the dirt floor of the garage. Corned herrings were cheap,
easy to keep, and nourishing, so we often had them for breakfast with cornbread
griddle cakes.

Since we lived near the coast, here in North Carolina, seafood was plentiful,
but we still had to buy the cheapest. Daddy would peddle his bicycle to work,
sometimes giving me a ride to the fish market. He's say 'Buy six pounds of
croakers' and hand me a quarter. I would buy them and walk the long trek back

home, all of six years old, with my newspaper-wrapped bundle. Mama would scale and fry them, with their heads on.

We children learned at an early age how to eat a fish. You eat all the crispy skin and flaky meat on one side, then turn the fish over and eat the other side. Then you start on the head. You pull off the jaws, one at a time, flip out and eat the good jaw meat. With the tip of your knife blade you remove the eyes and discard them with the bones. Then, with the knife handle you hit the skull hard enough to crack it, putting your lips on it and sucking out the cooked brains. The female's roe cooks up well with scrambled eggs for breakfast.

When our wealthier neighbors sent their maid outside to kill two chickens for their supper, she wrung the chickens' necks and left the heads in the yard. Mama sent my little brother to get the heads before the cat got them. Then, when the maid threw out the two pairs of lower legs and feet, my brother got them too. Mother scalded and cleaned them and made pie-bread dumplings for the soup. We had a good supper.

Wealthy people didn't want to be bothered by the poor. I recall once when we had some green onions and radishes in a little patch and Mama gathered a few, washed them and tied them in bunches. I was to try to sell them to neighbors for five cents a bunch. I washed myself, combed my hair and took the pretty bunches to a neighbor. The man came to the door and said 'You little bastard! Take your stuff and get off my porch...and don't you ever come back here again.' Needless to say, I never did. We had never bothered these people. We were poor but we were clean and mannerly.

Another time, another well-to-do neighbor received a shipment of potatoes. When he couldn't sell them for the profit he wanted, he dumped the whole load into the river. He didn't give a single potato to the needy.

Hilda Metzka
Chillicothe, Illinois

AS IF YOU WERE STRICKEN BLIND

I was born and raised at Tyrone, Texas county, Oklahoma and married a Kansas farmer in 1934, on Easter Sunday. Gray county, Kansas is just a few miles north of the Oklahoma state line so we lived in the heart of the dust bowl. Blowing dirt and those big black clouds of dust rolling in was as different as day and night. Masking tape was a common trim around windows and seldom-used doors. No matter how well the house was built, that trim was needed. For wider cracks we tore rags into strips and tightly packed them into cracks. Even wet towels or blankets wouldn't keep the dust out during the high winds.

In our part of Oklahoma in 1931 the rains almost quit entirely and that was the start of the drought. In 1931 the frequency of dirt storms started increasing until 'there were as many as 179 in 1933.' Those coming from the north or northwest were always black, 'arriving with a rolling turbulance, rising like a long wall of muddy water as high as 7,000 or 8,000 feet.'[1] Those coming from the south or southwest were lighter in color, sometimes red, with continuous winds as high as 60 miles an hour. They lasted for several days but weren't as vicious as those from the north. Even a light in the house wouldn't penetrate well into that darkness. Sometimes these dusters would last as long as twelve days and nights, with visibility being no more than two blocks. We felt lucky to see a quarter of a mile. People tried not to drive because the dust was bad on motors. Road ditches provided our guides for locating the road.

In the last of March 1935 we had a duster which destroyed most of the wheat crop in Nebraska, half of it in Kansas and a fourth of it in Oklahoma. It had so much static electricity it burned the wheat to a crisp brown before it continued all the way to the Atlantic ocean.

April 14, 1935 was a beautiful Sunday until mid-afternoon when the temperature dropped about 50 degrees and a rolling black demon approached from the north. Visibility was zero and no matter where you were it was as if you were stricken blind. It was frightening, specially to those who didn't see it approaching. Frank (my husband) and his father were in a shed working on machinery when the sudden darkness hit. They waited quite a while before attempting to get to the house. They started in the general direction, then followed a fence to the windmill near the house. From there they finally made it to the house.

This particular blackness lasted about four hours. I remember that to help keep the dust out of our food, we covered it with paper or a tablecloth, raising it just enough to get a bite.

One of the worst times in 1936 was in February or early March. Our oldest son was about two months old and for nine days and nights we kept him on a daybed with a sheet stretched over it for a tent. I crawled under that tent to nurse, change and bathe him. One of those days I had a sudden weird feeling while bathing the baby, so I hurried into the kitchen and turned off the burner under an oven on a gasoline campstove, which was our method of cooking. As the last flicker went out, the tank exploded, sending gasoline all over the kitchen and me too. I stood there in a daze with my hand on the knob of the living room door. When Frank came home a couple of hours later I was still shaking and whiter than any sheet in the house.

Instead of viral pneumonia, dust pneumonia was a problem. Coughing or blowing the nose brought forth mud. Hospitals were full and many older people and babies were dying. We had gone to Tyrone to my parents' place for the weekend and, since Frank had a congested cough, my dad said now was the time for a cure. He cooked a big iron skillet full of onions and put them in a sugar sack. He told Frank to remove his shirt and lay down. Dad put that very hot sack of onions across Frank's chest. After the first complaints of being burned alive, Frank endured the treatment and got over the pneumonia. To this day, however, he cannot stand the taste or smell of onions.

The little three room house where we lived in 1935-36 had no water. The well was unusable so we hauled water in a five gallon cream can, for all our needs. The washboard received almost daily use. I had no outside line so used a rope stretched across the living room on which to dry our clothes. When I would have the line full, two or three layers deep, the old oilburning stove would belch a time or two and soot would settle over everything...so back to the washboard.

When I mopped the kitchen floor ice would freeze behind the mop. Many nights we stretched sheets and blankets over our beds, making a tent for protection. If we didn't, we'd arise in the morning with a dirty face, the only clean spot being where we laid our heads.

We moved into Copeland eventually where we now had electric lights, water and gas for the stoves. A few years later we decided to move our house to the farm, four miles northeast of Copeland. We left what little furniture we owned still inside the house so, when it was set on the new foundation, we could start housekeeping immediately. About a mile out of town someone saw smoke coming from the roof and before long there was only a pile of ashes on the road—no house. As Frank was trying to push the refrigerator out the door, the roof collapsed on him and he had to be rushed to the doctor.

After that, our housekeeping was in an old, unused garage with a borrowed divan which made into a bed, no table, chairs, hardly any dishes or silverware, scarcely anything to cook in, no towels, clothes, money or anything else. After getting an emergency government wheat loan on the crop, a government permit to get building material, and a gift from friends, we planned a house on a paper napkin as we drove to purchase materials. Since it still wasn't harvest time that year, men were floating around looking for work and soon we had about seven men from Missouri and Arkansas to help build the house. I was cooking for all of them in that garage.

One day while getting dinner I heard a slithering noise and looked around to see three big bullsnakes enjoying my living quarters. I cautiously moved toward the door, grabbed a hoe and chopped down on all three, each trying to get into the same hole. Fearful that one would get away, I was afraid to lift the hoe for another whack, so I held it down with all my strength and cried, screamed and called for help. No one showed up until about 45 minutes after I had killed them. I was still shaking and angry and considered giving them bullsnake stew. The rest of the time living in that makeshift place was pure horror so moving into our unfinished house was delightful.

In the fall when the men could work on the house again, we moved our things into the new chicken house. The two or three chickens we had were a lot better company than snakes, even with the dirt floor and makeshift windows. By winter we were in our new house — three bedrooms with closets, living room, kitchen, running water, electric lights from our own lightplant. All this for what it would cost to build a garage today.

Rattlesnakes were as common as bullsnakes. The old cliche that if you have bullsnakes you won't have rattlesnakes just wasn't true. One morning Frank loaded his dad in the car to take him for a ride. Less than a quarter of a mile from the house they saw a rattler. Frank drove back to the house for a shovel and gun. Instead of one snake, he killed 48 in that one den. Within two weeks I was met at the front door one morning by two big rattlers. We never let one get away. They must have come for revenge. We could see them almost any place on the farm. At first only prairie rattlers but after the dam was built on Crooked creek not far from our house, some of the floods seemed to bring the diamondbacks.

We survived the depression, the dirty thirties, losing several hundred sheep in a flood, tornadoes, severe hailstorms, blizzards, losing a whole band of sheep in one storm, the loss of our house, and many other misfortunes but, all in all, we had it better than many people and are still thankful for even the small things in life.

As I write this we are celebrating our fifty-fourth anniversary.

Maurietta J. Patterson
Cleveland, Oklahoma

(1) 'Dust Bowl, The Southern Plains In The 1930's', by Donald Worster, Oxford University Press, Inc., 1979, pages 13 and 14.

LOTS TO EAT BUT NO SPENDING MONEY

We moved from the Roberts place to the Strawn vicinity in Illinois in the spring of 1932. People were planting oats the first of March and it wasn't very long before we got a road blocker of snow, from hedgerow to hedgefence. Everybody had to sow their oats again, some not getting them in until the first of April.

Then the Lindbergh baby was kidnapped and killed within a few days and we were all shocked by it.

The thirties were tough for all land owners, all of whom would have lost their land had it not been for government and insurance company loans. Schools seemed never to have trouble paying their debts, unlike schools of today.

I worked for a neighbor for sixty cents a day, putting in crops and walking behind a four-section harrow. In 1934, the dry year, I worked for $20 a month and was up at 4 AM and eating supper at 6 PM. Long days. So things were not sugar and spice.

That fall, September 30th was the last day of the Chicago World's Fair, which ran for two years. All the neighbor kids from sixteen to twenty years old, went to the fair in a covered stock truck for a dollar each. We left Chatsworth at 4 AM and got back at 4 AM the next morning. We were tired but it was an experience we have never forgotten. The very next day we started husking corn for a neighbor. It made only about 25 bushels an acre until we got to the low ground where there was some pretty good corn.

We took any job we could get because they were so scarce. We helped put in culberts on the roads and two neighbors and I helped shell one side of a crib for a dollar divided among us. We took that dollar and spent twenty-five cents each to get into a square dance, plus we shared a brick of ice cream for the other quarter. We had a lot of fun for that dollar. We had driven to the dance in an old Model T Ford running on two gallons of kerosene. It smoked but it did the job.

1936 was a very hot year but the corn was better and I think we sold ours for ninety cents a bushel. A neighbor stock buyer asked us to come over to see a hundred dollar steer. It weighed a thousand pounds, at ten cents a pound — so that seemed the start of better times.

We always had lots to eat but never any spending money. We were happy no matter what the circumstances.

The winter of 1936 was terribly cold and the roads were blocked half the time. I would walk over the snow banks two or three times a week to reach our neighbors to play euchre and other card games. We would all take turns having the neighbors in for cards.

We bought our first tractor in 1935; it was a used 10–20 International and we used it for a year before getting an new F-20 Farmall with a cultivator. We traded three horses and cash for it, which amount to $900 total. It was on steel and in 1942 I put it on rubber for traveling the road.

In the late thirties the little Ellis five-foot combines were the rage and we bought a good used one. A few neighbors were still threshing but it soon ended in our locality.

The weather in the thirties seemed to move from south to northeast and there were general rains. There seemed to be more lightning and thunder in the storms than had been usual. We had several storms that took down trees and windmills but not our homes. Then the Delco light plants came along to replace the Aladdin lamps which had been around since the twenties. The Delco plants brought life to the farmers.

They built the Norris Dam on the Clinch river in Tennessee (Ed.: not too far from Oak Ridge, Tennessee) and some of our relatives had to leave their homes to the rising waters. I had a good understanding of what life had been like in the valley before the flooding so I wrote a poem and sung it at reunions and other gatherings.

I remember the thirties well because they really shaped my life.I would have liked being a ballplayer, a radio singer, or a farmer; I turned out to be a farmer because I was a home body and didn't want to leave my family. I've never regreted it, even though it has been hard work with long hours. But is anything worth having unless it's obtained by sweat and honesty?

Carl Sharp
Chatsworth, Illinois

MOM'S SMALL PENSION KEPT
US FROM THE WPA

I was around fifteen and we lived at Arnold, Nebraska, a town about the center of the state. That year my dad planted more corn than he raised. That part of the country is good farmland and my dad was a good farmer.

I remember that summer so well. The wind blew every day from the south. Hot winds each afternoon. The sky would bank with white fluffy clouds everywhere but never a drop of rain fell that summer.

Big, black bugs took the garden, what there was of it, for there was no irrigation at that time nor were there any air conditioners. People went outside and sat in the wind, or jumped into the stock tanks for an afternoon swim.

One merchant in Arnold rigged up a car radiator in his store and had cold water running through it; I think it had a fan and it helped a lot; everyone thought that was quite an invention. He was a Jewish merchant and I've forgotten his name.

And tnere were the grasshoppers. The government furnished hopper poison laced with banana oil. It smelled so good. Dad showed us the poison and was very careful that none of us four kids touched it. It was a lesson in handling poison that we never forgot. It killed the hoppers. You could pick a man's hatful from each corn stalk—but there wasn't much left of the stalk by that time.

That year a snake, we thought, killed our best milk cow. There were many plagues. That place had a disease that killed the calves in a few months. It was later said that if you painted the umbilical cord with iodine you could save the calves. My family did not know that so we lost the entire calf crop.

My dad drove a 1928 model T Ford, open body, and that winter he took me to high school, about twenty miles away. We were so poor and I wore that old thin coat. I never did have a pair of mittens that was worth anything. I wonder how I ever took that cold weather. We surely could tell the value of a windbreak when we went by one. The air seemed warm.

I don't remember the dust. For miles around it was mostly grass land. There wasn't much we could do. There was no electricity, of course, just a broom. At that age who noticed a little dust. Or a lot of dust for that matter. We were a family of four living on a couple of sections and we played with each other because there were no close neighbors. We grew up to be a good family. We went barefooted in the summer with only two changes of clothes — one we called everyday and the other was Sunday best.

We always had something to eat. Mom was a good chicken raiser. Also she received a small pension from her brother, killed in World War I, which kept the wolf from the door. Roosevelt did have the WPA but, since dad and mom had that little $50 pension, dad couldn't get hired. Lots of people sent their young boys to the CCC camps because they didn't have enough food to feed them. One neighbor lady told us her son had to go to the CCC or starve.

We can think how terrible the thirties were, and all that effect of the stock market crash, but it turned out some really good people. Folks with determination, grit and the ability to make the best of a situation. I know that I could live without electricity, natural gas, air conditioning. I know the way and it really isn't so bad. However, I appreciate my nicer home and modern conveniences.

This year reminds me of the thirties. That awful hot wind, just like back then and no rain. Also I see clouds bank up every day and it tries to rain. I talked to an elderly relative and he says the same thing. Makes me wonder if we aren't entering another time, just like in the past. Only wise people in about 1937 and 1938 here in Nebraska started erecting dams. Here we have excellent irrigation for the farmlands. The higher grounds have sprinkler systems. Nebraska has a lot of wonderful underground water, good water. With the advancement in technology I don't think there will be a food shortage.

Deloris Stellman
North Platte, Nebraska

THE WEARINESS OF IT ALL

I am now 90½ years old.

During that summer of 1936 I was pregnant with my second child and we lived southeast of Big Springs, Nebraska.

The weather would be all right in the morning until a dust cloud would come over and it would be dark in no time.

We didn't have much outside protection for the animals. The cattle would stand in the shade of the barn because it was so hot. We bought feed from the valley near Big Springs where people could irrigate and thus raise crops. We also had a little feed left over from when crops had been good and we fed this to the chickens. They didn't lay many eggs but we had enough for our own use.

It was plenty hot.. We used a coal and wood range for cooking, had no electricty and no fans. We cooked in the morning while it was cool and sometimes ate bread and milk for supper. When we set the table we'd turn the dishes upside down to keep them clean until the next mealtime.

We carried all of our water from the windmill. We covered it with a towel to keep out the dust. That dust seemed to blow all day long, making us so dirty we took baths in a round, galvanized washtub at night. But that dirt was everywhere, a half inch thick on the floor. All we had to clean with was a broom, a goose wing, rags, water and homemade soap. When my first child was sleeping, I'd cover her crib with a little blanket to keep out the dust.

We tried in many ways to keep the dust out of the house. We hung sheets over the windows. We also filled old stockings with sand and laid them on the windowsills as a barrier.

I tried to raise a garden near the windmill. It was fenced to keep the chickens out; we watered with windmill water if the wind blew so it would pump water for us.

Life went on. I don't know how the mailman made his rounds, but almost every day he came by. There wasn't much entertainment. It was so dusty we couldn't see to travel. Sometimes we'd get together with neighbors at night and play cards. We'd all pitch in to buy some coffee.

Inez Daubendiek
Ogallala, Nebraska

FIRST FARM EXPERIENCES OF A NINE-YEAR OLD

As an eager nine-year old, I finally achieved distinction from the others in Miss Johnson's fourth grade class at Prescott grade school in Lincoln, NE. Mine was a unique quality which distinguished me from my peers. It was discovered in the fall on the first day of class when a visiting physician gave each student a cursory physical examination. He checked the usual and, as a finale, grasped each child's hands to examine them. He was startled to see that I had a real he-man set of calluses. Therein lies a tale.

A JOB

Early that spring, my Uncle Jake and Aunt Alta had offered me a summer job on their farm in the fertile Platte river valley. I was to receive my room and board and an occasional ice cream cone when we went to town. They were my favorite aunt and uncle and I was ecstatic. This was 1936 when grown men were begging for jobs. It was a thrilling experience for me and was also my first prolonged sojourn from home. Could I carry it off?

The first evening, Dean (the hired man) disappeared about 8:30 and Uncle Jake soon went to his bedroom. They knew what I hadn't yet learned—that 4:00 A.M. came early. However, I was tucked away in an upstairs bedroom and was allowed to sleep the next morning. Several things were wrong with that arrangement. Home air conditioning hadn't yet reached the masses, so it was stiflingly hot in my room. I also felt guilty about awakening so late and eating breakfast after the others had gone to work. The problem was accidentally solved the next night. We were enjoying a little breeze by sitting in the front yard. Being so tired, I soon fell asleep, and the others left me there. In spite of the fact that a litter of kittens found me about 3:00 A.M. and decided to play tag on my face, it was an improvement. This led to a compromise with my aunt insisting that I sleep on their northwest screened-in porch on what she called a sanitary cot. My fondest memories of that arrangement are of going to bed and listening to the cottonwood leaves rustle in the nearby tree claim. Cottonwood leaves are set on a flattened petioles and, like the quaking aspen, their leaves flutter in the slightest breeze.

The only time I really became homesick was during the weekly struggle when my aunt forced me to write my folks on a penny postcard. It dawned on me that if I were home this ordeal wouldn't be necessary.

PRACTICAL ECONOMICS 101

At breakfast the next morning I was enthusiastically attacking two fried eggs and some home-cured bacon when Uncle Jake asked if I liked the egg. Innocently, I nodded, careful not to break the rhythm of the fork in my right hand. 'That's good,' he announced. 'After breakfast I'll show you how to care for those old hens so they'll lay lots of eggs.' Thus I was introduced to the chicken chores. He provided me with two ten-quart pails and directed me to the pump at the hog pen. When the weather was hot I was to provide the chickens with fresh water three times a day. It took thity-six full strokes of the handle on the cast iron pump to fill each bucket. I was off to a good start in this farming business. Then came the stressful part. About 4:00 P.M. it was time to enter a darkened part of the hen house where I was shown how to gather the cackleberries. The red roosters had cured me of going barefooted several years before by attacking my bare toes. Some of the setting hens proceeded to be just as belligerent. Within a week I had an agreement of sorts with them and the eggs were dutifully deposited in a wicker basket each day.

A few mornings later as I was pouring a thin cream caught by rinsing the cream separator, my uncle observed 'You must like those corn flakes pretty well?' When I nodded affirmatively he remarked that those who like to drink milk and cream were expected to help milk the fifteen head of Shorthorn cows. I was shown how to balance myself on the one-legged milk stool, hold the bucket between my knees, and fill the bucket with rich, warm, foaming milk. If no one was looking I'd squirt milk into the barn cats' faces to feed them, as I had seen the hired man do. Unfortunately, my aunt and uncle and the hired man milked fourteen cows while I struggled with one. Occasionally, when I dawdled too long, old Spot (just to get even, I'm sure) would wait until the pail was almost full and then kick lustily at one of the many flies, catching the rim of the bucket in the process. Twenty minutes of my hard labor spilled on the barn floor! However, more than ever, I appreciated the whole milk and cream saved for the table at the cream separator. The cream to be sold was collected in a metal five-gallon cream can and the skim milk was fed to the bucket calves and feeder pigs. It was several weeks before I realized that Aunt Alta also saved about two gallons of skim milk daily, which was allowed to clabber (sour) and was then fed to her chickens, which evidently considered it a delicacy.

Soon after arriving at the farm I was introduced to the war against weeds. It was shown to me that a sharp hoe was important, so ours were filed down to a mere shadow of their original selves. Outside of hoeing our cucumber crop and saving a series of small pigweeds, it all went quite well. It was hot, boring and tiresome work. A team of black mules was hitched to a tongueless cultivator to plow the garden. This cultivator was the devil's own invention. A green team or a careless driver could turn slightly wrong and the whole contraption would collapse in a heap. However, those weeds my uncle couldn't get that way had to be hoed by hand. This monotony was interrupted when Uncle Jake handed me a half-gallon syrup pail filled with enough kerosene to cover the bottom. We went to the rows of potatoes and I was instructed to brush the red juvenile and the adult hard-shelled potato bugs into the kerosene pool. The day we dug new potatoes and picked peas, which were then creamed together for dinner, made it all worthwhile. I was fast learning where my food came from and what we had to do to put it on the table.

Our diet consisted of fresh and canned vegetables from the garden and fruit from the orchard. Alternatives were jellies and jams, pickles (how I loved those pickled cherries and watermelon pickles) and sauerkraut. Meat dishes alternated between home cured pork, canned beef, or a real treat of fried chicken.

That summer we had obtained some Leghorn cockerels at a bargain price. They were turned loose at a certain age and allowed to roam in the tree claim. When my uncle thought I was responsible enough, we made a deal. By mutual agreement, my aunt would fill the teakettle and build a fire in the cook stove. I would take the single shot, bolt action, twenty-two and go hunting. I could get within fifteen feet of an unspecting chicken. A well placed shot to the head wouldn't spoil any meat and then it was my job to scald it, pluck the feathers, and field dress it. The crisply fried chicken, mashed potatoes and milk gravy, green beans with a little salt pork, and fresh garden lettuce and onions made a meal fit for a king. A piece of fresh mulberry pie made a perfect dessert. We had very little money and no refrigeration, but we never went hungry.

REAL HORSE POWER

In that summer of 1936 my uncle had a team of very gentle, black, mollie mules named appropriately Maude and Molly. There was a spirited team of buckskin mules named Jenny and Josie, and finally a frisky team of bay horses named Bill and Flossie. The horses fascinated me. Their manes and tails were naturally wavy and Dean, the hired man, curried them until their coats shown like elegant hardwood furniture. In addition, a sorrel saddle horse named Daisy would be harnessed with a soft cloth collar and worked in an emergency. That, and an old Case tractor furnished all of the farm's horsepower. I have no idea what model Case it was. It had no muffler, but its exhaust stack was bent at a jaunty angle. It ran on tractor fuel which was sort of a cross between gasoline and kerosene. To start it, you opened petcocks to the cylinders and filled small cups with straight gasoline. There was a removeable crank which attached directly to the crankshaft which, in turn, was mounted cross-ways to the long axis of the tractor. Woe to the unfortunate operator who cranked until the pistons sucked tractor fuel into the cylinders. The dilution of the hotter gasoline with the less volatile tractor fuel spelled trouble with a capital T. The only other distinguishing feature of the tractor was that it had no seat for the operator. If you got weary, you sat on one of the metal fenders. The tiny steering wheel with its necking knob was attached to a worm gear. Everyone was too busy cranking to count the revolutions the steering wheel made to make a ninety-degree turn. Of course it came equipped with metal wheels. Its main function was to provide power for the threshing machine via a huge flat, canvas belt.

At the tender age of nine, I leveled the grain in the wagons as they were filled from the separator auger. In my spare time, I ran the tractor, ready to release the hand clutch at a moment's notice should anything go wrong. Usually this was limited to noon and quitting times.

MY KINGDOM FOR A HORSE

After a week I complained to my uncle that it didn't seem fair for me to have to chase after the milk cows in the evenings on shank's mare when that nice saddle horse was running with the cows and doing nothing. Uncle Jake agreed and, as Dean smirked, said that when I caught her I could go ahead and ride her. They would keep her in the barn and feed her with the work horses.

I couldn't wait. The next morning I got the western bridle from the barn and set off for the cow pasture. Call it beginner's luck but I cautiously sweet talked my way right next to Daisy. She even let me put the bit in her mouth. This was going to be easy! And then as I slid the headstall over her ears, to my amazement, the bit dropped out of her mouth and she lunged away. Dean had evidently lengthened the bridle when he had ridden old Mollie. From then on it was war. At first the men thought it was funny and then they agreed to catch the mare when she came to the barn with the milk cows. They had underestimated the enemy and Daisy thought it was great sport. She even eluded our trusty German shepherd, Blitz. After several days of this cat and mouse game, Uncle Jake, in exasperation, unchained Queenie. She was a full grown spayed pup out of Blitz and was kept confined to quarters except for special ocasions such as this because of her take-no-prisoner attitude. I was told to stay back out of the way with Aunt Alta and it wasn't long before the two men and the two dogs had Daisy in the corral. When she realized she was caught, she docilely submitted to having the bridle adjusted for her.

Thereafter, Dean would put the saddle on her every morning when he harnessed his team. At nine I couldn't do that but I would take the bridle off the saddlehorn and get her ready for the day's activities. After she drank at the horse tank I would lead her alongside the corncrib. Standing in the crib and grasping the reins and the saddlehorn with my left hand and putting my left foot in the stirrup, was Daisy's signal to start off with a brisk walk. I soon learned to utilize this to help swing me into the saddle. We were then off to carry a fresh drink to the men in the field, or to get the cows, or just to hunt for the noble red man.

THE LOVE AFFAIR OF EVERY AMERICAN MALE

As the summer wore on and the drought got worse, the milk cows were daily driven across the newly cut alfalfa to a luxurious stand of sweet clover which had been fenced off temporarily. As the cows learned the routine, it was my job and

Daisy's to shuttle them back and forth. One evening, my uncle suggested that we use the family car for that purpose. After opening the corral gate, I climbed in the car and we leisurely pursued the cows to the sweet clover. After shutting the gate, he asked me how I would like to drive back. Would I? You bet! The old '29 Chevie was ideal for this purpose. After explaining the three-speed transmission, my uncle warned me not to step on the accelerator. Instead, he adjusted two little ears next to the horn button. One was a manual spark advance, and the other was a hand throttle just like on the tractor. With the engine running at a fast idle so I wasn't likely to stall it, I scrunched down and depressed the clutch pedal and put the transmission into low gear. Easing out on the clutch as instructed, we started to move. I came up to peer over the hood and to steer it along the trail through the alfalfa. But it wasn't going to be that easy. Uncle Jake admonished me to get it into high gear. Sliding down in the seat again until I could depress the clutch again, I finally managed to miss reverse and to get it into second. Undaunted, as the engine revved up, I pushed the clutch in again, and high gear was easier to find.

With that out of the way, I came up for air to discover the car making a big circle across the alfalfa field. It was a proud nine-year old that drove the car into the yard that night. Needless to say, this became a cherished part of the daily routine, until it almost came to an abrupt halt one Saturday evening. As I drove into the yard with my uncle at my side, we were met by my parents who were just arriving from Lincoln. My mother was upset to say the least. After a hastily called family conference, it was decided that my driving lessons could continue.

THE YOUNG PATRIOT

The fourth of July was a big holiday in our family. My father had slipped a whole dollar into my hand the week before so I could celebrate appropriately. Uncle Jake and I went into a hardware store in Schyler which had a big display table laden with all kinds of fireworks. There were lady fingers, three-inchers, five-inchers, and even cherry bombs. The clerk hastened over with a brown paper sack as I directed him to give me a package of this and a package of that. Finally, when I stopped to ask him how much I had spent, I caught him asking my uncle if this little boy had that much money? Some grown men in the harvest field that year had worked for $2.00 a day. Unfortunately for the chickens, the pigs, dogs and cats, I could and did buy a whole paper sackful of firecrackers.

My careful experimentation showed that a three-inch firecracker under a number 9 bean can with the dirt carefully packed around it, would blow that can as high as the corn crib. But the five-incher, under the same conditions, would send that can to the cupola on the barn. It also caused a distinct bulge in the end of the can. Disappointingly, the cherry bomb simply blew the can apart. My father bought a sackful of Roman candles, sparklers, etc., for the night display. By my risky behavior, I surely did work my guardian angel overtime that day. Ah, but those were simpler times.

ALTERNATE ENERGY STUDY

Late in the summer, the community project of laying in the winter wood supply began on Bailey's island in the Platte river. Mr. Bailey offered any tree standing on the huge island for five cents under a sort of serve yourself arrangement. Access to the island was through Landis Dodendorf's farm. He was a huge man with twinkly blue eyes, a huge walrus mustache, and a wealth of stories which he told with a bit of an accent. Of special interest to me was the fact that he chewed tobacco which stained curious patterns on his mustache.

Earlier, Mr. Dodendorf had forded the south channel of the river with his old regular Farmall tractor and buzz saw. His rig stayed on the island until the rest of us were all finished. We took two-man saws, axes, and water jugs over on high wheeled, fifty bushel, grain wagons.

Two men with a cross-cut saw would fell a big, fifty foot cottonwood, trimming away the small branches with axes. They would cut the trunk into lengths and pieces that could be dragged to the buzz saw by a team, and man-handled onto the saw table by several men, where each piece was cut into stove lengths. If necesssary it would be split so it would be ready to burn after curing; then it was loaded on the grain wagons which were driven to the south channel where an extra team with their doubletrees were hitched by a log chain to the tongue of the wagon in tandem with the original team.

Our fording place was used every day, but no one really trusted the constantly shifting sands of the river bottom. Besides, all four horses had to get down and really lay into their collars to pull the fully loaded wagon up the south bank. All horses were then unhitched and everyone went back for the companion wagon. This was usually the last event of the day. The old story went around about how wonderful were those Nebraska cottonwoods. Each one warmed you three times — first, when you chopped it up; second, when you actually burned it for heat; and third, when you hauled out the ashes.

The last act of this project was to haul wood to the community church in the town of Octavia. As soon as Dean and Uncle Jake had their wagons safely on the south bank, I climbed on the wagon with Dean. He clucked to Bill and Flossie and we were off at a brisk walk. When we passed through the Dodendorf's yard and got on the county road, the horses broke into a trot. What a pleasure it was to drive them. The tighter you held the reins, the quicker their pace. The jingling tugs made soft background music to our conversation and soon we had covered the six miles to town. Unloading the wood down a coal chute to the church's basement was quickly accomplished and Dean offered to buy pop at Krueger's general store. I was nonchalantly lounging on the store's front steps with an orange Nehi when the next wagon pulled into town.

BRIGHT CITY LIGHTS

During the week Aunt Alta insisted we wash our feet in a wash pan in the yard. However, Saturday night was special. I was elected to pump water and Dean carried it a few feet to the wash house where he filled two boilers on an old cook stove. The hot corncob fire heated more than the water on those summer nights. We took turns bathing in a galvanized washtub in the middle of the concrete floor in that wash house. After cleaning up, dressing up, and loading the Chevie with the wicker basket full of eggs and two full cream cans, we headed for town. The first stop was at O'Halloran's dairy with our cream, so they could test the butterfat content and give us a check. The eggs were taken to the local grocery store and traded for those staples which we couldn't raise — such as sugar, salt and coffee. This weekly excursion had to be carefully planned. Hopefully the cream and egg money would pay for whatever we needed that night. If there were anything left over, we might get an ice cream cone at the dairy or, (somewhat guiltily) at that new drive-in on the way out of town. A girl would come out and take our order so we didn't even need to get out of the car. The cool breeze coming through the open car windows was often enough to put me fast asleep before we'd get home. The depression seemed far away at that point.

EPIDEMIC TO ENTREPRENEURSHIP

At breakfast one morning Uncle Jake declared that we were in big trouble. Doing chores he had found a second dead pig in as many days. We put the 25 pound pig in a gunny sack and headed for David City to see the vet. It was my first experience with a "post" as Doc deftly opened the carcass. As he worked, he explained to my uncle and me what pathology was present. Upon conclusion, he diagnosed the case as being swine erysipelas. We were given a gallon jug of purplish-black liquid which I now assume was a potassium permanganate solution (these were pre-penicillin days). We were instructed to make a slop of ground feed, water, skim milk, and a cup of this black stuff. We took a 55 gallon barrel and cut the end out and that was the receptacle for making this concoction.

In a week or so our pig count was down to ten or twelve chronics in a small pen. One day at chore time as my uncle and I were observing their progress, he stated that probably all of the remaining pigs would live.It was bad luck, he said, to give livestock to anyone, but he'd sell me one of those pigs, my choice, for a nickel. We'd ear notch him, and then if I'd do those extra chores, the feed for him would be free. You can be sure I stood right at the separator morning and night for a bucket of skim milk to feed them. They went on their regular diet after a while and I made sure they had all they could eat and drink.

Soon the summer drew to a close and I had to return to Lincoln to go back to school. The days slid into weeks. Halloween came and went. One day before Thanksgiving when I came home from school my mother announced that I had a letter from the Columbus sale barn. Puzzled, I hurriedly tore open the envelope and a check fell out. My uncle had hauled my now market-sized hog with his own to the sale barn and had sold it separately. It weighed about 270 pounds and bought about $7.00 per hundredweight. With the yardage and commission taken out, I was now richer by the sum of $14.67. Wow! That was the most money I had ever seen.

The farming bug had really bitten me and the old question of "How you gonna keep them down on the farm...?" just didn't apply to me. I simply hoped that Uncle Jake would let me grow some new calluses on my hands the next summer.

Walter E. Long, DVM
Curtis, Nebraska

THE SCHOOLS

NURSING SCHOOL FOR $100 TUITION

My parents had lost a lot of money in the years before 1936 and were hard working people where we lived on the farm in Van Buren county, Iowa.

I was graduated and went into nurse's training by borrowing a hundred dollars from my brother-in-law's life insurance. My tuition was a hundred dollars plus uniform costs. I worked to help meet costs.

My father cut down trees for the stock to have something green to eat but our pond was deep and we always had water for them. The men hunted rabbits and squirrels for food and we butchered. Thus we had meat for a time and cured and canned enough to last through the winter. We also dried apples on a window screen covered with cheesecloth to keep the slices clean.

Our diet at home consisted of green beans, potatoes and cornbread made from our own corn taken to a mill to be ground. Also brown gravy made from lard, burned flour and water. My mother baked bread two times each week on a three-burner kerosene stove with an oven. In the winter she used the old iron cookstove, heated with corncobs. Bread cost five cents a lofa, but there wasn't always money to buy it. We had banty hens for our eggs and, for an icebox, we dug a hole and put a wooden tub in it. It worked.

The folks bought flour in twenty-five pound sacks and washed the sacks to make dresses and aprons from them. We had no radio or electric lights but used kerosene lamps and went to a shanty in the back yard for a bathroom.

We bathed in a washtub or a large pan. In the summertime we heated water in an iron tub over a fire, to do the washing. In the winter we carried water inside and heated it on the stove. We had a wooden hand washer that had to be pulled back and forth and was very tiring to work.

After being graduated from nursing school I finally found a job for $75 a month and room and board. We worked twelve hours a day and did nursing plus cleaning rooms. In surgery we stayed in the hospital and was on call all night and often worked all day too. If we had a very sick patient, we put a big hunk of ice in a baby's bathtub with an electric fan behind it. It was surprising but it kept the room cooler.

In remembering, I think about how hard it was and how differently people live today.

Mary Yeager
Fort Dodge, Iowa

MARIE THE SCHOOLMARM

When dawn broke January 22, 1936, it was evident the snow and wind carried more than the usual clout of a winter storm. Marie Milder, a rural school teacher, ate breakfast early and prepared to travel three miles to Athens, her one-room school. Usually she went by horse and buggy but today her dad was driving her. Her monthly salary of $40 didn't allow her fancier transportation. Even though she didn't pay her parents for room and board, she helped her father in the fields during the summer. Also, she was expected to purchase some of the school supplies with her own funds. Also she paid a neighboring farmer to board her horse during the school day.

The snow was already fairly deep on the roads but normally blizzards didn't stop routine farm and country school activities. She could always get through with her horse and the sixteen students were all within a mile of home.

By the time she and her dad reached the Bill Pike farm, a half mile from the school, they were stuck. Bill and another friend helped dig them out and head homeward. Bill instructed Marie not to return to the school until he had called her.

There was no fancy snow-blowing equipment in those days. The summertime road maintainer was winterized by adding a V-shaped plow to the front and that is all there was. Sam, the man who ran the machine would try daily to clear the roads and daily the snow would fill them again. Soon there was more snow than Sam's machine could handle. Snowdrifts were as high as granaries and they covered clothes lines.

One farmer, Frank Kaalberg, quit using his truck and switched to a bobsled pulled by draft horses. He would go to town in the bobsled and get groceries and coal for several families. Each would meet him at the central crossroads to pick up what he had brought.

Most farms were self sufficient in those days. Each had at least one cow for milk and cream, chickens for eggs and meat. There were potatoes in the cold cellar and canned fruits and vegetables from the summer garden, so the needed groceries were staples like flour, sugar, coffee and crackers. If a housewife could not make yeast bread, biscuits or cornbread were good substitutes.

Some farmers had to dig tunnels through the snow from the house to the barn in order to reach their livestock to feed and water them, and to milk the cows.

When school finally resumed on February 12 not all roads were cleared so some arrived by bobsled, sometimes through a field rather than down the road.

Not only was there an excess of snow in 1936 but the -20 and -30 degree temperatures were bitter. It was difficult to keep the schoolhouse warm. The fire in the stove had to be built anew each morning before the students arrived and Marie, the teacher, had to run around the room, trying to keep warm; thus the children's feet could be warmed when they arrived. Long underwear was the order of the day but, because it was awkward to fold the underwear neatly under long, cotton stockings, the girls wore dresses. No slacks for girls in those days and the boys had only striped overalls.

From February 12 to 19, Marie stayed at the Pike farm near the school. It simply wasn't safe or practical to drive a horse every day in that bitter cold and snow.

When possible, neighbors would stop at the school at night and bank the fire with large hunks of coal so the fire would keep overnight. That would help keep the entire building a little warmer.

The roads were finally cleared February 12. Sam had a crew of four men scooping beside and ahead of the maintainer, breaking up the drifts so the machine could clear a path. The last house on the route was Frank's (the man with the bobsled) so Sam turned around in Frank's around-the-house driveway, then he and his four men (Albert, Ed, Alphonse and Jim) ate their lunches by Frank's furnace so they could get warmed up and dried off before the return trip to town.

Dolores Suchomel
Mt. Vernon, Iowa

COMING HOME FROM SCHOOL

I cannot write about my memories alone because I was born a twin to my sister Alice. We were born in a large farmhouse in Linn county, Iowa.

Our home had no conveniences as we think of them today. We had a wood and cob cookstove in the kitchen and a wood and coal potbellied stove in the dining room. That stove furnished the heat for our home. We had no furnace, no heat in the upstairs bedrooms, no inside toilets, no bathtub, no electricity, thus no refrigeration. We used kerosene lamps throughout the house. Our Saturday night baths in the big round wash tub were events, specially in the winter months.

I don't recall just when winter really set in, in 1935, but it was to be a major event during those days of drought and depression. I know it was an early winter, and a bitter one. Alice and I had to walk a mile to a one-room country school in Marion township. It was not uncommon to freeze our faces or fingers during that winter. Later in the winter there were many heavy snow storms. School had to be closed on several occasions. I believe it was in late January or early February when we were told we had to make up some missed time by attending school on a Saturday.

On the chosen Saturday a heavy snow began about noon and didn't let up so school was closed again. The first house on our route home was a quarter of a mile from the school. I really thought we wouldn't make it. It was difficult to keep going. We sank deeply into the snow with each step. There was a terrible blizzard raging and we were so very cold. By the time we reached the house we were really about frozen. We went inside to get warm and it was then discovered that Alice's and my legs were frozen, or frost-bitten, almost to the hips. Ladies and girls didn't wear jeans or slacks at that time, but thereafter our father did allow us to wear overalls over our lumpy cotton stockings which covered the long underwear.

Our bedroom windows were completely iced over nearly all winter. We couldn't see out of our upstairs windows. Jack Frost painted some marvelous pictures. We took a hot water bottle to bed with us and sometimes a hot brick wrapped in a towel. In the morning our covers around our faces would be frosty from our breath. Alice and I would grab our clothes and run as fast as possible downstairs to dress behind the potbellied stove.

Our roads were blocked several times. When the weather seemed to relent, the neighbors would get out their scoop shovels and try to open the road so mail could be delivered. I believe the farmers and youngsters, both girls and boys, shoveled our way out to highway #13 at least three times that winter. Dad had gotten the bobsled out of its storage area in the peak of the double corncrib and our two workhorses, Mirt and Maude, carried us across the countryside. We went over the fences which were buried under the snow, to church on Sunday and to town for supplies. We were wrapped well in blankets and curled up out of the bitter wind.

Our country schoolhouse was heated with a wood and coal stove. Our classes were held as close to the stove as we could get. I think the year Alice and I started school there may have been ten or twelve students. In '35 and '36 there were only seven or eight, including our two older brothers. Most of the time, Alice and I were the only ones in our class.

Each day when we got home from school our chores were to shell corn to feed the chickens, to feed the horses, to fill the woodbox by the kitchen stove with wood and cobs, and to gather the eggs.

There were occasional great memories during the winter. Lots of snow was provided for one of our favorite treats—snow ice cream. I don't know exactly how it was made, but I think it was with milk, eggs and sugar. We set it out on a brick area by the summer kitchen were we always cleaned the cream separator and made butter.

Alberta Cray
Cedar Rapids, Iowa

WORKING MY WAY THROUGH HIGH SCHOOL

I was an orphan whom an elderly widow had taken to raise. She had a small farm located one mile east of Middletown, Iowa; it consisted of 23 acres of farm ground and 32 acres of timber. This timber came up to the back of the barn, so it provided me with many hours of enjoyment.

"Mom" had moved back to this small farm, from Iowa City where she rented a house and kept student boarders who attended medical school. This was how she put her own three sons through school. When her youngest son was graduated and on his own she was free to return to the farm which she had inherited when her husband had died years earlier. I was seven years old in that year of 1926. Since Mom had very little money, she started by buying one milk cow and a flock of chickens. A neighbor farmed her 23 acres on shares.

By 1929 the old milk cow was getting old, would not breed and went dry, so Mom sold her and put the money in the Middletown bank intending to use it to buy a new, younger milk cow.

But. before she found a cow to buy, the bank closed. I remember Mom and I walked the one and one-half miles to Middletown where she tried to retrieve some of her money. The banker told her there was no way he could let her have any of it. Her entire savings of $400 was gone. Mom told her problem to the farmer who rented her ground and he told her he had a nanny milk goat that he would let Mom have for our milk supply until times got better. In turn Mom let him pasture his eight or ten shorthorn cows in our timber pasture. We had this old nanny goat for more than two years, maybe three. I do know a miracle was performed for us. That old nanny was never bred yet she continued to give enough milk to supply Mom and me with all our milk needs for that two-to-four year period.

Even though I was still a tad, I worked, driving the horses for area farmers who were putting up hay. Their whole outfit would straddle a windrow of hay and the loader would push the hay up to the back end of the hay rack where two men would load it evenly over the rack.

Sometimes I would ride on the rack and change from one front corner to the other, as the hay was piled up. Then, again, I would walk and drive. I rather liked the latter because we had one mean fellow who helped load the wagons and he deliberately would throw a big forkfull of hay on top of me, when I was on the rack, without asking me to move over to the next corner. I would have hayseed and itchy dust in my eyes and down my shirtback and really be miserable.

One day while driving horses for the hay gang up at the new dairy (which had 100 head of cows) they had a heifer calf born which was so weak it couldn't get up and nurse. The dairyman didn't want to fool with it and was going to knock it in the head and feed it to his hogs. I asked him for it, so he let me have it for fifty cents. I had an old bicycle with a basket on its handle bars and I hauled this runt calf home on my bike.

Mom babied this calf and fed it goat's milk and, lo and behold, it got well and grew up into a fine milk cow. This little calf eventually became our milk cow and we were able to give old Nanny the goat back to her owner.

I should mention that the foreman of the old C.B.and Q. railroad section crew, based in Middletown, had developed bleeding ulcers and the old doctor almost gave him up. But first he told this man to drink nothing but goat's milk. He bought some goats and he got well. There seems to be a certain healing element in goat's milk that cow's milk does not have.

In 1934 we had a very dry and hot summer. This was the year to go down in history, at least in our area, as the terrible chinch bug year.

Those chinch bugs became so thick that they invaded field after field of grain and corn. Of course this was in the days before bug chemicals. so there was no way of spraying to kill them. Farmers tried to pour creosote around the fences, or outside of their cornfields, but this idea failed because when the bugs developed wings they simply flew right over the creosote band. One day that summer as I rode my bicycle to Middletown general store the one mile on highway 34, cars would pass me and behind them would be waves of black chinch bugs, swirling around in the backdraft of these cars, just as snow swirls around behind a car.

I remember that Mom's corn crop was so poor that year and her hay crop had burnt, that she decided our farmer neighbor should cut all her corn and shock it. Then Mom and I borrowed a team of horses and wagon and hauled this fodder to the barn where we shucked the best ears (none were good because they were all nubbins) and feed this to the chickens. Our cows had the fodder for feed. Those poor beasts had a bad winter that year. The chinch bugs were dead in this fodder and it reeked with a foul odor and surely tasted just as bad to the cattle, but it was eat that or starve.

Since I was a kid and not given to worries, I acccepted life as it came and really didn't know we were poor and in bad times. We never knew any differently. We had no phone, no electricity, no radio. We lived on a dirt road. No car, no horses. I walked every day that one and one-half miles to school and Mom and I walked to church every Sunday, rain, snow or shine. We rarely missed.

Mom's neighbor, who had an old Model T Ford car, would haul groceries and hundred pound bags of chicken feed and oatmeal home for us. The smaller amounts of groceries I hauled in my bike carrier. We were too poor to have a cream separator so Mom would put the milk into crocks and let the cream rise. Then she would skim it off with a ladle and when she had her little two gallon cream can full, I would haul it and a few dozen eggs to the Middletown store to trade for such staples as flour, sugar and salt. Every fall Mom had the store man come and sort out her chickens. She would sell him the old hens and young roosters and apply this to her store bill. God certainly was gracious to Mom and me because it seemed we were always able to keep the store bill paid up each fall.

One of those years we also had an invasion of seventeen-year locusts. Since the timber was close to our buildings, there was a constant, unending supply of music put out by these locusts. I remember catching them and some would have the outline of a capital W on their wings while others had a capital P outline. One stood for War and, of course, the P stood for Peace. I do know that we had war about ten years later and it seems to me that most of the locusts had the W on their wings.

By 1935 I was old enough to work all my spare time for the dairy. I started by milking seven or eight cows morning and night. Also I would bottle milk and cap it, in the old glass quart bottles, all by hand and wash up milk equipment every evening.

About this time the boss decided I was old enough to help deliver milk to houses in Burlington eight miles away.

Every morning at 1:00 A.M. I would arise and ride my bike one-half mile to the dairy, walking if the road were muddy. I would back the panelled truck to the cooler room and load the cases or crates of milk onto the truck, then ice it down. Then I would walk quietly through the house, using my flashlight, go upstairs and call the boss in his room. He would come down, check the load, and away we would go to Burlington, by about 2:00 A.M. We would have completed the route and be back at the dairy by 5:30 to 6:30 A.M. The boss was proud of our record: we would average delivering one and three-quarters quarts per minute, which was very fast.

He had a board step built onto the back of the truck and I rode on this. I would drop off this step when he would slow down and get the houses on the right side of the street. He would drive up the street to a house on the left side and get it. I would run to catch up with him and try to be back on my step before he got back to the truck. I wore tennis shoes and would drop off this step when he slowed to ten to fifteen MPH.

When we returned to the dairy, I would bottle milk until time for me to run home, grab a quick bite of breakfast, change clothes and run back that half-mile to highway 34, where I met the kids I rode with to school.

One boy drove a 1937 Chevrolet and hauled five of us kids. We paid a dollar per week for our ride to school and back. This was high school in Burlington. There were no school buses in those days. Our school district paid our tuition but we had to find our own way there. Also we had to pay for our own book rental and shop fees.

Then when I came home from school, I would change clothes and run back to the dairy, where I milked my string of eight cows and then bottled milk and washed up buckets, etc. I would get back home between 9:00 and 10:00 P.M.

This left me hardly any time for school homework as I had to get up again at 1:00 A.M. I averaged no more than three hours of sleep a night. For all this work I got seventy-five cents a day. But, with this money I was able to pay my book rental, shop fees and rides to school.

Most of my clothes were hand-me-downs from older nephews of Mom's. *I never had a new suit of my own until I got married years later.*

Needless to say I never was able to attend any school activities or take part in sports. Also I almost got kicked out of school for sleeping in class.

Our schedule in the winter was easier on me because the boss changed to evening deliveries so people could get their milk out of the boxes before it would freeze.

Every evening after school, in winter, I would walk five or six blocks to a cafe to meet the boss. He would buy me a hamburger and then we would start our route. We would get done and be home between 9:00 and 10:00 P.M. I never had to do chores any more because the other men working at the dairy weren't busy with field work. I was needed only for the route delivery. However, my wages were cut to twenty-five cents a day.

The summer of thirty-six was extremely hot and since there was no air-conditioning, people would sleep outside on the lawn or on porches, wherever they might get a breath of fresh air. And might I add, some of the young women were not aware that the milkman was getting an eyeful, if you get my meaning.

I remember one family which took three quarts of milk daily which they wanted put in their milk box by the kitchen door. The only catch was that I had to enter a door on the porch and walk half the width of the house, across this porch, to the box by the kitchen door.

This hot summer it seemed that half the family slept on this porch on cots and mattresses. Also sleeping with them was a big buff-colored German Shepherd dog. He slept just inside this porch door and I had to step over him in order to get to the milk box. That dog permitted this and never made a sound or movement until I had the three empty bottles in my hand and stepped back over him. Then, without a warning, he jumped up and tore my pants, where he bit me on the hip.

The next morning it was the same thing all over again only this time when I stepped over him to leave, he jumped up and tore my shirt collar down to my shoulder. I was scared stiff and told the boss I would not deliver to that house again. He told me to put the milk outside the porch door and leave a note, so I did. The people then put the milk box outside and there was no more trouble until a few weeks later when the boss sent me to collect milk bills. This was one of them.

When I knocked on the door, the lady paid me for the bill and then proceeded to bawl me out unmercifully. The jist of it was that they had to get rid of their pet dog, because he got cross and bit people and *it was all my fault* she said, because had teased him. How do you like that? I never teased that mutt but I couldn't convince her of that. I almost lost them as a customer over that deal: that was when I learned the customer's always right.

Then came the winter of 1936. What a winter! It was extremely cold and snowed so much it drifted the roads shut. Burlington never plowed the streets in those days and the snow got deep and froze in ruts. You were okay as long as you stayed in the ruts but if, when turning on to another street, you did not negotiate correctly, you would end up crossways of the ruts and be stuck. People behind couldn't get by so they would get out and help push you back into the track. It was like running on inverted railroad tracks — only ruts instead of rails to follow.

That same winter an old neighbor was cutting fire wood on shares in Mom's timber and I would help him on Saturdays. This one bitter cold morning (twenty below zero) we had built up a brush fire to get warm and, as we stood there, we heard a loud crack or pop. We looked over toward the source and found a big crack in the trunk of a large white oak tree. When we examined it and others we found several cracked open this way. The cracks were from one to two inches wide, maybe four to eight feet in length up and down the tree trunk. In that extreme, prolonged cold the trees simply froze so hard they exploded. We had almost three weeks when the temperature never warmed above zero and it would get as cold as twenty-two below zero at night.

There was a family that lived a mile north of us on the dirt road. They were snowed in and ran out of food and fuel and had no horses. The man did not farm but worked in town. Luckily, they had a telephone and called for help, so the man who farmed our place made a V-shaped home-made snowplow out of planks with a place in front where he could hitch horses. He took one team of horses and got a sled wagon box full of coal and his model T Ford full of groceries plus six horses hitched to this snowplow. He rounded up several of us farm boys and armed us with shovels. So we started to break through drifts to deliver these supplies.

The road ran north and south and in places drifts would taper off to be no more than a foot deep on the east side of the road but very deep on the west side. One horse might be forced to walk through or over a deep drift while his teammate had little to walk through.

I remember one big drift. The left side horse started to walk over the drift which was caked so hard it supported his weight. Old Bud walked so carefully we thought he was walking on eggs and was trying not to break any. His feet were above his teammate's back at times. Rarely he would break through but he was an intelligent animal and well trained so he would stand quietly while we boys shovelled him clear so he could walk again. We eventually got it all to those needy people.

Mom eventually built a new bungalow and I remember many cold winter nights, sitting around the register in the kitchen, cracking and eating hickory nuts. Our old housecat, Fluffie, would sleep on the register and my dog, Rover, would usually sleep under the table, except in summer time when he learned about the cool basement.

We damned up a creek in the summer and made us a small pool where we learned to swim. Then when I was a teen ager we used to go to a natural "ol" swimmin' hole' in a creek about three miles away. After a hot day haying or threshing, one older fellow who owned an old Model T would gather up a bunch of us and we'd all go swimming. This hole was located where three creeks came together, all three emptying there at one time after a big rain creating a swirling action which made a good hole. It was always washed out to be as wide as fifteen feet and as long as a hundred feet. It was so deep one boy's western bronc horse would swim all around it.

When watermelons were ripe we usually ended our swim by raiding the patch of the farmer who owned this land. We were careful and never trampled or wasted any and he never seemed to mind because he always had a lot left and rotting in the field. One day when I was about twelve two of us ate our fill of melons then went swimming. Here came this old German man, the patch owner, who called to us saying "Come on, boys. I give you melons." We were already full but couldn't refuse. He would pick one and divide it and before we could finish it, he had another ready. "Here, boys, try this'n." I tell you we were two sick boys when that was over. I think he knew we had eaten some earlier and was deliberately teasing us. He sure cured us. I can't eat melon to this day — at least not much.

For a while there as a lad I rode the neighbor's pony to carry water to the men on the threshing run. That was a real fun job because I loved to ride and didn't have a horse of own. My job was to carry this old clay water jug, tied to the saddle horn, to all the fields where men were loading the shocks of grain on racks to haul to the threshing machine. It kept me busy going back and forth between the well at the house and the men in the fields.

I received no pay for this except that I was given my lunch free. That was a lot when one considers that in depression days a lot of people were hungry as well as unemployed. Did you ever eat at one of those threshing run tables? It was out of this world. They really fed you, especially those German families.

As I got older I graduated to being a pitcher, the man who pitched bundles to the man on the rack. Then came the proud day when I was deemed old enough to run a bundle, rack and load, and haul the bundles in and pitch them off into the hungry mouth of the threshing machine. There is a special knack in loading the bundles so one makes what is called a square end to the load. This entails laying the bundles certain ways so they tie or bind themselves together. We dove-tailed the corners together. But that is so many years in the past I can't remember how we did it.

Also we made a corn cutter sled. It was V-shaped and had scythe blades mounted on each side, about eight to ten inches above the ground. Two men rode this rig and a horse walked between the corn rows, pulling it. As it progressed, it would slice the stalks of corn and the men would catch an armful and yell "Whoa". It's a wonder that some one never accidentally stepped in front of the blades; it surely could have happened.

Neighbors worked together to harvest crops, to put up hay, to saw fire wood. Even to hitching up a team, putting straw in the sled box and bells on the horses and taking sled rides in the winter. We'd meet at someone's house for an evening of cards, games, coffee and cocoa for us kids. Those were the days.

Some time ago, we had an electricity blackout for three hours. We lit up the old kerosene lamp which we used when I was a kid. I couldn't even see to read by it. How did I study by it as a kid?

I still marvel at the courage and faith of Mom in those terrible days of the depression and hot summers and cold winters. Her faith and trust in God and seeing how He cared for us and we never went hungry, was the best witness for me as a kid. I have never doubted God's love and care for me. Even when in 1969 I stepped into a grain augur and lost my left leg. He was there to comfort and heal me.

I have never regretted growing up in those hard times. We had lots of friends and they all pulled together and shared. Sure, those were hard times but, as I look back, I believe they were also some of the happiest times of my life.

I must tell you one more story. Back when I was an eight year old, I sat watching the chickens and one old hen with her flock of babies. Suddenly a hawk dived down and grabbed one of those chicks. Do you know, that old hen flew up after that hawk and hit him so hard that he dropped her baby chick. However, the damage was done. The poor baby was dead because the hawk's talons had pierced its body. But that old hen sure surprised that hawk. The remarkable thing was that this old hen was a Rhode Island Red. They are a heavy breed and not given to flying. But she had lost weight while sitting on her nest. I know she flew up at least fifteen feet in the air and she was fast enough that she attacked that hawk, and he lost some feathers in the bout, as well as his intended meal.

Kids today don't know what they are missing by not seeing baby chicks hatched by an old hen. The old hen will turn those eggs every day. I know because I have watched them do it. Then, when danger comes, the hen will give a long, scolding sound and all the chicks will run under her wings, then turn and peek out, their little heads sticking out among her feathers. No wonder we have that wonderful old gospel song—'Under His Wings'. Watching an old hen and her chicks makes me think how God protects us and loves us too.

Mom used to sing an old song called "There's a Queer Little House and It Sits on a Hill". When the mother calls, the children all run to her. It is a story about a hen and chicks. I have the song and words but not the music, but I can still sing it from memory. I think it came from the old McGuffey Readers back when Mom was a girl in 1880. She had been born in 1874.

Ed Hahn
Oakville, Iowa

TEACHER BOARDED IN TARPAPER HUT

It was on a small farm in central Minnesota where I was born about five miles from Deerwood with its four hundred people. My father specialized in raspberries and made a fair living for us by producing almost all the food we needed. He also was secretary-treasurer of a large farm insurance company. But cash was always very scarce.

I was graduated from Crosby-Ironton high school in 1931 in the middle of the depression. Most of the people in Crosby and in the county had jobs in the iron ore mines at that time but, as times got worse, the mines closed one by one. Jobs for school kids were very scarce. We got together and picked strawberries and raspberries for farmers during summer vacation. We would ride in a truck to the patches, work all day and get paid two cents a box, sometimes three cents.

One summer I saved my wages and bought a winter coat (Chinchilla) from the Ward's catalog; I think it cost twelve dollars. Of course I had to buy overshoes, mittens, a hat to go with it. So my summer wages were well spent. My older sister worked at a nearby resort and did better because she made a dollar a day. That was a very good wage because it went so far when prices were so low.

After high school I attended a teacher training school at Crosby-Ironton. It was a one-year course and upon completion, could teach in an elementary rural school. We each sent applications to many schools and were offered wages of fifty to seventy-five dollars a month. Out of that we would have to pay room and board. We would stay with someone in the district and usually would have to walk to school, do the janitorial work such as starting fires and cleaning up after the school day was over. Not many had enough money to buy a car in those times.

I was one of the luckier teachers who was able to stay at home because I was hired to teach in my home town. I received seventy dollars a month the first year, which the board gradually increased to seventy-five by the third year. Some of my families were very poor and some of my wages went to help them when it was needed.

Wanting to try some new experiences I accepted a school in Palisade, Minnesota, my fourth year. I suppose it was a step backwards because I was paid only fifty dollars and I had to pay thirty-five dollars for room and board in a tar paper hut. The old couple who boarded me were terrific people who had homesteaded their farm, raised a family who, as they were married, just built on the same property. All of the extended family lived nearby. I didn't starve but I didn't have any money either. The school board didn't have any money for repairs or books and, although the school received some state aid, it wasn't enough; we had pie socials and basket socials to raise money. I taught two more years at other schools which were somewhat better but never did get back to the seventy-five dollars a month. Times were bad.

Clothing prices were not too high: shoes of real leather were from five to ten dollars a pair; overshoes, usually rubber, were about the same price; snow boots, nice warm ones, were a little more expensive; a simple dress was one to three dollars; dressy clothes were five to ten dollars; blouses were fifty cents to a dollar. A twenty dollar coat was very nice but one always spent from one to three dollars for a hat to go with the coat. As a teacher I had to dress like a lady and slacks were not for work. After school, walking home, I could wear a snow suit, which I really needed because the roads were not always plowed.

There were no credit cards then as far as I can remember. You could open a charge account at some catalog places but they had to be paid monthly. It was best to pay cash or to go without.

Churches were apparently run on love. The minister would receive a small salary; many times he would be paid in farm produce or in freshly baked bread. Most of the people who helped in churches, like the organist, for example, were volunteers.

Going to the movies was big entertainment. Tickets were from ten to twenty-five cents. Always there was popcorn in the lobby for five or ten cents a sack. Those people with money would go for a soda or sundae at an ice cream parlor after the movie. There were no hamburger or fast food shops.

Wedding dances were popular in some communities. The whole family would go — babies, children, grandparents — no baby sitters needed. Local talent would provide the music and the food was brought in by the people involved. Sometimes a collection was taken as a gift for the newlyweds. Otherwise it was free.

Appliances were few: wood and coal kitchen ranges; ice boxes for refrigeration; not too much indoor plumbing; no air conditioning. Most people had a radio and maybe a phonograph.

I think people as a whole were more friendly, more neighborly, because it was really necessary to know your neighbors. You depended on each other. People didn't travel as fast or as far from home as today. The world was smaller in those years.

Hazel Winquist Greenhagen
Minneapolis, Minnesota

RAIN PANICKED FIRST GRADERS

School had been in session in Texhoma about six weeks when one evening our friends Dan and Sue came across the street for a visit. The subject of dirt storms came up and Dan warned us that any day we could expect one. He suggested I go to the lumber yard and buy a roll of brown, sticky tape and tape all my windows and doors to keep out the dust. I had seen a dirt storm in Woodward county and disregarded his warning, thinking he had exaggerated.

The next Sunday we went to Sunday school and church as usual. About eleven o'clock it suddenly became dark. The wind was blowing very hard, lights were turned on in the sanctuary, and we could see the dirt pounding against the window panes. There was nothing visible beyond the windows. Outside it was as dark as night. A branch on a small tree just beyond the window couldn't be seen. The dirt had blackened out the sun and wind gusts made a frightening noise against the church building. The minister made some remark about the storm, simply to put us at ease and proceeded with his sermon.

At noon the storm was still raging so severely that no one could leave the church, either to drive or to walk. Everyone went to the basement to visit. Periodically someone would go upstairs and report back on the weather. By three o'clock the wind had subsided sufficiently to give ten foot visibility so, within thirty minutes, we all left the church. We had to drive no more than ten miles an hour and with headlights on.

When we reached home, we parked south of the house and went into the back door to the kitchen. To our amazement, we couldn't see the linoleum on the floor. The tops of everything was covered with dust. The bedroom was the same way.

Just the previous week we had purchased a new wool rug for the front room. When we opened the door, there before us was a floor completely covered with dust. The only way we could tell there was a rug on the floor was at the edges where the rug was higher than the floor level. It was brown, not green, and there was no pattern at all. We couldn't believe what we were seeing.

On closer inspection, we noticed small mounds of dirt on the floor near the baseboards. Soon we observed that there were several small nail holes in the walls, through which dust was coming and piling up on the floor below, much like water from a sprinkling can.

My wife dusted off the piano bench and sat down to cry.

The first thing I did after school on Monday was to go to the lumber yard and buy that sticky brown tape. Then I taped every window in the house. I even puttied the holes in the walls; I taped the hinge side of the back door in the kitchen. The front door I taped completely shut and nailed the screen door to the frame so no one could open it. These efforts took two evenings but we were now ready for another black duster.

This storm made another problem. Two weeks previously, I had purchased posts and woven wire and built a fence around our front yard, plus painting the tops of the posts. We were protecting our one-year old daughter from the busy street.

When the dirt storm came the Russian thistles began lodging against the north side of the fence. Dirt collected in them and began to build up in the row. More thistles lodged and more dirt piled up until the fence was completely buried, except for those painted tops. Then the thistles blew over the fence into the yard and the whole front yard was ruined. I spent any spare time available during the next six weeks restoring the area. I removed the wire and posts, hauled off the excess soil and levelled the yard, being convinced we didn't need a yard fence.

In the weeks that followed we had other dusters and the harder the wind blew, the darker the storm. The soil was powder dry. It had rained less than five inches during a three year period. Pastures were ruined. The wind had blown the soil away from the grass roots and finally the plants themselves were blown out of the ground. The fields were just mounds of blowing dirt without a plant of any kind alive as far as we could see in any direction.

With all the precautions we had taken, we still had a lot of dust in our house. Every evening we wet a sheet, wrung out the water, and draped it over the baby's bed to keep her from breathing the dust. Each morning our pillow cases were completely brown, except for a white silhouette where our head had lain. How so much dust could get into that house always remained a mystery.

One Saturday afternoon a black duster appeared on the northern horizon, appearing to be a rain cloud, but within fifteen minutes we knew what it truly was. It was rolling like water that had broken from a dam, and rushing down the valley with a front twenty feet deep. The sun was low in the sky and shining on the dust at an angle that reflected many colors. It was a spectacle, but a threatening one.

The calmness immediately changed as the wind became very strong. The storm was now overhead almost at ground level. Anna took our daughter into the house and closed the door. I stood on the back porch to watch it a little longer. Within two minutes it was so completely dark I couldn't see my hand when I placed it before my eyes. It was total darkness.

This was the worst storm we witnessed in the panhandle. It raged for seventeen days during which time we never saw a trace of the sun. It was light enough most of the time so we could see to walk and we continued having school, but no one could drive a car. Once inside a building with the lights on, business could be carried on as usual. People became accustomed to this pattern and learned to live with it.

I arrived at school earlier than usual one morning and found the custodian sweeping the hallway. There were three large mounds of dirt which he was preparing to carry outside with a scoopshovel. When he finished he stopped by to tell me that there were only seventeen scoopsful that morning. That's a lot of dirt.

Classes had begun one March morning when it began to rain. Several boys and girls in my room would look occasionally at the water running off the window panes. One made a remark about it. Soon another said "Mr. Aaron, water is running down the ditch in the street. It has been a long time since it has rained this much."

There was a knock on my classroom door. I answered it and saw Miss Bull, our first and second grade teacher. She said "Mr. Aaron, I need some help. Do you have time to come to my room?" I asked if she were having trouble and she replied "I surely am. My kids are all crying and I can't get them to quiet down. I've tried everything I know." I asked why they were crying and she replied "My pupils can't remember ever having seen it rain before. The rain hitting the window panes is scaring them to death."

We returned to her room and it was a serious problem. Everyone was crying and some were screaming for their mothers. I got the middle-grades teacher and the three of us worked for thirty minutes to quiet them and make them feel at ease. Miss Bull then started them playing games and Miss Kincaid and I returned to our rooms. Yes, you guessed it. All our children were standing at the windows watching it rain.

Later we were at Guymon for a parade and encountered another severe duster. Everyone rushed to get home but about three miles out of town we all had to stop alongside the highway. An hour later motors were started and we crept forward in a long parade. We were forced to stop at intevals to wait until we could see to drive again. It took us over three hours to make that twenty mile trip.

The next morning was a beautiful clear day so I decided to drive to school. The car wouldn't start and had to be towed to a garage. After school it still wasn't ready and the mechanic showed me the problem. Over two inches of silt was in the bottom of the pan. It had gone through the air filter and carburetor, down the cylinder walls, past the rings into the pan. The rings were completely eaten up by these small particles of sand and the cylinder walls were so scarred that they needed reboring. The crankshaft was flat. There was no choice. We had to replace the motor.

So these were our experiences in Texoma, a town twenty miles southwest of Guymon. About one-fourth of the town is in Texas and the rest in Oklahoma. An elementary school was in Texas and an elementary. junior and senior high in Oklahoma. It is a town of 1200 people and 28 teachers in the school system.

We liked the people and were happy with our jobs but, at the end of the school year, we'd seen enough of dust storms in the panhandle and decided to leave. Those were hard years.

Allen A.Aaron
Woodward, Oklahoma

LET'S NOT COMPLAIN OF LACK OF NICER THINGS

When we children walked miles over dirt roads to our one room country school (Mt. Olive grade school, district 37, Grant county, Oklahoma) we girls wore cotton print dresses and anklets. Our legs were bare and the hard winds blew sand until it felt as if it were cutting our skin.

The winds blew dirt relentlessly. Fields were swept bare and fence rows were piled high with drifted sand. Housekeeping was a continual battle; our home was better than many but doors and windows did not fit tightly and dust poured in during those roaring windstorms. Mother was an unusually particular house-keeper and battled the constant layers of dirt on floors, tables, cupboards, curtains — everything. Of course we had no electric vaccuum cleaner nor any of the conveniences we take for granted today. Mother heated wash water on the wood range in our kitchen, water that was pumped via a kitchen pump, drawn from the hand-dug well in the yard. She had a wringer Maytag washing machine in the car shed and that was where she did our laundry, hanging the clothes on lines strung across the yard. She had huge washings and this was forty years before disposable diapers. When we were babes she had lines and lines of flannel diapers. Ironing our starched cotton clothes required many long hours weekly, using the old sad irons heated on the wood range, usually with a dinner of beans sizzling atop the range and bread pudding and bread baking in the oven.

Our folks raised big gardens every summer and the entire months of June, July and August were spent cooking and canning. We canned all the vegetables, quantities of sand plums, peaches, apples, many being made into fruit butter to be spread between slices of homemade bread for our winter school lunches. These lunches were carried in syrup buckets or grape baskets because this was long before the day of school lunch rooms.

In the thirties there were some extraordinarily dedicated teachers to whom we will be forever indebted. Their wages were about ninety dollars a month for the eight months' term. They walked or rode horseback to and fro school, taught all eight grades, gave every test in every subject and issued monthly report cards. They did the janitorial work—carried in the coal or wood for the stoves, carried out the ashes, swept the bare wooden floors. They acted as doctor and school nurse for 25 to 40 pupils; they were the recreational planners, directors and participants, refereeing the basketball and baseball games we played on our dusty outdoor courts. They selected all the program numbers for our Christmas productions, for our box suppers, for the last day of school. Those dialogues, plays, recitations and musical numbers took lots of coaching, but we were always so proud and plenty scared when performing for patrons and parents. Special highlights of the weeks were Friday afternoons when we chose sides to have spelling or ciphering matches, or even geography games.

Back to the pie and box suppers. Our parents brought kerosene lamps or lanterns from home to light the school house and loaned bedsheets for us to hang up for stage curtains. The money raised from the auction went for classroom aids like library books, a globe, a new flag, or perhaps a new basketball. Our teacher furnished all the Christmas treats and end of school awards. She dealt with all the disciplinary problems and built lifelong friendships with us. We pumped our drinking water with a long handled iron pump from the well that had been dug on the north edge of our school yard. We felt rich to have a cement walk from the schoolhouse to this pump. On this nice paved walk we skipped rope, played jacks, marbles, hop-scotch and lined up to march inside when the bell rang.

On Halloween some young fellows always thought it was their bounden duty to push over the outhouses. Once they even put a skunk inside our schoolhouse.

Games that we children enjoyed playing at school or anyplace were blind man's bluff, black man, drop the handkerchief, last couple out, flying dutchman and Andy over. Protective grates covered the class windows of the building so we didn't inadvertently break any while pitching the ball over the roof.

Virtually every farm family had pigs to feed and butcher, cows to milk, sheep and flocks of chickens. They tried to feed the livestock from the supplies of grain raised on their land but in the thirties the women started buying chicken feed in sacks because these cotton sacks were printed in colorful patterns. We loved trading to get enough matching sacks to make our own clothing, lunch cloths and curtains. It required three sacks to make a dress for most of us but one neighbor lady was so large it took five for her dress. With feed at $5 for a hundred pounds, she boasted about her $25 dresses. That truly was a high-priced garment in those days.

The men chopped and sawed lots of wood to be used in the stoves. For us kids our evening chores included carrying in armloads of wood to stack behind the stoves, with a reserve amount on the porch, where it stayed dry in rainy weather. Around the warmth of these old stoves in the wintertime, many baby chicks were revived, as were baby lambs, pigs or an occasional calf. Our shoes were polished and set on newspapers to dry on the oven door, to be ready for school the next morning. School homework was done in the warm kitchen on winter evenings, and I still have Mother's old kitchen table on which I did assignments when dishes were done and food cleared away. That table was one Mother had bought at a farm sale for a dollar when she and Daddy were first married in 1915. Think of the tales it could tell if it could talk.

It took a great deal of bedding to keep all of us warm. Grandma Bartlett and Mother pieced large numbers of comforters and made beautiful quilts from every remnant of material available; they made all of our clothes. Many of their heirloom quilts have been passed down to their great grandchildren who treasure beyond measure those beautiful hand quilted items.

In the hot summertime it was hard to keep milk from spoiling because we had no refrigeration. Sometimes we carried the milk, cream and butter to the basement to set on the cool concrete floor. Some people placed them in galvanized buckets and lowered them into the well above the water level. Woe to them when the handle came loose and the milk spilled into the water. Grandad Bartlett constructed a dandy icebox by building a double-walled chest of wood with sawdust packed between the layers, as insulation. Grandma got lots of good use from this and further conserved the coolness by keeping thick canvas over the wooden top. She could even make Jello in it.

Combines were just coming into popular use by the wheat farmers in the thirties. Lots of wheat was still put up in sheaves, with binders, then the bundles were hauled via hay-racks and pitched into threshing machines. It required large crews and a lot of hand work during the blazing hot summer days. We wonder how the workers did it all.

Oh, how I wish the men and women who nearly gave their lives during the lean years of the thirties could have lived to see the conveniences and blessings we have today.

What a dream palace our modern five room bungalow would have seemed to my parents. I wish they could have known the luxury of our wonderful bathroom and indoor toilet, all the running water anyone could ever want, the furnace that requires nothing but a flick of a thermostat switch to keep the entire house warm and cozy, electricity for wonderful lights, an electric sewing machine instead of her old treadle model, the shiney propane cook stove with accurately controlled oven, the gleaming refrigerator and well stocked big freezer, warm, thick carpeting on our floors, radio and television. Our parents didn't have a single one of these.

May future generations never forget the patient endurance of the pioneer parents and may they cherish the institutions of our land, because they are truly blood-bought. The people who made these things possible gave their time and strength through days and nights of unremitting toil, fighting the battles inch by inch against the discouragements of nature, in many instances giving their youth and becominhg old before their time.

Before we complain of toil or lack of nicer things, may our lips be sealed, lest we stand as weaklings in comparison with the citizens of the thirties.

Genevieve Loop Wilson
Manchester, Oklahoma

TABLET PAPER FOR SCHOOL WAS A PROBLEM

In the early thirties I taught in a one-room country school west of Dunlop, Illinois, in Peoria county. The school was small as were the wages of $60 per month. I walked the one and one-half miles west facing the cold west wind in winter because we couldn't stretch the $60 to include gasoline; my husband was out of work. Five dollars bought our groceries for three for a week. Our rent was five dollars per month for a three room cottage. Electricity was one dollar per month. We had no telephone. The sixty dollars barely kept the wolf from the door.

There was one family in school with six children. It was hard for the parents to keep the children in tablet paper. My rule was that every word in spelling class had to be written ten times. The paper was brought to class to show it had been written. The lower class wrote the times tables ten times; they, too, brought the paper to class.

I knew it was hard to keep tablet paper for the six children so, when I went to town, which was Peoria, I asked for wallpaper books of samples no longer in use. I tore sheets from the books, folded the sheets in four pieces, and passed them out to the lower grades for arithmetic and spelling; at times the seventh and eighth grade students used them for orthography. I tried to make it as easy as I could for the parents.

These children carried a gallon Karo syrup bucket of cold pancakes to school. At noon the older girl divided them among the six children. The family lived in a rented farm house, the father being a barber.

The little old school had double desks with a pot-bellied stove for heat. The children brought potatoes and butter to school. I took one-pound coffee cans with holes poked in the top and we put potatoes in the cans and baked them on the top of the stove. For some that was all they had for lunch.

I hung a Sears and Roebuck catalog in the outside toilet, with a rope on a nail. This was toilet paper.

Water was brought by each child in a jar or bottle because we had no well in the school yard.

When fall rolled around I was at Teacher's Institute in Peoria and the family with six children moved into town, thus saving on gasoline. The year before there had been children attending my school who belonged to two other districts. When this one family of six, who belonged in the district, moved away, the directors decided not to keep my school open solely for those outside the district. So I had a school with no pupils. The directors paid me $300 for the school year. Suddenly I was out of a job and this was their settlement.

My dad lost his farm; he couldn't even pay the interest on the $10,000 he still owed, so the loan company took it over. He was then sixty years old. He found a job working on the highway, swinging a sythe cutting weeds for one dollar a day. My brother, a young married man with a wife and child, worked as a farm hand walking behind a hand one-bottom plow and harrow for fifty cents a day or twenty dollars per month. His house was furnished and he was provided with one quart of milk per day.

In spite of the hard times, we survived the depression. I pray to God we never go through those times again.

Grayce E. Kuhn
Henry, Illinois

FAMILY LIFE

Gas For Henry's Flivver
Keeping The Boys In The Home Town (PHOTO)
Wearing Adhesive Jacket In Boiling Weather
Our Best Crop Was Babies
Frying Eggs On Sidewalks
How Dad Added A Second Story
Doctor Delivered All Four At Home
Strenuous Life On The Prairie For Twenty Year Olds
One Hundred Years of Memories
A Sunflower For The Man From Kansas
A Bucket Of Icewater
Old Worn Out Truck With Kids Piled High Thereon
When Drought Ended Near Cumberland River
My New White Suit
Doctor Wanted To Adopt Our Baby
Bartering For Piano Lessons
Human Relationships Conquered Depression Conditions
Seattle Hooverville Remains With Her
Camping In The Orchard
Some Traitor Told The Girls
Knowing The Value Of A Dollar
Hoboes And A Baby Sister
Door County Orchard Home Provided Safety
The Soft-Hearted Constable
That's the Way it Was in 1936
Mother Canned, Patched and Prayed A Lot
Pie Paid Off The Dollar Bet Twenty Years Later
My Favorite House
Making A Five Dollar Bill Look Sick
Everything Was Canned, Sugared or Buried
Woolworth's Was A Real Five And Ten Cent Store
Not Dirty Thirties—Best Years Of My Life
An Icebox Made From Snow
I Remember Hunger
Brilliant Man Working Like a Slave
Do You Have Room For One More?
Four Room House For Four Hundred Dollars
Two Days of Hard Work

GAS FOR HENRY'S FLIVVER

I had just graduated from college and was moderately in debt for that period of times. Jobs were hard to find. People's funds were tied up in bank closings and there was little cash around.

I was living on the farm with my parents and younger brother. Since most farms had milk cows and chickens, food for the table was no problem. What did hurt was the low, low price of corn, oats and hogs. They didn't pay off the debts and mortgages people faced. Corn sold for seventeen cents a bushel, oats for nine to eleven cents and hogs three to five cents per pound; after paying the freight on hogs sold in Chicago, the net profit was very small.

In addition to all that, dry and hot summers prevailed and the chinch bugs swarmed over the crops, destroying many fields. This was a total loss in some instances.

Farmers began selling their livestock one at a time in order to pay their obligations. Even if they could have kept their cattle, there was very little roughage to store for the winter's use.

One fall I husked corn by hand for a neighbor for seventy-five cents a day and he supplied the gloves. I cultivated corn for $1.50 a day.

For that kind of money I couldn't afford to take my girl to the movie more than once a week, to buy a nickle sack of popcorn and five gallons of gas for Henry's flivver.

Rural mail carriers and school teachers fared pretty well financially, but those in business had difficult times collecting money owed them.

One good thing came out of those depression years. They brought farm families closer together, since most of us were experiencing the same problems.

The bottom line was hardship. Families lost their farms, their life savings in banks which paid a small percentage on deposits. By and by the cycle turned the other way and by World War II almost every one had forgotten the trials and tribulations. But it was too late for the older folks who couldn't get a second start in life.

If it had not been for radio's entertainment with Jack Benny, Fibber McGee and Molly, Amos n' Andy, I'm afraid some folks would have gone off the deep end.

Frank E. Clark
Rock Island county, Illinois

KEEPING THE BOYS IN THE HOME TOWN

Years ago, after World War I, the cry was "How do you keep them down on the farm after they've seen Paree?" (With apologies to someone who probably has that copyrighted.)

The same situation existed during the thirties—how could the small towns of America keep its youth at home? It had built good school systems, hired the best teachers for which boards were willing to pay, provided local activities to enhance the appeal of the old home town—but, still the high school graduates kept leaving for greener pastures.

Our little town of Boonville, Missouri, had an unusual man in George Morris, our confidant and I believe principal; he wore several hats. Among other things, he arranged local job training opportunities for us to experience different kinds of work. We did everything imaginable, sometime during school hours, as an exposure to clerking, or whatever. George was a futuristic thinker.

Along came the National Youth Administration (NYA) and the Civilian Conservation Corps (CCC) which provided make-work opportunities for young people. They put some people to work making a little money, building retaining walls, planting forests, binding books for the local library, all sorts of things. But, again, they were a drop in the bucket of unemployment.

We young men were facing a probable war in 1936; we weren't so naive as to fail to see trouble ahead. The old home town was old stuff where there were no jobs, no new girls, nothing but parents to suspervise our every hour. So, hit the road, Jack. We saw our elders riding the rails to California, going to some place where work was rumored, so off we went too. Usually we didn't come back. Eventually some went to war and were lost; others found a niche in life and stayed wherever the niche led. Some were placed with big corporations and became mobile managers, being relocated almost annually.

One of Boonville's activities was it's Boy Scout troop #67. It had been around for some time and was quite successful. A new Scoutmaster (Duane "Pat" Smith), a new Assistant Scoutmaster (Jimmy Farris) took over the troop, boosted an older boy (me) to become a second Assistant Scoutmaster and, with the help of a Mother's Club, this troop went to town. The mothers organized many activities and encouraged us as individuals to keep in Scouting and to earn those merit badges. They attended award ceremonies and helped the leaders build that troop to contain the largest number of Eagle Scouts in the state of Missouri. There were fifteen of us—all Eagles—including the leaders. That was an amazing accomplishment for any troop. The attached photo shows the Eagles only.

Here was a special segment of youth, trained in the high school to work locally, trained with special skills by the Boy Scouts of America—and now, about fifty years later, only two of them still live in the county. One is deceased and others have been absorbed by the rest of the country. What a tremendous investment in education, in time and love, to lose all of that talent to the home town.

This probably wasn't unique to Boonville, which is today still a fine town. It probably occurred in similar county seats all over the country and the situation is probably true today. We educate for the benefit of other communities. Did Boonville, in return, benefit from an influx of well-educated people from other towns? Probably, but it is always a terrible loss to see youth have to leave home to find a place in life.

WEARING AN ADHESIVE JACKET
IN BOILING WEATHER

My summer of thirty-six began on March 31 when I was brought home from school with a very high fever, breathing problems, severe headache and painful sore throat. I was just twenty-two days short of my fourteenth birthday.

A doctor was summoned and my illness was diagnosed as being diphtheria. My life hung in the balance for about two weeks and I developed pneumonia and fluid collected in my right lung.

My mother, sister and nurses cared for me around the clock. My father had died when I was eight years old. The doctor was very attentive, even to the point of staying at my home throughout one long night when he thought I might not live. Also, I was important to him because he was new in town and he'd had only one other seriously ill patient, who had not lived.

When it became evident that surgery would have to be performed for the empyema (Editor: Webster defines this as "the presence of pus in a body cavity.") I had to be carried to a hospital twenty-five miles away from my home in Russellville, Alabama. My doctor was new in town and had not yet become affiliated with the local hospital.

Following the surgery I went home and was confined to my bed for almost three months. In order to keep my lung free of fluid it was necessary to have a tube in the incision and it was connected to a collecting bottle. I had several layers of adhesive tape around my chest, from my waist to my armpits.

The summer weather was almost unbearable. We had no airconditioning and I believe no fan. We didn't have an electric refrigerator and could afford to buy ice only twice a week. There was no rain, the street was not paved, and dust was like fog at times. Nights were equally uncomfortable. Water was scarce.

Of course it was necessary for my room and my bed to be sanitary at all times. My mother and sister worked diligently to keep the bed fresh so I could be as

EAGLE SCOUTS IN TROOP 67 — BOONVILLE, MISSOURI

First row, l to r: Deering, McMillan, Sam Cochran, Jr., Johnny Hosford, Billy White, Joe Rochus, Jr., Eugene Scholle and Jimmy Farris, assistant Scoutmaster.

Second row, l to r: Bill Hull, assistant Scoutmaster, Quenton Oertly, G. W. Norris, Jr., Gilbert Chamberlain, Eddie Mueller, Carl Schupp, Jr., Billy Huber and Duane "Pat" Smith, Scoutmaster.

cool as possible. That required frequent bed linen changes. Laundry was done by hand and the linens had to be boiled. Mother was using up her savings to pay for the accumulating hospital and doctor bills. Our only income was my sister's meager teaching salary. There was no money to hire domestic help.

Eventually prickly heat broke out underneath the adhesive jacket and I suffered from itching and perspiration. The blisters broke and my body became raw. Removing the adhesive was not advisable but the doctor eased a small bit open at the top so air could reach my body and help dry up the blisters.

When it was safe to begin taking off the jacket I couldn't bear the pain. It had to be removed layer by layer and when the last layer was reached I was in great agony. My body was too sore to use ether to loosen the tape, so they didn't remove all of it. The summer got hotter and I was in greater pain. I began loosening the tape about an inch at a time until I was able to get it all off. This took about a week. What a cool relief—still hot and sultry—but at least I was not imprisoned in an adhesive jacket any more.

There was a polio outbreak that summer and because of my weakened condition my visitors were limited to coming no further than the door of my room. As I began to show signs of gaining strength, I looked forward to going places again. However, because of the long illness I had to be restricted from places where there would be crowds of people, like movies and churches. All children twelve and under were restricted, because of the polio outbreak, and I resented the restriction because, after all, I was fourteen.

Finally, in August I was allowed to leave the premises for short times. On the day I took my first visit from the house I walked about one-half block to a neighbor's house. When I got back home I went to the doctor's office to get an injection for whooping cough. The doctor had said I couldn't endure a disease of that nature. I was the first person in town to be given this new vaccine. While I was there with him I mentioned that I had a pain in my side and, after a blood count, I underwent emergency appendicitis surgery.

By this time the doctor had built his own clinic and hospital so I didn't have to go to another city for this surgery. It was still hot and dry and in the hospital the windows were raised to allow as much air as possible. It also let in dust and noise. My window was directly opposite that of a friend who lived about 200 yards from the hospital and we could call to each other. That helped pass the time.

This surgery left no ill effects and when school began I was back in the saddle again. I had to take a reduced course load for a few weeks—just until I had my full strength back.

Do I remember the summer of 1936? You bet I do!

Ouida Quillin Thompson
Sheffield, Alabama

OUR BEST CROP WAS BABIES

Anyone living in Harrison county, Iowa, in 1936 should be able to write an interesting hard time story. I became a farm bride in 1930. Crops and finances had always been lean and our best crop was babies—good ones—a boy in 1931, a boy in 1932, and a lovely, longed-for little daughter in 1935. With plenty of milk, chickens and eggs, they all thrived. But in 1936 another baby was on his way.

Each summer day got hotter and drier. The 160 acres we were renting was very rough and had golden yellow ground. The spring had been good and the seeds sprouted and grew. By Memorial day the heat and dryness were becoming intense and from that time on every day was damaging. The normal looking corn began to shrivel. As if that weren't enough, chinch bugs and locusts invaded the area.

There was enough reserve hay and grain to keep a cow producing milk for the family and I had started baby chickens.

The fryers had grown fine. Each Saturday morning I dressed three chickens, took them eight miles to town, received a dollar for each and could buy enough gas, groceries and other necessities to keep us surviving until the next Saturday.

We had only dirt roads, with high banks on each side as we went over the hills, but that was the year we would have been glad to be stuck in the mud.

But the children grew, bless them. Relatives were kind to give me old clothes to salvage the useable parts from which I could make more clothes.

There was no refrigeration. The milk came in warm, was strained, put in a gallon pail that could be covered securely and hung in the well. It was good for supper. Can't remember how we got enough cream from it to cool and make butter.

That summer it was also a problem to keep the bread dough cool enough to rise instead of keeping it warm enough. I remember one afternoon while the bread was baking in the old cook stove that the thermometer got up to 112 degrees in the kitchen.

So the children could be comfortable enough to sleep in the afternoon, I would dip a sheet in a pail of cold water, wring it out and hang it over the south door opening.

Praise the Lord! In mid-August the rains came. Temperatures became normal after seldom being below ninety; the grass turned green—and we were given notice to move. Grass looked greener on the other side. In February we moved, via truck, to Guthrie county and baby number four was born two weeks later. Yes, there was another tag-along. They are all healthy and normal and have blessed us with sixteen grandchildren.

G. Cleo Smith
Des Moines, Iowa

FRYING EGGS ON SIDEWALKS

It wasn't at all unusual to see and hear of people frying eggs on the hot sidewalks. Anybody, but anybody had either done it themselves or watched someone else doing it. It was so commonplace as to be ordinary knowledge that when it was over a hundred degrees, that an egg placed on a downtown sidewalk would sizzle and simmer just about like at home in the skillet.

Hogwash, I think.

At least I never saw it completed.

In fact, I've tried to duplicate it on our electric skillet. I prewarmed the egg by leaving it at room temperature for a couple of hours; then I gently oiled a warm skillet and set the temperature at 150 degrees. When it had time to warm sufficiently, I broke the egg gently into the skillet and left it alone for an hour. Cooking all the time.

When I checked it occasionally I could see no change. At an hour I threw it out.

Now, how hot does a sidewalk actually get? Surely no more than 150 degrees. But there are people who will swear that . . . .

Once I did see them frying an egg on the street in Boonville. I believe it was in front of Viertel's garage—out in front for the whole world to see. Probably Dick was the one who placed it on the sidewalk and created a barrier so no one would step on it. As I went home from school, sweating like an animal, here was this raw egg waiting to be cooked. The sun streamed down on it; the paint peeled off the autos parked nearby; ladies swooned politely; it was hot. Somewhere between 105 and 1000 degrees F.

Here it was midafternoon and I couldn't wait forever, so I had to go on homewards, determined to check it out the next day to see how it fared. How thoroughly did it cook?

The next morning, on the way to school, I rushed up to the spot. No egg. No sign of an egg. No barrier. I asked Dick "What happened to the egg you were cooking yesterday afternoon on the sidewalk?"

"What egg?" he said. "We didn't cook any egg, kid."

I still don't know.

William H. Hull
Edina, Minnesota

HOW DAD ADDED A SECOND STORY

Having been born in 1928, I well remember the summer of 1936. I was born in Anamosa, Iowa, the third child of my parents. My father was a blacksmith. Farm prices had been depressed long before the crash of 1929 and since 90% of my father's income was derived from farmers, we had faced poverty for a good long time.

The incident that I so well remember began when Mother decided that we should own our home and stop paying rent. Dad, unable to stand her constant harping, finally gave in. He borrowed $2,000 from Grandpa and brought a four-room house in the wrong end of town. The house consisted of a living room, two bedrooms and a sort of tar paper kitchen tacked onto the back. There was running water in the kitchen but the traditional two-holer was out beyond the lilac bushes in the back.

Dad agreed to pay Granpa six dollars a week on the $2,000 debt but, since he only made $20 a week, we were now down to $14.

No sooner had Dad bought the house than Mom started complaining that it wasn't big enough and that we really needed an upstairs. Dad couldn't conceive of tearing off good shingles to build a second story so the argument went on until I was eight years old.

At long last Dad came up with a plan. All the plan needed for success was dry weather. No rain had fallen since April and it was now the first of July. The grass was brown and hurt your bare feet when you walked in it. The heat was unbearable. Mom would wring out sheets from cold water and hang them in the windows to cool what air was moving. At night we slept in the yard and the mosquitoes were almost as unbearable as was the heat.

Dad decided to go ahead with his plan. He set two telephone poles in the ground—one at each end of the house. He hooked a big pulley to the top of each pole and then put ropes through the pulleys and somehow attached them to the roof.

The morning of July 4 dawned as bright and hot as it had been all summer. Dad got up early and cut many 2 X 4 uprights on the ground. Then he climbed up and cut the roof loose from the house. With help from the crowd of people who had gathered, he began pulling on the ropes, a little at one end, then a little at the other. When the roof reached the proper height, the uprights were put in place and the roof attached to them.

By dark Dad and his crew were exhausted but the roof was in place and he could now build the upstairs under it.

We went to bed with visions of our new upstairs dancing in our brains. About midnight it began to thunder and by 1 A.M. all hell broke loose. The rain came in sheets, driving into the house whose roof was eight feet above its walls. We fought the wind and water all night, trying to hold up old canvas tarps to keep dry. But by the light of dawn we saw that the roof was still there and Dad's plan had worked.

The house still stands at 106 South Alderman in Anamosa, Iowa — a lovely two story house!

The summer of '36 passed only to be followed by the winter of '36 — but, then, that's another story.

Helen M. Gray
Center Junction, Iowa

DOCTOR DELIVERED ALL FOUR AT HOME

I was farming in Missouri, having started in 1929. I started with big ideas — four good mules, five cows and a hundred white leghorn hens. Things weren't too bad then but by 1934 the big dust storms hit and it never rained all summer. I had sixty acres of corn, which was quite a crop for one man then.

You couldn't see the sun in those 1934 days because the dust was so bad and the temperature was 105 to 110. We even had hot winds at night.

We cut down elm trees for cattle feed. In 1936 many cows were lost from broken bones, sliding into ditches. My brother and I lived well that winter. People asked us to dispose of their injured cow and we'd shoot it, sell the skin for $6 or $7, and butcher a good hind quarter.

In 1935 rain fell until July 4. What corn we got planted never even got to roasting ear stage until frost got it. In 1936 the cinch bugs and grasshoppers ate everything.

My wife and I lived on mush, cornbread, rabbit, ground hogs which we called "Hoover Hogs". We couldn't get on relief because I was farming. People in the cities were worse off than we were. Nobody had any money. My neighbors and me would chip in to make ten gallons of corn whiskey, trade it to the merchants for beans, flour and sugar to make more moonshinte. We didn't have any money but we did enjoy life and helped one another. We did have it better than city people. We cut our own wood, had our gardens and milk.

I built fence ten hours a day for a loan company for seventy-five cents a day. I sent three Angus steers and one short-horned steer weighing seven to nine hundred pounds to Kansas City and received a check for $75. Today they'd bring $700 to $800 each.

We had two boys and two girls. The doctor came out in the country to deliver them right at home for twenty-five dollars. I paid him with beef or hog meat. Once I paid him with a hundred fence posts and two loads of wood, ten quarts of blackberries. I don't know how people in the city did make it. Those that had jobs in the cities didn't know what a fifteen minute coffee break was, working for up to ninety cents an hour.

My boys make more money now in one week than I used to clear in one year. They think I'm lying to them when I tell them about those times.

I'm 83 years old and have seen it all...and am pretty well banged up.

John R. Brackett
Troy Mills, Iowa

STRENUOUS LIFE ON THE PRAIRIE FOR TWENTY YEAR OLDS

Marrying in June 1934 we were immediately involved in a battle against the chinch bugs. We fought them with a drag hooked to the team of horses and creosote which burned our eyes and skin. But they and the drought took all the crop anyway. In 1935 lots of the corn was flooded out but pasture and hay were good so we gained a little. We lived on a rented farm two miles from Oakley, Iowa, and twelve miles from Chariton, our county seat.

The first snow of 1936 started on New Year's evening and little did we realize as we returned from a family gathering that evening how long it would be before our Model-A Ford roadster would travel those dirt roads again. We were twenty (Martha) and twenty-five (Paul), in our second year of marriage and expecting our first child in February.

Blizzard after blizzard continued and it was bitter cold. Our house was old and drafty so we moved our bed into the living room, nearer to the heater stove and several mornings awoke to a small snowdrift across the bed. Our only other heat was our one extravagance—a big Kalamazoo wood kitchen range, which I loved dearly and still do where it is now in our basement. It weighed 540 pounds and we'd paid $84.76 for it, including freight. On it we cooked our food, heated the kitchen, always had a reservoir of warm water, and we bathed the baby in front of the open oven door.

Among the other furniture, we'd saved $150 and I remember we spent a little of it on four unassembled kitchen chairs from Sears Roebuck for eighty-nine cents each.

By January 24 Paul became so concerned about my condition that he hitched his big team to the sled, bundled me into it with blankets and hot rocks for my feet and away we went across ditches, through fences (which he later repaired), wallowed the horses through snow banks for the two miles to Oakley, where he put me on the train bound for Chariton about twelve miles away; there my family, our doctor, and the hospital were all located. I was a sorry sight, wearing his gloves over mine, my three-buckle overshoes, a wool stocking cap and all the sweaters and coats I could manage over my bulging figure. I carried a knapsack with a few baby things and clothes for myself. I stayed there in town with my sister and brother-in-law because the weather was too dangerous.

For three weeks Paul stayed on the farm alone, caring for the livestock and the house, being outside so much he couldn't tend the fires well, so he moved the cream can behind the heater stove, but it froze solidly anyway.

On February 14 my sister sent word to Paul that they were taking me to the hospital. The call was relayed from the Chariton operator to the rural operator in our neighborhood, then on a different line to our house.

Paul dressed and arranged with neighbors to tend the chores, and started walking all the way. It was twenty-two degrees below zero with snowdrifts up to the barn eaves. After several miles he came to the C.B.& Q. railroad tracks which was better walking. He arrived at the hospital at about 8:30 A.M. very cold with two toes so badly frostbitten that he was required to wear felt shoes for several winters.

At 3 P.M. our seven-pound son arrived, well and healthy. During our ten-day stay in the hospital the weather broke, temperatures moderated with some thawing in the daytime and refreezing at night, but the roads were still impassible. The baby and I stayed in town another two weeks until we boarded the train on March 4 homeward bound. Paul met us in Oakley. The neighbors had driven cattle over the muddy road the previous day and it was still sufficiently frozen for our little car to make it; we bounced, clattered and banged the two miles to home.

By the last of March warmer weather had melted the huge drifts and the roads were settled enough that we felt the baby should have a checkup and we should buy some much needed groceries. Crossing the creek over a big rattling bridge which had been condemned two years previously, the water rushing underneath was nearly touching the bridge. I was so frightened I refused to cross it again so we drove twenty-three miles just to go around it.

Spring came early with new calves, lambs and pigs. We seeded oats, planted corn and had a few chickens and a garden.

We had no electricity and our water supply was at the foot of a steep hill. To avoid carrying all that water up the hill Paul made a drag which held two barrels and brought it up with the team of horses, for laundry and bathing. For cooking and drinking, we carried it in buckets.

By mid-May we were having some unusually early hot days. I recall one day while doing the laundry in the smoke house, on a washboard of course, I noticed the sky had darkened and, shortly, glancing out again, it was obvious that a bad storm was brewing. The sky was terribly black in the northwest and heading our direction fast. Closing the smokehouse door and windows I raced for the house, closing windows and doors as I went, then snatching the sleeping baby from his basket, grabbing a small kerosene lamp and running for the cave. As I rounded the corner of the house I saw Paul had unhitched the horses from where he had been working in the field and was heading for the house on a dead run in a swirl of dust and wind. I too felt the wind as it slowed my steps. To this day I don't know how I got the two cave doors raised, my cargo down in the entrance and the doors closed again. But I did, and managed to light the lamp. Paul came from the empty house to the cave where we all waited out the storm.

It was a severe storm but we had no permanent damage—only our oat crop was laid flat and never recovered.

By July it was dry and hot, reaching a hundred degrees or more nearly every-day, with no modern facilities. Baby spent a lot of time paddling in a little water in a dishpan on the kitchen floor. At night we slept in the yard on a fold-out sanitary cot and mattress. Baby was in his basket with cheesecloth to protect him from bugs.

Crops began to dry up; then the grasshoppers moved in. There were clouds of them. The ground would move with a grasshopper carpet when you walked. They ate holes in some of the laundry on the clothesline, ruining one pair of overalls. They chewed on the pitchfork handles until they were rough—the men would bury the pitchforks in the hay to hide them. My garden became a stubble because they ate off all the leaves, from everything even including the weeds.

Our three cows couldn't produce a lot of milk because of lack of pasture, so a small weekly check from cream and a few eggs was our only means of buying groceries. Believe me, we were careful to buy only essentials. We were fortunate to have a three dollar check. If we had as much as five dollars, we could buy two big sacks of groceries. There was no such thing as baby food so I prepared Baby's cereal by cooking oatmeal to a gruel, then forcing it through a sieve. When he got teeth he could eat chicken liver and gravy and all vegetables cooked soft.

One hot summer day I decided to go to town for some supplies. Putting the baby in the crib beside me, I took off in the Model-A for a five-mile back roads trip to town. Then I felt the thump, thump of a flat tire. What to do? No help for several miles. Since Baby was asleep, I got out the tools, jacked up the car, pulled off the tire and patched the tube. Then I put it back on, pumped it up and, since I didn't hear any air escaping, I put the tools away, got in and went to town and home with no further problem. This was a first experience for me but I had seen Paul do it many times. With no money for new ones, even though a tube only cost a dollar, we patched them until the patches sometimes over-lapped.

By fall the grasshoppers plus the hot, dry summer had taken their toll with the hay and the pasture. The corn was badly damaged and we decided it would be best to chop it for ensilage except that we had no silo. To meet that need we converted a hollow tile garage into a silo and placed some on the ground. Chopping ensilage by hand is one of the worst jobs ever to be done on a farm. It was a matter of neighbor helping neighbor. When our turn came we had to charge some groceries at the Oakley store in order to feed these men two meals a day for two days. That $9.62 bill gave us much concern until we could pay it from money from the next bunch of hay we sold.

By mid-November our livestock feed was very short and Paul bought a pile of ensilage from a neighbor who lived three miles away over hilly, ditchy terrain. The weather turned colder, it started to rain and freeze and we soon had four to six inches of ice over everything. Paul needed that ensilage so he chained all four wheels of the Model-A to pull the wagon over to get the ensilage. On the first hill he slid backwards and jackknifed. Then he managed to get the main pulling team of horses shod on all four hooves with spikes. Even then the horses would fall and stumble, skinning their knees. But they made the trip every day until it was all hauled. So the livestock wintered very well.

Thus ended our remarkable year of 1936.

Martha and Paul Peterson
Chariton, Iowa

ONE HUNDRED YEARS OF MEMORIES

My husband, Ras, was transferred to Milwaukee — he was representing a drug company. One of those wholesale firms, outside of Chicago. I travelled with him during those years. We covered Minnesota and the Dakotas. This was about fifty years ago. I was in my forties then — a great time in my life. Of course I'm 100 now, having just observed my birthday on June 30, 1989.

We were married and the kids were grown by the nineteen-thirties. Ras had four boys and one girl and I had two girls and one boy. We were a family of ten when we were married in 1921. His oldest girl got married when she was only 18 and later died of cancer. His oldest son died of cancer as did Ras himself. We were married during the years when all of this was happening. His youngest son, Ken, was with the Greyhound bus company as a tour guide when he was killed. He was out for dinner with one of these boys at the Dyckman hotel and when they came out, Ken was going back to work. His car was found still down by the Dyckman but his body was found up between first and second avenues in the alley; we never found out why it was so far from his car. That was in thirty-three.

I was travelling with Ras out of Milwaukee in 1934. We stayed in hotels although there were motels then. It didn't cost much to stay in a good hotel in those days. He used to pay nothing for me. Travelling men never paid anything for their wives or for any other woman they happened to have along. The single rate was about a dollar and a quarter a night. They did have good restaurants too. And we travelled with his sample cases loading up the car.

What were the roads like? Some were pretty good and some were terrible. In some spots they were pretty well paved but sometimes out in the Dakotas he got stuck in the snow—oh, and lots of times stuck in the mud. But he had chains for the tires. He used to drive with something he put under the rear wheel—a piece of mesh-like stuff. He'd slip it up to the wheel, then get the car wiggling back and forth on it and then he'd get going. But you never let anyone stand behind that thing because it would come swooshing out from under that wheel like a big knife.

No, he never had a special kind of car. He got a new one every two years—a different car. But Chrysler really was his favorite car. After he passed away I bought nothing but Chryslers—I always had a white Chrysler.

I have never been quiet. My father would see that we always went to church. I'd comb his hair and he'd pay no attention to me as a child. I could pull his hair, comb his hair, love him, crawl around at his feet, mess with his papers and magazines on the floor or at church and it would never bother him. He never once said a thing to me. The people in church would bring their company to watch us—saying they wanted them to see what went on in church. He was so patient with me.

I'll never forget how I learned to ride a bicycle as a child when we lived in Napanee, Ontario. We had a great big lot and I had a cousin who used to ride in to school. She'd leave her bicycle at our place. I taught myself to ride when she left the bike there. Oh, I was a little devil.

What stands out in my mind about travelling? We used to stay overnight up in Michigan where we could play the machines—the one-armed bandits. We had them in northern Minnesota not too long ago too. We had them here in Minneapolis too and we used to go down and play them. There was a nickle one, one for dimes, quarters and even silver dollars. Yes, that was more fun than playing bingo. I went out there in California and my daughter-in-law and I drove up some place, took the bus and went to one of these gambling places. I would win and then I'd lose. I never ended up with anything but I'd only take so much with me. My son would give us each fifty dollars but I'd just keep that and not lose it at those tables.

I went overseas on one of those big ships, right after World War II. We'd dance until twelve o'clock; then we'd go downstairs and gamble and have something to eat. But we had to get up in the morning to eat at nine o'clock. If we weren't there for our setting, we just missed breakfast—that's all there was to it. The ship I came back on had the same arrangement.

Yes, I've had a busy life. I surely have. The only thing I regret is sometimes people say I shouldn't have spent all that money travelling like I did. But what would I want that I don't have here (pointing out her comfortable apartment in an exclusive neighborhood). I wanted to know what was going on around the world and I saw a good part of it. I got into Italy—oh, boy, ever, did I have a good time there. That was in 1950. Of course the war was over and I had a regular circus.

Upon being complimented for looking so youthful: I think it was because my dad and mother always acted young too. They were always kidding each other, even when they got older. My mother passed away in the fifties.

Oh, yes, yes, I remember the dust and dirt of the thirties. We didn't have it just here in the midwest, but in Manitoba too 'way back in the years we lived there. That was in the 1910s-1913s. My oldest daughter was born in 1910—the next one 1913 and my son in 1914. They're in their seventies now.

We had dust in Florida too. I was working down there in the alterations department. A friend and I worked at the same store and shared a place to live. We took the blankets and hung them at the windows so the dust wouldn't come in. That was as recent as the fifties.

My parents really gave me something when they gave me my great attitude toward life. But you didn't get sassy with my dad. When we lived in Ontario we had a beautiful home. One day when we were eating dinner I saw a girl go by and I waved to her. Her mother used to be a washwoman. My father said to me "You have your nerve talking to that kind of people." I said something about she being just as good as we were—and I lit over there in the corner just like that. He tossed me across the room—just kind of pushed me. Of course he didn't really hurt me.

When I first went to school I came home and was scratching and scratching. My father said to mother "You'd better look at her hair". She did and sure, I was lousy. My father put the teakettle on, out in the summer kitchen, of course, got the water hot and took me out in the back yard. He took a whole cup of kerosene and poured it right on my head, then washed it. That got them. He sure got rid of the lice.

I have no reason to complain about life at all. None whatsoever. I guess I've made it happy. When I think of some of the things that I did when I was a kid—I'd steal apples off the neighbor's tree and could eat green ones by the bushel and they'd never bother me. I can still do it. I can eat anything and do—at 100 years of age. I have a good stomach.

My father and mother were very fussy. We ate three meals a day and we ate good ones. Of course breakfast. Very seldom we had anything else but oatmeal porridge and maybe a little toast with it if you wanted. No bacon and eggs. And we always had fruit of some sort. Sometimes my dad would buy the regular wheat porridge and fix it like oatmeal. I haven't seen the wheat porridge for years and I just loved it. But that Cream of Wheat stuff—I can't stand that. Mother would never cook it.

When it came noon we always had dinner. My father would come home for dinner and unless we were going to have company at night we'd always have everything—meat and potatoes all the way through—and dessert. If I didn't clean it all up I got no dessert. My father waited on the table and I'd get a little of everything and if I wanted more of something I could have it.

When it came to dinner at night, if we had dinner at noon, for supper we'd sometimes have some left overs from noon but we always had fruit. My mother was very good at always fixing up something special for us. We always had a good meal—and I think that is the trouble with our children today. They eat any time they want to.

We always had a roast for Sunday dinner. Mother would put it on the top of the stove in a pot before we went to church. Then when we'd return home she added the potatoes. She cooked a leg of lamb the same way in just a regular iron pot. It would be browned and just as tender as it could be. A pot roast is one of the finest foods a person can eat. But—it was all healthy food.

At Easter my dad always bought a suckling pig. He had a roaster made the size of the oven. You could just barely get it in. The pig had the head and tail left on it and it was stuffed with dressing. He cooked it, always for company of course. It was brought in standing up because father would put wires in the legs to hold it up, an apple in the mouth—and bring it in. It was about fifteen inches long. I always served some of these same things to my own family—veal or pork—but I never had that big pot in which to cook the suckling pig.

When there were ten of us at home I would have to spend as much as ten dollars to get a roast big enough for all of us. It probably was 15 pounds or more. And how much we liked those roasts with the tenderloin in them. I've forgotten the names of them.

Ethel Rasmussen
Edina, MN

A SUNFLOWER FOR THE MAN FROM KANSAS

Where is that little sunflower pin? It has a border of yellow felt, cut to resemble the petals of a sunflower—and in the center it says something about Alf Landon. He was the presidential candidate (R) running against Franklin Delano Roosevelt in FDR's second term in 1936.

I've looked everywhere for that pin, starting in my two former cigar humidors; they now collect pertinent and nearly pertinent things I just have to have around. In other words, junk.

Then to my downstairs office desk. It wasn't in the center drawer which has everything "from a big red wagon to a candy cane" in it. Nor was it in the special drawer where I keep a few worthless antique coins and personal mementoes.

Aha, I thought. maybe it's in my box of boyhood medals. Seven Junior Division National Rifle Association medals—up to Expert and Instructor—and Senior Pistol Expert rating. Here's my original AAA School Boy Patrol badge— looks like a G-Man's shield. And, oh, yes, a ring made from a black walnut shell. Typical boy stuff.

But where's that Alf Landon pin I've kept for 51 years? I know it's here someplace.

Why do we hang on to all this stuff? Here's a boxfull of hand-made handkerchiefs from my dear Mother, God rest her soul. They are antiques but probably worthless at a sale, but money wouldn't replace them. Perhaps the daughters and granddaughters would find them meaningful. They come from the era when ladies had never heard of Kleenex.

Alf Landon was overwhelmed by the juggernaut of FDR's power and action. He carried only two states, and obtained only 8 electoral votes versus Roosevelt's 523. Born in 1887 he had been an Independence, Kansas, bookkeeper, a distiguished professor at Kansas State University, a first lieutenant in the chemical warfare service, two term governor of Kansas, but he couldn't stop Franklin Delano Roosevelt.

William H. Hull
Edina, Minnesota

A BUCKET OF ICEWATER

The year was 1936. It was still the aftermath of the depression for us. Although father had just gotten a job as a laborer making $15 a week, taking care of a family of seven was not an easy task. Need I say that many years later the scars are still present.

The weather was as bad as the economy. I don't ever remember being kept home from school because of inclement weather but I vividly remember dressing warmly with a wool cap and scarf and even knit gloves which had been darned and made like new, then trudging off in my galoshes—boots were unheard of at that time.

I would follow the path to school with snow over my head on both sides. The more I walked, the further away school seemed to be. I remember some kind person took me by the hand and led me to my home where I thought I'd never thaw out completely. My mother said that if I'd walked faster I'd have made it to school. Although I felt defeated, she made me hot cocoa with water. What a treat!

Spring and summer wasn't much better because 1936 was a winner because it was hot and dry. However, I'll take summer over winter anytime. Air conditioning was unheard of and very few people could afford the luxury of electric fans. Hence everyone used hand fans, which could be anything from a piece of cardboard on up. Living in the city made it even hotter for there wasn't any place to go swimming and very people had cars and there was no money. Seashores were out of the question.

The days in school were almost unbearable. I remember that each afternoon someone brought a clean bucketful of water into our classroom and each row would take turns going forward for a drink from the agate dipper. We couldn't afford paper cups. No, we didn't worry about germs. It was so refreshing, especially before the ice melted.

We were lucky. We had food and never went hungry. Relatives and friends helped one another. We were proud to wear used clothing if it were clean.

While I never became an artist, each Christmas I received a set of cheap paints (they cost 15 cents) and coloring book, a stocking filled with a few hard candies, nuts, an orange or sometimes an apple and a monkey on a stick. I never had a doll of my own until I had children. Now I have five.

I remember in '36 going to the corner store for neighbors and getting two or three pennies. I saved those pennies and at the holidays I was able to buy everyone a ten or fifteen cent gift. This made me happiest. To this day I'd much rather give than receive.

Most of this happened in Philadelphia, PA where I was born. Later, when I was married, I moved to New Jersey but still my wish was to live in a warmer climate. That wish came true for I now live in California.

Mrs. Camille Alcott
Danville, California

OLD WORN OUT TRUCK WITH KIDS PILED HIGH THEREON

My husband, Ray Powell, was born and raised in Bucklin, Kansas, near Dodge City. Since he was born in 1920, he would have been 14 to 16 in those bad years of 1934–1936. So he well remembers the drought and depression years.

Ray tells me how hard his father farmed a small wheat ranch, about 1 ½ miles from Bucklin, and how he almost lost it due to the drought, except that an angel in disguise, unbeknownst to Ray, paid off the mortgage and saved the farm. That angel was Ray's brother who had made good money as a banker in Wichita.

My husband also remembers how the dust would blow so hard and be so thick that it looked at times as if it were dusk. His immediate family stayed through the dust, drought and depression but some other family members did not stay. Ray remembers how they drove into the family yard looking like "Grapes of Wrath" people, an old truck loaded down with worn out furniture and kids piled wherever there was a spare spot. To show how times change, one of those kids is now a favorite relative, living in Anacortes, Washington, as a retired army colonel, has a nice big boat, airplane and a summer home in the beautiful San Juan islands. Some days when we visit them in the islands, the two men recall the old time days back in western Kansas, when things weren't so good. I'm sure the hardships they both endured have "stood them well" throughout their lives.

Mrs. H. Ray Powell
Portland, Oregon

WHEN DROUGHT ENDED NEAR CUMBERLAND RIVER

The worst drought I have experienced in my eighty-two years of life occurred in 1936 — and the two worst floods and winters. We had an early winter in 1934, early snow and very cold. There was a great flood on April 15, 1936. Rivers and creeks were out of banks and then it turned very hot and dry. Farmers used horse power in those days and the ground became so hard they couldn't prepare it for planting crops. Those that did get their crops planted found it was so dry that corn began to parch and dry, dying for lack of rain. Grass land would burn over. Springs and wells on the farms began to dry up. Farmers began to haul water wherever there was a spring running in September.

I drove a car from Tennessee to Glasgow, Kentucky, taking my mother and sister with me; as we passed through Burkesville, we stopped for a visit with my mother's sister who invited us to stop for supper on our way back. I drove on through the fertile Marrowbone valley. Grass fields were burnt; corn crops were all lost. I drove along the banks of a large creek that flows through the valley; it had dried to an occasional pool of water.

We arrived back at Burkesville late in the afternoon. After taking supper with mother's sister we started for home, crossing the Cumberland river on a ferry boat just at sunset. Dark, stormy clouds were in the south of us; as I pulled off the ferry boat a few drops of rain hit the car.

The more we advanced the harder the rain fell. The road was lighted by lightning while thunder shook the car. The drought had ended. We passed cars stopped because of the rainstorm, the road being more nearly a creek than a road. We arrived back in Tennessee about ten o'clock at night because of a dirt road. We had to cross a creek that had been dry all summer and I knew I couldn't drive the car to my own house under those road conditions so I stopped at a friend's home where I left my mother and sister to spend the night — and started walking home. When I arrived at the creek that had been dry all summer, the rain had flooded it out of its banks; I removed my shoes and started to cross. I could feel rocks bumping my feet as they drifted down the swift current; I arrived home at eleven o'clock that night.

We had an early winter starting in October and continuing until late spring. Very cold sleet and snow covered the ground almost every day.

Quinn Davidson
Pall Mall, Tennessee

MY NEW WHITE SUIT

As a high school senior I lived only for a white suit. There was an actor named Sidney Greenstreet, a big man who always wore white suits in the tropics. He must have been an idol. The very end of gentility, the supernova of being well dressed was to own a white suit.

I saved my money from work at J. C. Penney and stretched every dollar I could stretch to afford that white suit. Of course my parents told me how impractical it would be, but you know kids, nothing could disuade me. I had to have that white suit. Finally I got it.

What a thing of glory it was — all three pieces. Pure white! Clean white! The most attractive, most sexual thing in town. My WHITE suit.

I well remember the first night I wore it. It was to a show at the Lyric theatre — an antique building approaching the century mark. The beautiful old edifice which was and is today the oldest continuously operated theatre (legitimate) west of the Mississippi. Four huge columns of brick outside, a lofty ceiling inside, used as a stable during the war for union troops and horses in the basement. A place with a capital P.

The show seemed late and I was walking home up Main street. It seemed very dark and very ominous — probably because I had seen something like "Dr. Jekyl and Mr. Hyde". Anyway, I felt insecure. To say I was fearful would be to face the truth and no one wants to do that. Besides, I was off to college at the end of the summer — to be a college man.

It was midsummer and the mulberries were in fruit. If you've never tasted a sweet ripe mulberry you have missed one of nature's true delicacies, which it heaps upon a big tree almost to the groaning level.

Blackbirds also are very fond of mulberries.

Now blackbirds came into town to roost at night in the trees on main street. Particularly after eating mulberries all day long.

You're ahead of me, aren't you? Me and my white suit!

As I approached home, I started whistling. How stupid of me. I've always liked to whistle and been fairly decent at it. But it didn't occur to me that it would excite the sleeping blackbirds in the trees directly over the sidewalk.

I whistled and whistled.

And every blackbird in the county simultaneously shit directly on me.

William H. Hull
Edina, Minnesota

DOCTOR WANTED TO ADOPT OUR BABY

I had my first child delivered at home on May 8, 1936, a Monday. The doctor brought a nurse, an anesthetist and enough sterilized sheets to cover everything in the house. All of this for $35 which included taking care of me for the full nine months. He charged what he thought you could afford to pay. He was a specialist and at that time had adopted eleven children. He asked to adopt our girl too, saying "What can you ever do for her?" We kept her.

That summer the pavement softened from the heat. There was no air conditioning but we managed to buy a fan for $1.98. I hung damp cloths over the sides of the baby's crib and let the fan blow across to an opened window. She slept well and had no heat rash like so many babies had that summer.

My husband made $13 a week working in a chain of grocery stores six days a week, 14 hours a day and every fourth Sunday he and others took inventory of about 17 different stores. The man he worked for invented grocery carts; I believe his name was Sil Goldman.

Our icebox had a drip pan; every other day we got fifty pounds of ice delivered. Also we could get laundry picked up, washed and returned wet for forty-nine cents. I hung it up on a clothes line.

On the plus side we could get a wonderful plate lunch for thirty-five cents, a cup of coffee and a piece of pie for eleven cents. Men's trousers could be cleaned and pressed for fifteen cents.

We had no car to be an expense. My husband rode a street car to work.

In 1942 we moved to Texas but we'll long remember the nightmare summer of 1936.

Nettie Mae (Isham) Harding
Dalhart, Texas

BARTERING FOR PIANO LESSONS

The depression of the thirties affected everyone, specially the arts — music, painting, sculpturing, etc., because people decided these could be discontinued and maybe renewed later.

As a piano teacher I well remember the 1936 year as well as a few years before. People did not have money to buy even the necessities of life, let alone luxuries or piano lessons. My expenses for room, meals and every day items became more than could be provided by fees from a few students.

Some parents who really wanted their children to continue their piano lessons began to offer services in exchange for lessons. One lady offered to do my washing each week for her daughter's lessons. Another did my ironing. This was before polyester fabric was available.

A lady who was an excellent cook baked pies and cakes for her daughter's lessons. I could have a party any time just by telling her the kind of cake I wanted or the number of pies needed. Another patron, who lived on a ranch, brought me freshly dressed chickens and fine ham. Their daughter was a lovely girl and quite talented. She married and when her children were of school age the family went to Switzerland where the children were enrolled in private schools of renown. What a change! I have often wondered if the children were ever told that their grandmother brought me chicken and ham to pay for their mother's piano lessons.

There were four sisters who were taking piano. Their parents owned many sections of land, the taxes on which amounted to quite a sum of money. They asked if I would accept a beautiful crocheted bedspread for two months' tuition, so they could use their ready cash to pay the taxes, after which they would then pay the regular tuition. I agreed and the bedspread was a beauty which I have enjoyed using for many years.

Public school teachers had to accept vouchers instead of checks; some merchants were able to accept these vouchers as payment for groceries, clothes, gasoline, but usually at a discount. I remember one teacher found a good small farm and paid for it with his vouchers. A few years later oil wells were brought in on his land.

Women stood in line to buy a pair of hose. Even bobbie pins were scarce, as were many other things.

Doing without didn't hurt or destroy us. Instead we became more grateful and thankful to God for our blessings. Should another such depression or recession ever occur, I sincerely believe that the American people have sufficient faith and hope to pull through such a time graciously and victoriously with the help of God.

Gertrude Rasco
Memphis, Texas

HUMAN RELATIONSHIPS CONQUERED DEPRESSION CONDITIONS

Although I now live in Utah, I was born in South Bend, Indiana, on April 29, 1936. Mother was from a farm in Wheeler and Dad was the second son of a building contractor who had been wiped out in the crash of 1929. They were living in the construction company office, which the receivers of the company property allowed, partly to discourage looting and vandalism.

As time came for my arrival, Dad and Mom had no money for doctor or hospital bills and food came from my mother's folks on the farm. Extra food was being traded around through our extended family, friends and neighbors. This provided variety. Everything was used. Some extended family members subsisted almost entirely on pumpkins, like my grandmother's family in Ionia, Michigan, which was too far away for us to help effectively.

About the middle of April that year Dad found a job installing landings and a fire escape ladder on the three-story Jefferson street hotel. The job would pay $50.

When Dad got the job there was a ruckus because unions were organizing to provide scarce jobs for their own members. A group of three leaders told Dad that he would have to join the union, pay the initiation and dues fee of about $15 or he wouldn't be allowed to start the $50 job. Dad told them he wasn't going to join because he needed all the money the job would pay.

The job was started by going to the hotel roof, placing two 4 X 8 beams over the flat roof edge, and by sandbagging the roof ends of the beams to hold them in place. Then the third story platform or landing was hoisted up, using ropes and pulleys, to be under the upstairs hall window. A 2 X 4 was placed across the inside of the hall window and the platform tied to the 2 X 4 with rope so it wouldn't pull away from the outside wall. Dad crawled outside on the platform to lag and bolt it to the exterior of the building.

While he was on the platform, star-drilling anchor holes in the brickwork, a man believed to be a union enforcer, reached out, pushed the platform away from the wall and attempted to topple Dad down to the ground. Dad tried to jerk him onto the platform but the man jerked away. Both ended in the hallway in a deadly fight, which continued down the two flights of stairs with my Dad's economic desperation winning the day.

Dad completed the job and collected his money the day before I was born. Early the next morning Mother was admitted to Epworth Memorial hospital in South Bend. Since our family doctor, Dr. Helman, was out of town, they grabbed an intern to help in the delivery. He was going off duty and was wearing a white shirt. The shirt became soiled during the delivery and I am told Dad paid him $5 for a new one.

He also paid Dr. Helman $5 for prenatal care and the hospital bill of $40. I understand that Dr. Helman was provided apples and potatoes as his fee when there was no money available. He was one of the most important and respected people in the family circle. His medical pamphlets were always in great demand.

By the time I was two weeks old, Dad had a job building two houses on the south side of Angela boulevard, two blocks west of Michigan street. There was no money to pay for someone to care for me, so I was placed in a bassinet and hauled to the job site. Dad did the heavy work and Mom tied the reinforcing bars together with mechanic's wire. I looked on from my bassinet, all bundled up in the early morning cold (as attested by photographs.)

The family pulled together throughout the depression, grew in numbers, and redeemed the family construction company property on North Wilbur street.

I grew up to be the shadow of Dad and Grandpa on their construction sites. I had to behave or I got paddled. Somehow, all the oldtimers on the jobs had the right to paddle me if I didn't behave. I was puzzled as to why Dad and Grandpa tolerated, befriended and employed the bewhiskered grizzled codgers. Some of them ate cow and pig brains, kidney, liver and stunk from loose bowels and limburger cheese.

I noted that as a pre-schooler I was welcomed at the Hoosier brewery, Drewey's, where Grandpa sometimes rebricked the boilers. Also at other places like O'Brien Paint, Wheelabrator company, Notre Dame and Saint Mary's universities and about any place I wanted to go if with my parents. By the time I was five I could sneak away from Mom, flag down a strange driver of a concrete truck. ride for a couple of trips and be delivered back to our house. Mom would be in a dither. Later I learned that the concrete plant was owned by a group of Dad's friends.

It took many years to realize that strange things had been happening from 1929 to 1936: family relationships had held up; there was sharing with friends and family, Broken and worn out saw blades had been converted into knives with ebony handles cut from a log of that material. The knives had been bartered with local farmers for chickens, pigs and produce. Material and work was bartered and shared. It was important to know somebody who knew somebody from whom one could get a favor or help. One dealt, trusting that the bread placed upon the waters would return. Old unemployed construction workers would stop in at the shop from 1929 through 1940 just to use equipment to mend or repair personal items.

I well remember how, at the shop, they would sort out and cut rotten or scrap lumber and stack it by the barbed pyramid chain link fence next to the street. Good lumber was moved far to the back of the property. Every night this cut wood was "stolen" and taken over the fence. Grandpa Charlie would appear at the office about 8:30 in the morning. If it were cold, he would look to see if smoke was coming from all the chimneys in the neighborhood, or just a few. If the chimneys of widows were not smoking he would go on a rampage to the adjacent houses, accusing them of being thieves and telling them he wouldn't mind the thievery so much if they'd at least take enough for the widows. Then he would return to the shop, start up the belt-driven table saw to saw more wood to throw against the fence for the next night's raid. Some uncut boards were also thrown there in hopes that the thieves would do some of their own wood cutting. That woodpile was maintained for years as my family's contribution to the neighborhood. The pile was kept high enough so a ladder on the outside of the fence would provide easy access.

I finally realized that I had been born at a special time. The grizzled codgers (or grandpa's cronies as my dad called them) were people who had shared adversity and help. There was a special respect for each other. Although I saw many wear the tatters of street people, they were indeed considerate princes.

The summer of 1936 was a point in time when human relationships conquered depression conditions. That year marked the point of successful human bonding. I found myself being given special consideration by people who were total strangers to me but who knew my family.

Years later I would see the fruits of those times. Grandpa Charles would upbraid me severely when I was driving him somewhere and did not pull to the curb and stop when a funeral cortege approached. I was told in no uncertain terms to show respect for the dead, partly because they had gone through trying times. I tried unsuccessfully to challenge him on the basis that he didn't know the person concerned but that didn't matter; he respected the toils and hardships of his fellow man.

When Grandpa Charles (Karl August Jordan, his immigrant name) died in 1953, among the mourners was a threadbare old man who went to the casket to pay his last respects. While doing so I saw him slip a fifth of whiskey into the bottom half of the casket.

When my mother, Evelyn, died in 1976, her cousin came to the funeral from Appleton, Wisconsin. The cousin left the Indiana toll road and asked directions to the Hay funeral home. The toll booth operator asked which one since that firm has several locations. When the cousin mentioned my mother's name the booth operator stated that "Ev's viewing" (her nickname) was at the corner of Jefferson and Ironwood streets and then gave the cousin detailed directions.

If a depression ever comes again, we need to emulate the noble nature of those who perfected their love for their fellow man in the trials of 1929 through 1936.

John Jordan
Spanish Fork, Utah

SEATTLE HOOVERVILLE REMAINS WITH HER

I was only eight years old in 1936. It's interesting what you remember having seen through the eyes of a child.

We were riding in our new 1936 Hudson, the one with the shifting mechanism on the steering column, which was a new and radical departure from the gearshift on the floor. Unlike the stick shifts of today, this had a little mechanism operated with the index finger. Our new car was black and shiny and the most beautiful auto I'd ever seen. I remember the front and back door handles were together, thus making a very dangerous situation should the rear door be opened while the car was moving. This happened to me as my father was accelerating and I tried to close the open door. My mother's screams quickly brought the car to a screeching halt before I was dragged out of the car.

As we rode along the Seattle waterfront we passed about a hundred shanties built from pieces of scrap metal and packing crates. The tenants were huddled around small bonfires as the perpetual Puget Sound rain drizzled down. This area was called Hooverville locally. Herbert Hoover had wanted a chicken in every pot but these people didn't even have a pot, cooking or otherwise.

We lived in a modest home; my father worked for the city street department; it was a good steady job but not lucrative. I can remember him being paid in warrants rather than with a check. These warrants were like promissary notes which could be redeemed for cash in the future when the city coffers were replenished. They didn't, however, make the payments on the new Hudson nor put food on the table, nor pay the rent. I can remember living in constant fear that our family would be relegated to the Hooverville area. My grandmother, a widow, lived with us, and my uncle and his family of four, lived with us for a while that year, until my uncle got a job with the Works Progress Administration (WPA). It was basically a welfare program but those receiving benefits had to put forth some effort, which is much better than we have today.

Our clothes came from the Salvation Army Thrift Store. I don't recall ever having a new store-bought article of clothing until I was sixteen and got my first job. For my birthday in 1936 I received a beautiful, newly painted, two-wheel bike from the Thrift Store. I couldn't have been more thrilled or excited if it had been brand spanking new. I have a lovely, expensive ten-speed bike now but I don't like it half as much as I did that second hand one I got for my eighth birthday.

We seldom had chicken in our pot but we did have a lot of beans and potatoes. I don't remember ever being really hungry or going without food. But anything that was put in front of me I ate and relished when reminded by my mother of the plight of the Hooverville residents. I even remember mentioning in my prayers of my gratitude for a real roof over my head and a warm bed in which to sleep, and asking Him to help those less fortunate.

I often think fondly of that 1936 Hudson, used eight years later when I passed my first driver's license exam and five years after that, polished to look like new, as it chauffeured me to my wedding.

Those of us who lived through those troubled times, when the livin' was far from easy, have a resilience and ingrained grit the likes of which my children have not seen. Any one of them will tell you they have heard all about it as I, like my mother before me, threatened them with their own private Hooverville any time they were inclined to waste or not finish food on their plate.

Belle Weight
Provo, Utah

CAMPING IN THE ORCHARD

It was always hot. Sweat came to the brow and under the arms easily during the thirties. Everyone seemed to smell of sweat. Clothes became stale easily. Housewives didn't have electric washing machines so handy to day, and to keep the family's clothing free of dirt and smelling sweet was a backbreaking job.

Tom and I were always working on some merit badge or the other. Always thinking ahead toward that day when we'd be Eagles. We knew we would make it sometime. But it took work.

We decided in the spring to qualify for our overnight by sleeping out in an orchard on the hill on old 40 out of town. It was a hot night and we knew we wouldn't need much except our pup tent and we'd sleep in our underwear. The problem was that we didn't know there was a chance of rain.

Rain! Hell! It never rained anymore. But that night we cooked our small rations over a little fire, using my very small skillet that must have been a World War I relic from Uncle Seb or someone. What a tiny thing it was. Anyway, we ate a bite and then pitched our tent.

Now like all good Boy Scouts we knew everything there was about pitching a tent — or so we thought. We pitched it on the slope in the apple orchard with lots of good ol' trees around us. And we knew enough to ditch it all the way around — just as a token — because no way would it rain. Suffice it to say we only dug a little ditch, so small it wouldn't have handled dew. Then we went to bed, talked until exhausted and went to sleep, snug in that darned little pup tent.

In the middle of the night we were awakened by a strong wind, flashing lightning and a downpour. That rain came down like it was going to bring the last four years' average up to date in thirty minutes. And it all came rushing down that slope where we were located. Water was everywhere.

We had water running into the tent from holes in the top; there was water rushing across the bottom where our blankets were strewn and water inundating us. "Hell", one of us said, "What the devil are we doing out here?"

At nearly that precise moment a terrible crash and nearby shock of lightning made us jump nearly out of our underwear. But nothing seemed to have occurred

Well, we stuck it out but we'll never forget that night. We finally went back to sleep for a while to awaken stiff and cold, wet to the skin. We had to climb through the branches of a downed apple tree directly across our tent opening. That crash of the night before had been a direct hit within ten feet of us!

You can imagine how our folks felt when we came straggling in early in the morning, a pitiful sight for two future Eagle scouts.

I've often wondered where we borrowed that junky pup tent.

William H. Hull
Edina, Minnesota

SOME TRAITOR TOLD THE GIRLS

North-central Wisconsin, being a wooded, rolling landscape, was spared the effects of the awful dust storms of the states west of us. But it surely felt the drought and depression of the thirties.

In 1936 my parents had already lost their eighty acre farm eight miles east of Merril, the Pine river district of Lincoln county. So they were more or less in limbo at that time. I, at 15, was working as a hired hand on a neighboring 200 acre farm owned by Ben and Martha Rajek. Their 16-year old son, Benny, was my best friend.

January started cold, with much snow and at mid-month a roaring blizzard hit us for a day and a night. The next morning was totally still with the mercury holding at 58 degrees below zero. Later we were told it had been-60 at the Merrill courthouse. While getting the milk to the cheese factory, just a mile away, Benny and I froze our noses, little fingers and toes. For six weeks the temperature stayed below zero. Then one morning about the first of March, the older Ben awakened the household at 4 A.M. saying "Boys, do you hear anything?" We listened and then we heard it — the sound of water running off the eaves. It was 47 degrees above zero outside. So quickly does the Chinook come!

Spring broke beautifully but unseasonably warm, with massive floods. Creeks were over their banks. The Pine river. normally a placid forty-foot wide stream, became a wild two hundred-yard torrent. Benny and I hiked two miles upstream and found a big pine log hung up in some gooseberry bushes. It had been hollowed out and its ends covered with tin, undoubtedly as a watering trough by someone upriver. The two of us, reckless young smart alecks, pulled it loose and, with makeshift poles, eased it into the current that was raging down through the trees inland from the main river. We must have ridden that shaky craft for three miles before we found a flat area sufficiently shallow so we could jump out and wade ashore.

I remember well the invasion in the early thirties of a newcomer from the prairie states farther west. It was a small ground squirrel known to mammologists as the thirteen-lined spermophile, but to farmers as the striped gopher. It was a pest. It was everywhere, thriving well in the drying land. Benny and I accounted for numbers of them with our slingshots but, by 1936, we had graduated to single-shot twenty-two rifles and then our inroads were noticeable. I recall that in a two-month period, in spite of our busy workload, we depleted their numbers by sixty-seven. But, by 1940, with the return of the normal, wetter climate, the gophers, I learned, were scarcer than hen's teeth.

The summer grew so awfully hot that by day's end our thoughts were on only one thing — making a run for the swimming hole about a mile downriver. We'd build a big bonfire — a smoky one to ward off mosquitoes — and then hoot and holler, diving off the high bank and a leaning tree until far into the night. All skinny-dipping, of course, until some traitor told some neighborhood girls how to find our swimming hole — but that's another story.

By August the hot sun and the accompanying furnace winds made life miserable. Corn, that much-needed supplement for winter-fed dairy cattle, was already stunted and soon withered on the stalk. Oats attempted to reach maturity but was soon barely hanging on in the 120 + degree heat. It was bleak.

Late in the month our family packed ourselves and some belongings in and on the family car, a 1926 Chevvie, and caught up with the caravans of dust bowlers heading west, hoping to find a better life in Oregon's Willamette valley. Things were tough all over.

The drought apparently peaked in 1936 but it was a number of years before the economy rebounded enough to be of real help to the farmer. Like the advent of World War II perhaps.

Donald R. Jole
Vancouver, Washington

KNOWING THE VALUE OF A DOLLAR

Many people slept on their lawns, as did we, even making a soft spot for our three-month old baby son.

To help with the housework, we hired an unemployed lady who only wanted her board and room but, after some private juggling of figures, we insisted she take two dollars per week, which we felt we could spare from my husband's meagre monthly check.

We could never make ends meet on that slim check but felt lucky that we had it, considering how many of our friends had no income at all. We had to borrow from time to time, getting three or four dollars from our parents to tide us over until the next check.

It was interesting how folks learned to economize when it was really necessary. We women learned to take apart paper tissues to make them last twice as long...and to use them only when visiting or shopping. We cut our own hair or had a friend do it. We wore anklets to eliminate the expense of stockings. My father-in-law owned a shoe last and when our heels became worn on one side, he removed the rubber heel lifts and switched their positions, putting off the repair job to a more distant date.

We lived in Winona, Minnesota, where the meat packing plant hired many workers. But who had enough money for gasoline to get to work? It was needed for food. The solution was simple...everyone used a bicycle. My husband, a government meat inspector, bought a bicycle and, along with hundreds of plant workers, pedaled his way to work, leaving the car in the garage.

I watched him from the window of our furnished rooms (we didn't call them apartments); the street leading to the plant was choked with bicycles and any automobiles present had to slow down if they didn't want to bump into a bicyclist.

I remember the choking dust which seeped into our home from under the front door. We dared not open the windows for air; we would only get more dust coming from the dust bowl states where valuable top soil was being blown into neighboring states.

I still have on hand an expense ledger for the years 1932–1937. In June, 1936 we paid $3.44 to the milkman for a month's milk, $7.22 for gas and electricity, $2.00 to have the car brakes adjusted and our monthly grocery bill was $9.90. Even that ten cents was considered a savings. It may all seem like peanuts now but every cent had its value then.

There was humor in our difficult times too. One day I washed a pair of my husband's socks and hung them on the clothesline, conspicuous because nothing else was on the line. My neighbor quipped "I suppose your husband has only one pair to his name, so you have to wash them out often."

Our slogan was: "We must hold on because a better day will come." We did and it did.

The depression years taught us much. I am self-sufficient today at age 79, but I still turn out the lights of an unused room. I still look for bargains at rummage sales, andI still shop for groceries on sales days. It is sad to see the younger generation placing articles in their shopping carts without even glancing at the prices. Having enough money is fine, but knowing the value of a dollar is better. The summer of '36 had its educational virtue.

Jean Schmidt
Siren, Wisconsin

HOBOS AND A BABY SISTER

I recall vividly the hobos or bums that came to our door on the west side of Provo. The Union Pacific, the Rio Grande Western, and the small guage Heber Creeper (a local line that hauled cattle, sheep and sometimes people) all ran near our home. All kinds of men would come to the door asking for something to eat. Mother would always give them a big slice of home-made bread with preserves or jam and a glass of milk. We are Mormons and do not drink coffee, tea or alcohol and had none of these to offer. They would be expected to chop some kindling in return, which they always did. I suppose our house was marked by the hobos. They didn't get a whole lot but they never left hungry. We'd often talk with the hobos about where they were from and where they were going. We weren't allowed to open the door by ourselves — one parent always had to be there.

My folks showed a lot of compassion in the thirties. Mother was the tenth of thirteen children, born and raised on a homestead dry-land ranch in Spanish Fork, Utah canyon, where her father was killed by lightning when she was seven. So life for her mother had been a struggle. Dad was the last of eleven children and his father died on dad's seventeenth birthday on the farm in Springville, Utah. Both of my parents were college graduates.

There were "hope houses" everywhere in Provo. The footings and foundations were in and the floor joists covered with a flooring and tar paper. In effect, people lived in the basements, hoping they could finish the upstairs eventually. There are still some around but more often those awful tin and aluminium trailers.

Almost everyone made a living in agriculture. . .and everyone hunted deer in the fall, eating all of the venison. Dad's job paid him regularly and only rarely did he receive script paper. The teachers at Brigham Young university often went for months without any real money for their services. They were paid in chickens, wheat, flour and anything available. Students paid their tuition with "like or kind" which meant anything they could get their hands on.

We all wore hand-me-downs. Little Orphan Annie and Jack Armstrong were our heroes, along with Charles Lindberg and a guy named Ab Jenkins who drove the Mormon Meteor on the flats of the Great Salt Lake—and Jack Dempsey, who grew up in Manassa, Colorado and Provo. His mother was a Mormon also.

Jeanette, our baby sister, came to live with us on March 3, 1936. Of Mother's five boys, three died almost immediately because she had something they called "Milkleg"—I believe it is called edema today. (Editor: Webster defines milkleg as being "a painful swelling of the leg at childbirth caused by inflamation and clotting in the veins.") Neighbors said Baby Jeanette was a door step baby, an unwanted child that someone left on our doorstep, knowing it would receive love and care. Mother and Dad always said they arranged to have her through Dr. Cullimore, our family doctor. Anyway, we named her after Jeanette McDonald, a great singer.

We were never poor.

Dad taught biology and agriculture at Provo high school, making about $600 a year. He also refereed athletic games on the side to keep the WHEATIES on the table and to make life better for we three kids at Christmas time.

Dad worked every day of the depression. His school job ran from Labor day to Memorial day and he worked for the National Park System seasonally at Zion, Bryce or Grand Canyon each summer.

The day after school was out we'd all pile in the old 1928 Chev and head south for the parks, kids and groceries all of us going along at 27 miles per hour. We knew that at exactly 28 mph the front wheels started to shimmy.

I can still smell the old car with canned and bottled goods wrapped in newspapers and stacked everywhere therein. We often got carsick and dad would stop while we took turns throwing up.

We made this pilgrimage every summer from 1931 through 1936. Dad received $75 a month that last year which was good money then. Thus we had food: chickens and access to a cow when we were in Provo. Then my dad was offered the principalship at Provo high if he'd go to Stanford at Palo Alto during the 1937 summer.

At Zion national park we lived in seasonal housing built by the Civilian Conservation Corps (CCC). They had wooden plank floors. They were pretty crude. Visualize half-inch cracks in the floors, roll-up canvas windows, canvas roof over 2 X 4 boards, temperature over a hundred degrees. The bath was a tub and the refrigerator was an icebox that everyone used. There was a tap of running water outside and a common privy. Mother would get upset at people using the privy and then going to the icebox without washing their hands.

Once one of the affluent Californians dropped her camera down a canyon and my brother and I went after it—almost straight down and back up again. She gave us a five dollar bill which we gave to Mom. The next time we went to Cedar City or St. George we received a new shirt and some candy.

We also got to know the wrangler very well, partly because we were always hanging around the horses. When there weren't enough dudes to ride all the horses up Angel's Landing or through the Narrows, we'd get to ride the extra horses. However, it was strictly understood that we didn't run them. Of course we often went in the other direction and did run them. I remember once when it thundered and rained very hard. Of course Mother had instilled a lot of fear of lightning since her father had been killed by it but we didn't have any that day. However, the horses spooked as the thunder cracked and the cloudburst came. We really had fun that day.

I went back as a college student and drove a bus for the Park System. Dad went back in the fifties, along with Mom, to be honored as one of the very first Park Rangers—a pioneer. I still have old people come up to me in Provo and say "Are you Ken Weight's kid, Joe?" When I say yes, with a smile, they always say "He was the very best teacher I ever had." That's when you get paid for being a teacher.

Joe Weight
Provo, Utah

DOOR COUNTY ORCHARD HOME PROVIDED SAFETY

Too cold to let the little girls go outside, even for a ride around the yard on a sled. Too cold to do anything but stoke fires and exist the best we could. Things had not been easy. Still, we were some of the lucky ones. We had a place to live—in the farmhouse on top of a hill on the orchard place that had been the old homestead. My husband's grandfather had established it after arriving from Valders, Wisconsin, and originally from Valdres, Norway. He had served in the 15th Regiment in the Civil war, served in 1871 as an assemblyman, came to Door county, Wisconsin in 1873.

The original log cabin he had built had been sided over and additions built on both sides. It had stood unoccupied for many years, then Sven's son Albert bought the land and planted a cherry orchard. He lived in town, on the Sawyer side of the bay, driving up twice a day in winter to milk the cows. In summer he worked the orchard which began bearing in 1925.

The cellar under the kitchen addition could also be reached from outside steps. There was a long driveway to the road, through the apple orchard, and the tracks of the Green Bay and Western ran through the land. The big barn, tool house and implement shed and the granary were grouped around the yard like covered wagons in a semicircle. The pump stood proudly in the middle. The outside toilet was back of the granary.

As a town girl and country school teacher I adjusted quickly to the inconveniences. My girlhood home hadn't had electricity until I was thirteen. Sewer and water didn't come down our street until I was about twenty. The telephone was installed when I was about twelve. For the first few years after our marriage in 1928 we had city conveniences. When we moved to the farm/orchard we were still lucky. My husband was unemployed for a couple of years—even had six weeks work on the WPA. We paid no rent, an important factor, but helped in the orchard and on the farm. We got through the depression as our ancestors had done before us. Now, in 1936, luck was with us. My husband got work at the feed elevator just a month before our second girl was born in 1934 and we proudly handed the doctor $15 of the $25 delivery fee he charged for the delivery, which was at my Mother's.

That winter the house was banked with straw, the big open back porch closed in with mismated storm windows and a storm door. Wood was piled in there under cover. Everything essential was moved into the kitchen or dining-living room. Beds huddled together, piled high with wool comforters. An old black range did our cooking; a long stovepipe connected with the chimney to the Heatrola to help warm that huge kitchen. On the other side of the wall, the winter bedroom, an old time baseburner kept our breaths from becoming frosty at night. Sometimes we took hot water bottles or well-wrapped sad irons to bed with us; other rooms were closed off.

At first it seemed like an adventure—pioneer days and memories of blizzards in Nebraska or the Dakotas. But the novelty soon wore off with more of the same every day and our routine settled down to keeping fires going, keeping clean, keeping fed. Luck was with us again. No variety, but vegetables and canned fruit and apples stored in the cellar and in the closed off pantry there was a long table, towel-covered with cuts of beef and pork for which we'd bartered, and which kept frozen all winter. We ate well. The big oven was ever-ready for loaves of crusty bread, gingerbread or cakes, cookies, baked beans, baked or scalloped potatoes, fruit cobblers, pies, while soups or stews cooked at the back and bread toasted in screen racks over coals.

Baths were taken in a washtub in front of the range. Water for washing on the washboard was carried in from the pump in the yard, or snow melted in the copper boiler. Bathroom facilities were outside behind the granary and a covered pail was kept for night use and for the children.

We learned to conserve water. Water from washing vegetables went on the window plants which were protected from the quarter-inch crusted frost by layers of newspaper. Steam from the teakettle provided humidity to the room. Ice in the yard covered the top of the foot high layer of snow like a skating rink. One had to dig down to get snow to melt. Other beauty hints were cream for chapped hands, home made shampoo of Ivory soap jellied and salts-of-tartar added, Saleratus (baking soda) for teeth

Entertainment was reading, Atwater-Kent battery radio, recipes and home-talk. Mail brought in the evening when the man of the house came, parked the Ford at the end of the long driveway, walked up and brought news and groceries. We were a family again.

Grace Keith Samuelson
Edgerton, Wisconsin

THE SOFT-HEARTED CONSTABLE

I've sat on the road and chewed road tar and watched the WPA men work and lean on their shovels. I've sold milk bottles to get money for the Saturday matinee. I've seen my folks excited when some young man was accepted for the CCC. I've gone with Mom on Saturday afternoon, after she received her check, to pay a little to the doctor, the grocer or the dentist.

The morning ritual at home was to get ourselves ready for the day. Mom put our shoes, the scissors and a sheet of cardboard on the old cupboard. We drew around our shoes, cut the shape and slipped the cardboard inside the shoes. What a great feeling. It covered the holes and would last most of the day if it didn't rain.

I wouldn't have missed the Great Depression for the world. My happiest memories come from those years. It was a teaching experience to be raised in a time when you learn that money isn't necessarily the basis for a happy childhood. It all depends on the parents.

I was raised in the Moultrie county seat, a block from the square, one block from the court house. We could spend hours there climbing the stairs in the beautiful old building and looking down from the rotunda at the people below, and spitting on the design in the tile on the main floor. You could get a kid once in a while if he didn't know you were hiding up there.

The statues on the court house lawn made wonderful mountains to climb and the old cannon became a beautiful black horse that stood perfectly still while we tried to run and mount the way we saw Buck Jones do at the matinee.

Times were hard, I suppose, but in those days kids were never burdened with the problems of an adult world. It must have been difficult for adults at that time. Everyone was in the same boat. No one tried to keep up with the Jones' because there weren't that many Jones' to keep up with.

Both of my parents worked "up town". Dad ran a pool room (off limits to me of course) and Mother worked in a small variety store. Even though they both worked, we had access to them so, if someone broke an arm, the dog got hit by a car, or the house was on fire, we were only a block away.

When the six o'clock whistle blew, all the kids gathered their bikes, scooters and dogs, and headed for home. The evening meal was a wonderland of stories of the day at our house. Dad always had stories to tell and his flair for making everything funny was something to hear. Mom chimed in with her daily experiences and we all laughed and talked together. Never gossip or adult secrets, just fun.

We were gathered at the table one night and Dad was unusually quiet. Finally he announced that he had accepted the position of town constable. While Mother sat there with a frown on her face, we kids were excited and took turns wearing his badge and prancing like big time law officers. Mother's concern was that the job required him to serve papers on people who couldn't pay their rent and even setting their furniture on the street if payment weren't made.

Dad knew and liked everyone in town and many of these people were his friends. In Mother's wildest imagination she couldn't believe that my Dad could handle such a situation. Dad reminded her that he would receive five dollars for serving the papers and that such news might be easier coming from a friend. He assured Mother that he would explain that it was not his doing if he had to serve papers on friends.

It wasn't a week before Dad announced at the supper table that he had to go serve papers on an old buddy, Slim. Now Slim had about a dozen kids and a red-headed wife. So, after supper Dad told my brother and me that we could go with him to serve the papers. Mom didn't want us to go because Slim had such a violent temper but she relented, insisting that we stay in the car and, if there were any problems, to run for help. Maybe she thought we were protection. How could anyone shoot a man with two kids in the car? Surely Slim liked kids—he had so many.

We drove to the worst neighborhood in town and stopped in front of a house that today would be condemned. There was a dirty little face peering from every window, if you could call them windows because the glass was broken out and gunny sacks hung therein to keep out wind and rain.

Dad crawled out of the car and went to the door. Slim answered the door and invited his friend inside. George and I crouched in the car, waiting for the inevitable. Soon the door opened and out came Dad, Slim, his red-haired wife, and a bunch of stair-step kids. They stood in the yard, laughed, slapped each other on the back, spoke of how hard the times were, and Slim had the papers in his hand.

Dad sang and joked all the way home. George and I looked at each other. Kids didn't ask questions in those days.

Time ran out. Slim didn't pay his rent. Dad had collected his five dollars for serving the papers and now the furniture and family had to be set out on the street, a not uncommon act in those days.

The next evening, at supper, Dad told Mom that he had gone to Slim's at the insistence of the owner and had set Slim and his family out of their home. It hadn't taken long. There wasn't much. Some broken down cots, an old table and a couple of chairs, plus some tattered bed clothes. Dad assured us that they would be fine. The weather was nice and he had put everything under some trees in the front yard.

We went out to play and Dad stretched out on the daybed for his after-supper nap. Mom quietly went about clearing the evening meal dishes with no help from any of us.

When it was just about dark, Dad got up and announced that he had to be gone for a little while. He had something to do. My brothers and I sat on the front porch and wondered what it could be. It wasn't long until we heard the old Model A coming around the corner and here came Dad with a big grin on his face. We ran to find out where he had been.

As he strolled into the house with his back ramrod straight and a twinkle in his eye, he said "Well, I had to go help Slim and his wife move their furniture back in."

I think I loved my Dad more that night than any other time in my life.

He had followed the law to the letter. He had served the papers. He had set the family out. Who said he couldn't help a friend move back in?

He didn't wear his badge the third trip.

Betty Sanner
Bethany, Illinois

THAT'S THE WAY IT WAS IN 1936

We were before television, before penicillin, the pill, antibiotics and frisbies. Before frozen food, nylon, dacron, Xerox, Kinsey. We were before radar, fluorescent lights, credit cards and ball point pens.

For us time sharing meant togetherness, not computers. A chip meant a piece of wood; hardware meant what you bought at the hardware store; software wasn't even a word. Back then bunnies were small rabbits and rabbits were not Volkswagons.

We were before Batman, Rudolph the Rednosed Reindeer, and Snoopy. Before DDT and vitamin pills, vodka made in the United States, and the white wine craze. We were before disposable diapers, Jeeps and the Jefferson nickel. Before Scotch tape, M and M's, the automatic shift, and Lincoln Continentals.

We were before pizzas, Cheerios, frozen orange juice, instant coffee, and McDonalds. We thought fast food was what you ate during lent. We were before FM radio, tape recorders, electric typewriters, word processors, Muzak, electronic music and disco dancing. We were before pantyhose and drip-dry clothes. We were before men wore long hair and earrings and before women wore tuxedos. We got married first and then lived together. How quaint can you be?

In our day cigarette smoking was fashionable; grass was mowed and not smoked; Coke was a drink and not a drug; and pot was what we cooked in. We were before coin vending machines, jet planes, helicopters, and interstate highways. In 1936 "Made in Japan" meant junk and "making out" meant how well we did on an exam.

In our time there were five and ten-cent stores where you could actually buy things for a nickel and a dime. For a nickel you could ride a streetcar, make a phone call, buy a Coke, or buy enough stamps to mail one letter and two postcards. You could buy a new Chevy coupe for $600 but who could afford that in 1936? A pity, too, because gasoline was only eleven cents a gallon.

The differences in the sexes had already been discovered in 1936 but we were before sex changes. We just made do with what we had.

That's the way it was in 1936.

Bernice Erickson
Glasgow, Montana

MOTHER CANNED, PATCHED AND PRAYED A LOT

When Father's wages were cut to fifteen cents an hour he knew we were in deep trouble. Raising five small children and paying off a house mortgage called for more than just thrift.

How was this managed? No new clothes were bought—all were passed around as hand-me-downs. We started the school year with one set of passable clothes and wore them every day until we outgrew them.

A very large garden and the chicken house provided most of our food. Even with the give away prices at the store we had to make do without buying things. Any available money had to go for school, shoes and the ever-pressing mortgage payments. Mother canned everything in sight, patched our worn clothes and prayed a lot.

When any local farmer butchered, my father would offer to buy the head for a few coins. It was a horrible sight to look into the big kettle on the stove and see that head simmering but it made a lot of good eating if you forgot the source.

Breakfast was mainly oatmeal or cornmeal mush. This was simmered on a wood and coal cook stove which also served to heat the kitchen. For lunch we usually ate apple butter spread thickly on bread. For the evening meal we would have whatever could be scraped up. A chicken was divided into seven pieces. A twelve cent ring of balogna was also cut into seven pieces. Baked apples were also a favorite. A live grown pig could be bought for seven to eight dollars. Since my parents were former farmers, they were able to use every ounce except the hide. Anyone still hungry after the table was bare was told to fill up on bread.

As we boys grew older we all got paper routes. For about a dollar a week we peddled in the cold, the rain and the heat, spent most of the dollar on bike repairs. In summer we tried selling our garden produce out of our little wagon but sales were usually poor because no one had much money.

Our attitude toward life was never poor because our neighbors were living much as we were living. However we ate better than most people because our father threatened us with spankings if the weeds were not pulled and the potatoes hoed. Nothing can be more boring to ten to twelve year old boys than working in the garden when the other kids had some kind of game going.

We dressed in front of the kitchen stove and took our baths there since the coal furnace in the basement was permitted to go out at night to save fuel. This situation also allowed the pot to freeze in the upstairs bedrooms. Yet it was better to use a cold chamberpot than to go to the outhouse. No bathroom. We never bought a roll of toilet paper because catalaogues and papers were free.

During hot weather we would buy a cake of ice for fifteen cents for our ice box. This never lasted long because we kids would keep chipping at it for slivers to suck on. This was our treat. For Christmas we received a big bag of hard candy which was doled out one piece per day. Presents were some clothes and, in a good year, a fifteen cent toy.

My father was a master mechanic. For a few dollars he would pick up an old car which wouldn't run anymore. He could always get it running, but we couldn't afford to buy gas, so we all walked, except on Sunday.

We children never regretted the lack of new clothes, or riding old beat up bicycles. We would have liked a few more dimes for going to the pool or to the movies. We managed the latter by scraping up enough money for the oldest brother to go to the movie. When he got home he would have to tell the rest of us the whole plot. He did a good job and eventually ended up as one of the best story tellers in the country.

We seldom complained because my mother would tell us we were blessed. When she had been a young girl about 1900 the neighbor kids were limited to one-half an egg a day because the rest of them had to be traded at the store.

When I became thirteen I was getting enough odd jobs after school and in the summer to have that coveted dime in my pocket- so the bad times had ended for me.

Gil Vandre
Rochelle, Illinois

PIE PAID OFF THE DOLLAR BET 20 YEARS LATER

I cannot write from either the perspective of what it was like on the farm, nor working in cities, nor living in crowded conditions. I can only speak in anecdotal terms of impressions of a small boy in a small Illinois town.

My mother was a kind person. Almost daily we would have tramps come to the door for food. They were the thirties' version of street people. She would observe them as they approached and if she didn't like their looks she simply wouldn't go to the door. On many occasions, though, she would fry an egg and fix some toast. As recompense she would extract conversation from these men and wheedle from them as much of their background as possible, thereby learning of abandoned families and shattered careers. Often, whether to escape the clutches of her conversation or to appease a conscience molded by the work ethic, the men would offer to do some task to pay for their meal. Hence leaves were raked, trees trimmed, chickenhouse cleaned, all of these things that needed doing. Often I heard her lament in the midst of egg frying that yonder train whistle meant her efforts were for naught because her beneficiary would be long gone before she finished.

I can remember my folks starting a savings account for me and then one day the banker came to our house with papers for me to sign. They were waivers. He explained that by signing them I was really signing away half of my five dollar savings but if I didn't sign them there was a likelihood of losing the whole caboodle. I signed.

Being an only child I was not the beneficiary of hand me down clothing as were so many of my contemporaries. I do remember Mom bleaching flour sacks and cutting and hemming them so I'd have an ample supply of handkerchiefs. I'm not sure whether it was depression related but family togetherness was enhanced when we would buy a hog to butcher. My job was to cut slabs of fat into little squares but I'm still not certain what happened to the little squares.

Other sights and sounds that come to mind are my walks downtown to the post office and seeing the men congregated in the park awaiting the WPA truck to pick them up to go dig holes—or to fill in holes—depending on which day it was. How could anyone who was once a small boy possibly forget the awe with which he regarded the CCC boys from down the road when they came to town and "murdered" the local stalwarts in softball?

Money wasn't easy to come by for small boys in small towns. One time I managed to land a job distributing the weekly paper published by the Townsend Plan, that economic panacea for the ills of the downtrodden. I bet my friend, Pie, a quarter that FDR would beat Landon in the presidential election. Later I offered to double the bet on a Roosevelt landslide. Pie accepted but collecting my winnings was another matter. He offered to change the bet to double or nothing based on his clear superiority in ping pong. If he beat me five straight games the score would be settled. If I beat him only once I'd be into him for a buck. Well, he won four straight games but on the fifth the stress must have gotten to him and I won. Some twenty years later when I visited the old home town I reminded him of the bet and he paid off.

It's sometimes difficult to separate events which relate to the depression from those that simply were part of growing up. I'm tempted to tell about people being arrested for moonshining, or about some of the town gossip, but those events predate the depression years so I'll omit them.

Roy S. Coon
Pebble Beach, California

MY FAVORITE HOUSE

My parents never owned a home. We moved several times while I was growing up, probably because we couldn't afford the rent.

One house I really loved. It was the only place that ever felt like home. I must have been about seven years old when we moved there. It was a big place with stairways in both front and back of the building. The third floor even had stairs in the center and was finished into one large room. This is where we played in bad weather. My older brother also had a wood lathe up there and we watched him work with wood. We put up blanket curtains and staged elaborate plays up there. Sometimes the big boys would put up a boxing ring and have boxing matches.

This house has lots of memories. My best friend was Josephine Hannah. We loved to play paper dolls together. We would cut whole families of dolls from the Sears catalog and put them in shoe boxes. Our favorite play place was under her dining room table which had four feet running from a center support. These were our dividers, usually for different sections of town. I lived in one section with my families and Josephine in another, with all her families. The other sections were where our daddies worked, or playgrounds, or shopping. At night Josephine and I liked to sit on the porch swing and tell ghost stories.

Every day in my favorite house was laundry day. This house was modern in that one inside room contained a flushing toilet. Nothing else—just the toilet. Plus a cold water spigot on the back porch, over a rectangular sink with a wooden counter top about two feet long. A lattice-work wall behind it gave us some privacy from the street. This porch is where Daddy washed up every day after work and left his dirty overalls by the ever-present washtub for Mama's daily laundry.

Mama seemed to enjoy doing the laundry. She sang the whole time, mostly sad songs like "Girl of The Belfry", "Give My Love to Nell", and "Row Us Over The Tide." But it was hard work.

Mama had three big galvanized wash tubs. One was for scrubbing the clothes in hot sudsy water with P & G white naphtha bar soap on the old wash board. The water had been heated in a big lard stand (can) on the kitchen stove and carried to the porch. Clothes were washed this way all year around. After they were washed the white clothes were boiled and washed a second time, as were the work clothes. Colored clothes could not be boiled because they would fade. They were boiled in an empty lard stand which had probably held a hundred pound of lard at one time. Mama bought lard and molasses in those large cans for this purpose.

We didn't have store-bought wash cloths, dish cloths or dust cloths. We had rags. Wash rags, dish rags. Our duster was a real goose wing. When they were first married Mama and Daddy had a goose which they ate, using the feathers for pillows and feather beds and keeping the wing for a duster. It was excellent for that purpose.

We never bought toothbrushes either. Mama showed us how to take a twig from a sweet gum tree and make a brush. We simply chewed on the end of the twig, gently, until it formed bristles like on a small broom. Then we wet the brush, dipped it in baking soda and cleaned our teeth. We once had a neighbor who used this type of brush to dip her snuff. She'd leave the stick sticking out of her mouth (she had no teeth) and I kept expecting her chin to hit her nose as she chomped on that stick.

We never had enough dishes to go around either. We just made do with what we had. Some of us had plates, some had saucers, others a blackened pie tin. We used canning jars to drink from. Milk was an unheard of item in our house, as was fruit. Some of us sat on an up-ended orange crate or a lard stand, but we thought nothing of it.

When I was sixteen I bought Mama a table setting for twelve people- a set of dishes, glasses, and stainless steel silverweware. And I paid for it all myself. Of course I was very happy I could do it.

Eventually we left my favorite home, going to another place temporarily then out into the country. I had never been in the country after dark before. I never knew night time was so dark. No outside lights anywhere. No neighbor houses. No street lights. Not even any house lights because we had to use kerosene lamps. And we only had two of them. No electricity. No plumbing. We had a hand pump outside and an outhouse out back. Daddy was now working for the WPA and things were truly tight.

Nobody in the family owned a pair of gloves. We heard of a farm where cabbages had been raised that summer and in the field some plants were sprouting. It was winter now but Mama gave me a sharp knife and a gunny sack and told me to go to that farm and cut a mess of sprouts for supper. In spite of the bitter cold, my cotton dress and a worn out jacket I knew I had to go. I had to break the ice off the plants with bare hands before I could cut them, but I did it and we had a good supper that night.

School soon started and my peers were cruel to me. They taunted me because they were established, had always lived on a farm and had grown up together. They ridiculed my clothes, my poor little sister and brothers who rode the same bus. We truly did look poor by now because times were so hard. Maybe I looked worse than I thought too. I had only two homemade cotton dresses (wear one, wash one). The other girls had sweaters and skirts. I tried to be friendly but I was rejected. Soon I stopped going outside at recess and would eat my cold biscuit lunch in my home room.

I began visiting the outhouse at home at school bus time and deliberately missing the bus. Mama really yelled at me but I knew she wouldn't understand. She got on my case, telling everyone "Hilda thinks she knows more than the teachers and she doesn't have to go to school." That hurt. Nobody understood that I couldn't face all that taunting at school. I had no decent clothes, no friends, no home life. So I quit school and started working at a hot dog stand for three dollars a week. I had an appendix problem, was deathly ill for about ten days, didn't get paid and didn't go back. I took a live-in job caring for twins; this turned out to be much better until the husband made a pass at me and I ran, frightened. They never paid me either.

The following year I went back to school. School lunch cost five cents for a sandwich or for lemonade but if you bought two sandwiches the drink was free. I knew a girl who had no money so she brought six eggs in her pockets. At lunch time she went to the nearby grocery and sold the eggs for a dime, then returned to school and bought her lunch. I still was eating cold biscuits.

There was a little white church which I loved to attend for as early as I can remember. Mama said she didn't go to church because she didn't have clothes to wear or money to give. A little girl who lived near us in town, Mary Midgette, a playmate, went to the Calvary Baptist church and asked Mildred and me if we'd like to go to church with them. We were delighted and went every Sunday, staying for morning worship services. If Mrs. Midgette was ever ashamed of the way we looked, she certainly never showed it. Neither did anyone at the church. We were even invited to sing in the choir of both adults and children, which we did. I was in the Christmas plays. Mrs. Chory was my Sunday school teacher and I loved her. Singing Sam Davis was the superintendent, a beloved man of God, whose love for God and for humans radiated from him and blessed those around him, even the children.

When we moved around I went to other churches but this one remained very special to me. When the time came for me to be married, I told my beloved that I would like to be married in this church, and we were. That was over forty-six years ago.

I survived the depression, World War II and many heartaches I have not mentioned. But I prefer to live in the present, to forget hurtful things, to forgive those who knowingly or ignorantly caused me hurt. After all, Jesus is our example and no one was ever hurt like He was. People spat on Him, pulled His beard, taunted Him to come down if He were the Son of God (He could have, you know, but Thank God He didn't). But He endured the cross, despising the shame, but He endured. And He said "Forgive them, Father, they know not what they do."

Now we have our own home, my husband and me, and we have four children and seven grandchildren. We are blessed.

Hilda Metzka
Chillicothe, Ilinois

MAKING A FIVE DOLLAR BILL LOOK SICK

My parents were central Illinois farmers, scrabbling hard to make a go of it during the thirties. We were no poorer and certainly no better off than anybody else so, while Mom and Dad were overworked and frightened by the times, I grew up a pretty happy kid. My parents gave me their time and their love, and they let me help with the never ending chores which had to be done. It was riches enough for me.

Being an only child meant that I drove the hayfork during haying like a son would have done and then went inside and waited table for the menfolk like a daughter should have done. I learned to pick wild grapes when there was precious little else for jelly. (Boy! Were they sour! But Dad liked it that way.) I also learned to work in the garden, to help make my own clothes (Mom was an exquisite seamstress) and to fix supper while my parents did evening chores.

In return Mom took me to the creek to swim—I could never go alone. She also read me stories and helped with homework. Dad taught me to drive a team of horses and the Model T before I was ten. He made me stilts and taught me to walk on them, and joined me in whooping war dances around a bonfire of leaves in the fall. I was a full partner—smaller but always included. As long as I could be with them, life was rich and full and secure.

When I was about five my father decided to try making a little cash with a small dairy. It seemed that it should have been pretty easy to collect five cents a pint and eight cents a quart for milk with thick, rich cream far down on the next of the bottle. Well, it was easy to get customers, but collecting was something else. Especially in a small town where everyone knew what jobs had disappeared and which families were hurting. My father never could bring himself to shut off the deliveries just because the bill hadn't been paid for a few months or even for a few years.

"Those children have to have milk," he'd tell my mother who, truth to tell, was as soft a touch as he. "Especially," he always finished, "when they have mighty little of anything else to eat."

Some of the bills, eventually, were paid to the penny, but all too often, when work did reappear, the family found a new milkman and started fresh all around, ignoring old debts as part of a bad dream from which the family had finally awakened.

Farmers in the thirties were three times cursed for several years. To go along with the terrible prices, there came a drought and then the chinch bugs came in a veritable Biblical plague. I remember families digging trenches and post holes, pouring in creosote which was later burned in an effort to stop the insects. But nothing really worked, and the precious crops were swept away.

Looking back I still ache with pain for my mother who one day shared with me her loneliness for her family only 55 miles away by Illinois Central railroad.

We had made the trip fairly often in the good years but one summer, frightened by the terrible times and longing for her mother, her sister and brothers, she confided how much she wanted to "go up home." Afterward, seeming to feel some disloyalty at even mentioning her wishes, she said resolutely, "That trip would make a five dollar bill look sick." So there was no question at all of going. How desolate I felt, for once realizing how vital money could be when it just wasn't there.

Within a year or so Dad managed to save up ticket money for her and for me to go along. And my Aunt Laura, bless her, had acquired some passes for the Century of Progress, the 1933-1934 World's Fair, in Chicago. So for a full day we walked until we nearly dropped trying to pack all the wonders into that magical free day when we saw the Temple of Jehol and the Travel and Transportation building. We even saw the marvelous sky ride making its way across the hot summer sky, just as content that we couldn't possibly afford the tickets for a ride on that scary old thing. I even had ten cents to buy a souvenir, a little penny bank. I still have it to this day, a memento of a day too incredible to believe.

Dad never did work up any enthusiasm for traveling out of reach of his own bed each night but many years later, for her eightieth birthday, we persuaded Mom to go with us to San Francisco to visit our son who was spending the summer there as a college student. She spent the nearly four hours of the flight with her nose against the tiny window peering hopefully for the Rocky mountains and nearly collapsed from excitement when she finally saw them. And she took to Baghdad on the Bay with boundless enthusiasm, toiling along with us as best she could and content to sit on a bench and watch the ships go in and out under the Golden Gate bridge.

It sure did make a five dollar bill look sick, Mom, but it did a little something to help me ease the pain of that heartbroken moment in the thirties.

They were a gallant generation, those parents of the great depression. As one neighbor put it, "We just took a piece of wire and fastened it together and kept on going." And their spirit kept their children going. We can only try to pass it on.

Mary Ellen Cohon
Morton Grove, Illinois

EVERYTHING WAS CANNED, SUGARED OR BURIED

In 1934, after the Century of Progress Exposition of 1933 in Chicago (commonly called the "World's Fair") we were let down. The radio described the many exciting things happening all over the world, from one country to another. Here we had so much that we would have shared but didn't know how. We sophomores were ready for junior years and expecting a lot.

All the kids worked gardens after school and sometimes I was lucky and sold tickets at the Avon theatre. I worked for a Greek family and received free passes to the show for us kids. The Greeks owned two theatres and confectioneries. I had a job making ice cream bars and worked in a cooler with boots and a coat. I sat at a table with a hole in it and a square full of chocolate. I dipped the overhead ice cream bars in the chocolate. Good!

We young people walked every place. Our shoes were always in the repair shop. Also we skated on the sidewalks until we were run off by other people. We used our bikes when we wanted to go any distance. The library area was always full of bikes because we had so many reports to make at school.

One summer my best friend and her brother, who were older, and me, who didn't want younger ones always tagging along, built ourselves a hideaway. We tore down our back fence and made a play-house to have some peace. We had four hinges on the door and you had to know how to get in. We also dug a tunnel to keep boys out. It was a secret place. We didn't have radios, or television or record players. At home we did have player pianos and record players. Some records were cylindrical, not flat. Mainly play was up to us and our imagination.

After Sunday school and church we had big picnics and went to beaches to swim or for a boat ride. Fortunately, we had a big excursion boat that went all around the lake.

People gathered at the church and at the parks. Kids and men played ball or tennis and we had a sunken garden with lots of flowers we always went to see. We were interested in what was blooming. They also had goldfish swimming there. We had many retreats too in those days. We sang church songs, did crafts, had sermons all day long and evenings too, with three or four speakers preaching all day.

Men worked seven days a week for ten to twelve hours and if they brought home fifty dollars that was very good.

Of course you know that Henry Ford made a car which sold for five hundred dollars. It had big shiny wheels and when you got stuck in the mud you pushed it out; folks often walked out. You always carried a shovel and a bag of gravel or sand.

When you went fifty miles from home it took all day so you always had to be prepared to stay at least overnight.

People got their highs by putting lemon extract in fountain Coca Cola.

My grandparents planted everything to eat and it was either canned, sugared or buried. We made our own sauerkraut and we robbed the bees for honey.

Our laundry stove used Kentucky-Illinois coal to fire it and to heat laundry water. We got up at 4:00 A.M. to start the fire and used a wash board with Fels Naphtha soap. Because we got up that early, we went to bed by 9:00 P.M. A lot of people had to walk three or four miles to work, taking along a lunch bucket of food. There was no food at work places unless you brought it.

People were always close and friendly. When there was a death, people were there. Not much money but always helping hands. Men friends would dig the grave and people stayed at the cemetery until the burial was complete. My first experience was at my grandmother's funeral. I can still hear the drop—drop of the clumps of earth on her coffin.

It was a happy time but sad too. When a person reached seventy he was either dead or would just sit around. I'm seventy, drive a van, gone all the time to hear men talk, do my laundry at the laundromat, have freezers, refrigerators, electric lights, television. A far cry from my grandmother's coal oil lamp which she used very carefully.

Some people call them the good old days. Maybe they were. I enjoyed them. But we had our sorrowful times too. People don't take time now to enjoy their families and friends and to smell the trees and the flowers.

Dortha Mitchell
Thibodaux, Louisiana

WOOLWORTH'S WAS A REAL FIVE AND TEN CENT STORE

The depression was when we appreciated a ten cent gift for a birthday and sometimes all we did was sing the popular song "Happy Birthday to You." This was in Brokaw and Wausau, Wisconsin where we lived.

There didn't seem to be the crime we have today. You could enjoy a walk in the evening and not worry who might attack you or rob you of your purse. Even little children played under a street light until dark or perhaps nine o'clock.

Nylon stockings were a rarity. Cotton house dresses sold for a dollar and when you didn't have the dollar to buy one you sewed your own. You could get two yards of material for a quarter and sometimes remnants were a dime.

We were lucky to have a battery-powered radio, which not only played enjoyable music but stories of mystery and love. For instance "The Shadow" or "Ma and Pa Kettle" or "George Burns and Gracie Allen". There was no television.

Many homes didn't have water inside; we had a pump and pail and dipper. There were tubs to be filled half full on wash day and water heated on a wood burning cook stove. We washed clothes by rubbing them up and down on a washboard. Even took baths in the wash tub and used an outside toilet because there wasn't any plumbing in the house. We also used pages from a Sears Roebuck catalogue because toilet paper was too expensive.

People would walk the railroad tracks to pick up bark and coal to burn in their stoves for heat.

Also people went to bed early and got up with the chickens because of lack of electricity. We had oil lamps and some people had gas lights. Of course there wasn't any air conditioning and we blessed the shade trees.

Everybody had a garden, saving seeds each year to plant the following spring. Children learned to pull weeds and get a penny as a reward.

If the family needed a baby sitter, it would be a relative or friend and it was done as a favor, or sometimes for a meal. People helped one another more than they do today.

Many newly wedded young folks lived at home to help on the farm, which always needed the extra hands, and when a baby was due there was a midwife to help deliver; doctors were scarce and there was no money to pay them.

The best thing that happened to our young boys to take them off the streets and give them work was the CCC camps where they became young soldiers. Also they worked each day fixing up parks, doing roadwork and repairing country roads. They were paid a dollar a day and room, board and clothing and were required to send twenty-five dollars a month home to the folks. Also there was WPA where husbands were put to work at minimum wages.

A dollar was really a dollar. Coffee was twenty-three cents a pound, bread twenty cents a loaf if you didn't bake your own, vegetables ten cents a can. If you helped a farmer you'd earn a few pounds of whatever was available — onions, peas, beans, corn, potatoes, even share some beef or pork when he butchered.

Kids would go to the woods to pick berries for mothers to make sauce or jelly. Many people raised their own chickens and rabbits. Ice boxes held twenty-five or fifty pounds of ice and kept things cold, but not frozen.

Woolworth's was a *real* five and ten cent store. There was also a Kreske which had things up to twenty-five cents and a McClellan's which sold items up to a dollar. We did most of our shopping in these stores.

Men who smoked had to roll their own for ten cents a package of tobacco and papers. Some fellows chewed the tobacco for twenty cents a can.

Restaurants were far and few between and mostly found in hotels or depots. The hamburgers and hot dogs sold for a nickel. They also carried ice cream cones and bottles of pop.

In winter we wore long underwear, not the nice insulated wear we have today, and we covered up at night with home-made quilts or feather ticks to keep warm in bed. At the foot of the bed would be warmed flat irons or hot water bottles.

In spite of these problems we were happier and far more appreciative then than children and grownups are today with cars, bicycles, clothes of every kind and all the modern conveniences. I also think that when the father worked and brought home the paycheck and the mother took care of the home and family, people were far better off. Now it takes two to pay the expenses and there's less family togetherness.

Lillian Edwards
Chicago Heights, Illinois

NOT DIRTY THIRTIES — BEST YEARS OF MY LIFE

My brother was born in 1925 amd I arrived a year later. Those were thriving years in Rockford, Illinois. Furniture building was the major industry and the machine tool business was rapidly growing to meet the demands of furniture factories' needs for more modern, sophisticated manufacturing methods.

When the depression came in 1929 the factories closed and many of Rockford's finest craftsmen were out of work. When our income disappeared, my father entered my brother and me into a children's home and he, too, disappeared. My mother returned to an empty house after a futile day of job seeking. After a day of frantic search for her family, she hiked the twenty miles to her parent's home south of Byron for advice and comfort.

My grandparents were survivors of the first degree. He was the youngest of nine children, descendants of one of Ohio's pioneer families. She was the oldest of the five children of Ezra D. Pendleton who had taken his family west in a covered wagon in 1888. Ezra lost his wife in childbirth in Kansas and my grandmother, at the age of eight, became the mother of the younger children. The infant survived and an Indian squaw was hired to suckle the newly born babe until the family was able to return to Ohio.

Grandmother went through nurses training and grandfather became a carpenter. Their pioneer spirit took them west to Illinois shortly after marriage. They bought twenty acres of raw land and a three-room cabin. He cut timber to build a barn and corncrib and dynamited the stumps to make a cornfield. His reputation as a carpenter grew and the surrounding farmers' demands helped finance the improvements on their land. She worked for a Byron doctor who made house calls in a horse and buggy. The couple had the one child.

When my mother arrived in 1929 with the news of the disappearance of her husband and children they contacted authorities who located us in the children's home. My grandparents applied for legal custody and I spent the depression years on that twenty acre tract of sand and limestone under the protection of my grandparents.

In hard times one does what one must do. Grandfather had built a chicken house 100 feet by 40 feet, dividing it into three portions. One area was for laying hens, one for raising young chicks, one for storage. They bought a 200 egg incubator from Sears, which was heated by kerosene. They went into the egg production business and, as the business grew, he built two more chicken houses. The incubator was a permanent piece of furniture in their bedroom and we children were allowed to peek but never to touch. During the years of 1935 and 1936 we had a thousand Leghorn laying hens.

We had no horses or machinery to raise the corn to feed the chickens. We hired a neighbor to plow and plant in the spring and everything else was done by hand. Our one-room country schoolhouse was a mile and a half across the fields and woods. Our route home included a pass through the cornfield. In the fall grandfather picked the corn and shocked the stalks. We children would shoulder as much corn fodder as we could carry each night on our way home. We would also fill our dinner buckets with wild berries or crab apples for the winter's jelly supply.

We eventually bought five cows which we milked by hand. My job was to shell the corn for the chickens and carry the cobs to the house for starting fires; they produced quick heat for cooking. We had a hand-cranked corn sheller and feeding a thousand chickens seemed an endless chore for a nine-year old girl. To this day my right (cranking) shoulder is larger than my left. In summer I would spread the corn on the ground into arcs, circles and alphabet letters just to see all those white hens make a design on the sand.

Grandmother had a friend in Chicago who contacted a large store to market the eggs. Grandmother sent the eggs by mail in 30-dozen crates and her friend would mail back the empty crates with a money order inside. We would trade eggs at the local store for staples, such as sugar, flour and coffee. We had a large vegetable garden and fruit trees and grapes. Our dirt cellar was abundant with winter supply of canned fruits and vegetables, potatoes, onions and a crock of sauerkraut which my grandmother had produced. The cows had calves which grew up to be beef and the sides of beef hung in the milk house in the winter, frozen solid. Grandmother would saw off a few days' supply at a time and keep it in the icebox.

Our utility bills included ice for the icebox, kerosene for the lamps and gasoline for the Model T Ford truck. Gas was five gallons for a dollar and five gallons went a long ways.

In 1936 we bought a radio which was operated by a battery, since we had no electricity. Grandfather would take the morning milk to the cheese factory in Byron, then bring the truck battery to the house to listen to the radio. We only listened to the news and my brother and I had to maintain complete silence while the news was being broadcast. As the years went by and Hitler's power and the European crisis grew, the radio was used more and more. Grandfather had to devise trips to town to recharge the battery.

We were considered country hicks and yet our city acquaintances soon came to understand that we had what they couldn't have. Self sufficiency was not in their grasp. Grandmother was very generous and every Sunday the kitchen of our three-room cabin was filled with hungry friends from Rockford. Fried chicken was always in abundance. With the incubator producing 160 to 200 chicks every thirty days, there never was a shortage of chicken. Every hobo that walked down the road was brought into the kitchen and fed, then sent off with a pocketful of sandwiches. My mother had learned to hunt and trap fur-bearing animals and fished in the nearby Rock river. This provided a bit of variation from the ever-present chicken.

On Saturday night we went to town. Our grandparents would do the weekly shopping while we children went to the free movies. They were always cowboy films, projected on the side of the dentist's office which had been painted white, for a screen. Our seats were blankets on the lawn. Rain or shine, we saw the free movie on Saturday night.

We had no insurance. There was no need for it. If a building burned, everybody banded together and rebuilt it. We had no telephone but we had neighbors who really were neighbors. We were all indispensible to one another.

Our washing machine was powered by a gasoline engine. We washed one day a week. Water was pumped by hand from the cistern which collected rainwater from the house roof via home-made wood eaves and troughs. We carried it in pails to the wash boiler on the wood cookstove. Summertime saw the kitchen as a steam bath on washday. Every Saturday morning the furniture was carried out and the house got a thorough scrubbing. The kitchen floor was concrete and Grandmother would scrub it on her hands and knees with a stiff brush. We didn't know what vermin was until we got into high school. We never had lice or bedbugs but a lot of kids in school had them.

Several years ago I accidentally found my father, who was dying of cancer. He apologized for abandoning us and confessed he had gone west, hitching rides on freight trains. He worked for his board and room in the wheat fields and returned to Rockford when the factories started producing again. He still went through hard times because he was a hand-finisher and upon his return found that all the finishing was done by machine. He learned that we children were well taken care of and didn't try to contact us. Of course I forgave him for abandoning us because I felt we were far better off because of it.

Many times through the years I have used the skills of self-sufficiency learned during the depression. It enabled my husband and me to raise seven children on his wages alone, and they have all turned out very well. Through their own self-sufficiency, five of them have put themselves through college: the other two have obtained positions through apprenticeships.

Many have called them the dirty thirties; I call them the best years of my life.

Gertrude A. Jones
Pecatonica, Illinois

AN ICEBOX MADE FROM SNOW

There were a couple of years when the snow would block us in for several days. Snow plows didn't operate like they do now. The men in our family hauled snow by the bucketful and packed it into an empty cistern. They washed their overshoes well and walked around on the snow, packing it well. They filled the cistern to the top so we had an icebox all summer where we could hang the milk, butter, and cream. That packed snow was also used for icepacks if necessary but never for drinking. Before that we had a hole in the ground lined with large drain tile that my brother and I had to keep filled by pumping water. It was our substitute cooler. Of course we didn't have electricity or the money to buy ice, except for rare occasions like when a threshing crew was working at our place.

We were quarantined one time, as I remember, for the old German measles. We didn't feel specially bad about it, because everyone else had it too. I remember the sign that went on the door. Also I remember that the neighbors brought in groceries as we needed them. Some of them were very ill too. I couldn't stand the smell and Mama found an empty perfume bottle that I held under my nose for a long time.

We had lots of fun! Most of it we made ourselves. When my oldest sister reached her eighteenth birthday, she received a guitar. Somehow she never learned to play it but the rest of us started playing around with it. We sang and strummed guitars at school activities and at a little fair. We would audition the various acts and name them after their genuine program. For instance, my oldest brother was Arkansas Woodchopper, my sister and I were the Flannery Sisters. We sang in harmony because we never had a music lesson in our life; how our parents ever put up with our constant barrage of music I don't know but my father was a peacemaker. He didn't want us to fuss and quarrel so we sang and made music. Such as it was. We would get out on our porch and yodel away. The neighbors could hear us when the weather was right. We sang songs by Lulu Belle and Scott, Arky the Woodchopper, the Flannery Sisters, Gene Autry, Roy Rogers, and the Carter Family.

One time we were asked to sing at the closing of school picnic and we made up verses about each family in the district. It was well received because it was funny. We adopted a theme song which we used even years later. It was the Carter family's "Keep On The Sunnyside".

We had a rough time financially, but can't forget the consideration with which some people treated us. The chinch bugs hit us badly one particular year and wiped us out. We had a payment due on some land in Canada—it seemed everyone had bought some cheap land in Canada in the twenties—and my father was so discouraged he was about ready to turn it back to the insurance company mortgagers. But my mother wrote them a letter, telling them of our plight, and asking for help. They sent a wonderful letter telling us not to worry—they would even pay the taxes on the land so we could keep it. They did just that and, in a few short years, we paid it in full.

My husband Wesley's father was sold out by a local bank during those years. One of his friends who ran a local gas station, went to his safe one day, opened it, in front of Wes's father, and said "How much money do you need, Henry?' He helped him buy back a few implements and a tractor to be able to continue farming.

These are the things you remember.

We still had a horse drawn hack in the thirties. Two people could sit on the seat in front and it also contained seats along the side in the back. When the weather was bad, my father or the hired man would drive us to and fro school in this hack. One day the hired man came to get us in a slushy, muddy snow. All the kids who lived down our way rode in the back and I didn't want the others to get the best seats so I ran to the hack wearing just one overshoe, carrying the other. You can imagine the mess my dirty shoe made in that overshoe when I put it on. To avoid a spanking I told my parents a tale about a neighbor boy who had run off with my shoe and I had to chase him to get it back. My mother wanted to call his mother immediately but my father, always the peacemaker, calmed her and said to let it go that kids would be kids.

I didn't want to go to school one day because a certain arithmetic lesson was too hard, so I played sick. In those days the first thing you would do for an illness was to take a physic. We call them laxatives now. Anyhow, the taste of Epsom salts and the results of a good physic made me decide it would never be worth while to stay home again. During those days Wesley had a bout with pneumonia and, even though he was delirious, he had to take a physic, and be up on the chamber pot many times. It's a wonder more people didn't die just from the various physics.

Eventually a fellow came around to have us sign up for electricity because the REA was coming to our area. This was a dream come true for farmers. We had two meals a day—a late breakfast, a late dinner and something like popcorn at night. It was about 2 P.M. when this man came and caught us at our meal. There were eight or nine of us around the big table, some on chairs with no backs and a bench on the back side of the table. Papa invited him to eat with us. He was very impressed with our family and thought we must have been born friendly;

then my father said' No, you have to cultivate friendliness, no matter what your circumstances.'

Madie L. Klehm
Chatsworth, IL 60921

I REMEMBER HUNGER

I remember hunger. I really haven't been hungry since the mid-depression days and suppose I should consider myself lucky for having had that experience. But when you are a growing boy, it takes a lot of food to fill you up—and we simply didn't have it.

We ate a lot of cheaper items and supplemented the food on hand with whatever we could find.

I remember in the spring how my mother would go hunting greens. She would pick all those wild things like – I can't even remember their names – and would bring them home to make a big plateful of wild greens, overcooked of course. They were good because of the balance of the mixture she was able to find. And, with a little vinegar on them, and perhaps a little hot sauce, they were as good as spinach, or collards, or any of the cultivated greens.

She also cooked a lot of flake hominy, something I haven't even seen on the market for 45 or 50 years. Apparently it was made like regular white corn hominy and then flaked and dried. It looked more like soap flakes than anything else, but it surely tasted a lot better. Cooked in fresh grease or lard, gently salted and peppered, I remember it as being fried fairly crispy and quite excellent.

Of course we all ate chicken. So much chicken that I'm surprised people my age still eat it. Fried chicken, chicken and dumplings, chicken sandwiches. chicken everywhere. They were easy and cheap to grow when let roam and would fill the stomachs of all of us.

Meat in the smokehouse was like money in the bank. I can still see Uncle Pete stringing up a squealing hog and cutting it's throat, then the not-so-repulsive part of scalding the carcass to loosen the bristles and eventually cutting it into chunks to take in the smokehouse. We could go into that smokehouse in the middle of the summer, empty of meat, of course, and still smell that delightful odor. The hickory that we used in northern Aarkansas truly clung to the building.

Sometimes flies would get to the meat before it was properly cured. Not enough salt or enough smoke yet. This didn't happen too often because the smoke would be so heavy it would repel the insects. But when they did get to it, maggots would occur. An unpleasant thought, a picture that still nauseates me, but I can remember seeing my grandfather, and my mother, removing the maggots before we could cook the meat. Nothing was wasted unless it was truly spoiled.

I had a friend who was raised in the bayous in Louisiana during those times. Several times she has spoken of how they snared birds for food. They would toss a few bread crumbs or cracked corn onto a flat piece of well worn soil surrounded by a looped string. When a bird landed within the loop to eat the food, a quick jerk of the string resulted in a catch. It didn't seem to matter what kind of bird. Just any bird would do—and it would go into the soup pot.

Of course we gardened. If we hadn't done so, we simply would not have lived. Fresh vegetables for the summer and things to store either canned or in the root cellar for the winter, were practically a guarantee of making it through the year. I hope we never again have to see so many people actually hungry. There are enough out there right now. Personally I'd rather see us put more money into feeding the poor right here at home than send it to the poor in some other country. When you've once been hungry, once been poor, you never forget it.

Anonymous (Name withheld by request)
Arkansas

BRILLIANT MAN WORKING LIKE A SLAVE

I won't forget the year 1936 because it was the year I was graduated from high school. It was the coldest winter and the driest. hottest summer ever. We lived on a farm in the northwest corner of Sherburne county, Minnesota, just out of St. Cloud. This sandy loam, about six inches deep, produced good crops when there was water. but it had been dry every summer since 1930.

The drought, combined with the depression, made life very hard for all of us. I remember my father coming in from the field for dinner, covered with dust until his face was black. He had been cutting oats with a mower when it was only four to five inches high. I remember feeling so sad because here was a man with a brilliant mind and a university education, working like a slave just to make ends meet. I also remember my beautiful, small, thin mother, carrying pails of water from the wash rinse to her sweet peas. As a teacher in St. Paul she had met my handsome father on the tennis court at the Ag college in 1917.

I was seventeen the summer of thirty-six, the oldest of three—a sister and a little brother.

When we cultivated corn the soil was so dry we had to scrape the shovels at the end of each row. But we all worked together. The whole family put up the oats hay. Dad and Grandpa Hibbard pitched it on the hayrack while Patty and

I stamped it down in preparation for the hay fork which would carry it up into the hay mow.

We would make homemade ice cream for picnics and many times it tasted like ragweed which the cows were eating for lack of grass.

Our cream check averaged about three dollars a week from the ten cows. From that money we had to buy flour, coffee, sugar but not much else. The rest came from the garden and the farm animals. We got so tired of chicken and pork — and sometimes a veal calf — that we often sold them for cash to pay taxes and insurance.

Car licenses were cheap, and so was gasoline, but it all mounted up. We had no electricity so we read by lamplight and listened to radio which ran from a car battery.

Today I would give anything for a good farm-raised chicken. I feel that some of the farmers who are going broke now could raise a garden and chickens to get by like we did, but I guess they wouldn't know how to do it.

Tears always come at my most poignant memory of Dad and I walking to the road and sitting on the big rock to watch the sun go down, each silently praying for rain.

Times got better. The rains came and dad made money in the forties and fifties. He lived a good life, got a government job, travelled to foreign countries and lived to be eighty-nine years old.

Sylvia Hibbard Kubes
St. Louis Park, MN

DO YOU HAVE ROOM FOR ONE MORE?

If in the nineteen-thirties some relative had said to you "Do you have room for one more, or both of us?" what would have been your reply? Would you have said "No" point blank? I hope you would have said "Sure, we have; we'll move over. You come right over, both of you."

Most people would have given the we'll-move-over answer. There are some very gracious, loving people who can't say "no".

I'd like to tell you of these young people who already had six children in school and four little ones at home. The twelve of them lived in a rented farm house with three bedrooms. The house needed paint and a couple of window panes needed to be replaced. They had stuffed two pillows in the hole made by the children's ball. Yes, this house was sadly in need of repair but the landlord said he could make no repairs because times were so hard and the land produced poor crops.

One fall day a car drove up to this home of L. P. Jones with Grandma and Grandpa with all their worldly possessisons in paper bags and boxes. They were welcomed with open arms. Sure, they had room. The youngsters helped carry in the meagre packages and were glad to see these fine people who called themselves Granny and Pappy. The three older children gave up their bed; they each got a gunny sack with oats in it for a bed that night. They slept with the other children in the big room which their mother called the dormitory. Indeed it was—for ten gunny sacks half full of oats on either side of the room, leaving the center of the room for dressing and undressing. They were a happy group and as snug as bugs in a rug.

Yes, poor but happy. Many an evening after supper Granny lead the singing of familiar songs and hymns, every one singing, even the small ones trying too. Word soon spread among the family members of how comfortable and happy this expanded family was. Uncle Willie and Aunt Mae had to give up their home and, being old and destitute, they asked their neice and nephew,the L. P. Jones family, if they could come to live with them. The reply was "Sure, come on over. We'll move over." And move over they did.

They put another old iron bedstead in Grandma and Grandpa's room—they were willing to share too. So the original family of twelve had moved over to give four more relatives a roof over their heads and a table to put their feet under. Everyone had given what little money they had to put in the pot. With good management there was always food on the table. Summertime saw a large garden feeding the family. The two older men, each with a hoe in his hand, kept the garden free of weeds. The ladies helped with the canning for winter food. Sure, they were old but they could pod the peas or snap the beans. They washed the dishes, even helped with the bread baking and rolled out the big sugar cookies to be baked in the coal stove oven. Of course it now burned cobs but it did the job. The milk cows supplied milk and the chickens supplied eggs.

One day at schooll in the fall of the year, the one girl came to my desk and said "I tried to wash myself this morning but there was no soap. I brought a rag with me. Can I wash my face in the anteroom?" I said "Sure you can. I'll get some water warm for you. Don't tell the other children." I brought in the rest of the family one by one and helped wash their faces and hands. The next day I bought each of the six children a bar of ivory soap so they could wash at home. They showed their gratitude by bringing me a little bag of black walnuts which they had hulled and dried. I accepted them as graciously as I could, knowing they wanted to repay me.

One day one of the girls said "Last night mama baked a big, big pumpkin and put it in the center of the table for supper. We each broke off a piece to eat and put salt and butter on it."

Another time she said "Last night mother made a big spider (Ed.: a cast iron pan) of milk gravy. She put it in the center of the table. We all sopped our bread in the gravy." That was supper plus a glass of milk. The grown ups sat at the table while the children stood up and squeezed in wherever they could.

Yes, they were poor but happy. This family (whose name really was not L. P. Jones) could always move over for one less fortunate than they.

Grayce Kuhn
Henry, Illinois

FOUR ROOM HOUSE FOR FOUR HUNDRED DOLLARS

Bessie and I were married in 1936 and started keeping records- lots of records to which we return many times.

We spent our first winter in a nice rented house in Tamaroa, paying rent of ten dollars a month. In 1937 we purchased a solidly built four-room house on a half acre lot in town for $400. The taxes that first year, paid in 1938, were $13.21 for real estate and $4.67 for personal property. For the year 1938 our total bill for electricity was $15.58 — for 194 KW. That was lights, toaster, iron, washer, radio and a fan. Heating with coal cost us $13.72 for the winter of 1937–38. Groceries for the entire year of 1937 totalled $139.60.

Our utilities cost nothing since we had a well with a bucket and rope for drawing water. Also an outhouse. WPA had begun in 1935 and one of its projects was to install modern, safe toilets. The property owner could have the installation completed solely for the cost of materials, with WPA furnishing the labor. Many of these WPA privies are still in use. Previously, privies were at the rear of the lot, along the alley. For a fee a scavenger would periodically come along at night with his wagon and clean it out. Old Sears catalogs were plentiful and toilet paper rolls rarely seen.

As to the house, such things as underpinning, insulation or storm windows just weren't around. A coal burning stove was set up in one room, banked at bedtime, usually with one or more lumps of coal; the first thing in the morning, someone had to shake down the ashes and carry them outside. Then small coal was shovelled in and heat was set up for the day. If, perchance, the fire had burned out during the night, it had to be started all over again.

Water was carried from the well fifty feet in the rear of the house and kept in a wooden bucket, usually with a dipper in it. On many cold winter nights ice would form therein. Dishwashing was done in a dishpan and the water carried to the back door and hurled into the yard. Garbage and refuse were burned with the accumulated cans and glass being carried away occasionally. Later, when a chicken pen and house were built, garbage was thrown into the pen.

Baths were taken in a number three galvanized tub, also used in laundering. In cold weather the tub was placed next to the heating stove. Laundry water was heated in a copper boiler on a two-burner kerosene kitchen stove; sometimes it was heated outside over a wood fire.

Cooking was done on a three-burner kerosene stove. For baking, there was a portable oven that was placed over two of the burners and the cakes and pies from that set-up are reported to have been better than those we get today from our modern electric range. For the year 1939, 116 gallons of kerosene were used, costing a total of $12.11. The private line telephone cost $2 per month.

In 1937 a tonsillectomy cost $20, in 1940 a gold crowned tooth was $9 and in 1941 two teeth were filled for $3, a haircut was 40 cents and a new Crosley Shelvador refrigerator cost $131. Prior to getting this refrigerator, an ice box was all we had. It held 50 pounds of ice which was delivered every few days by the iceman. Water was caught in a pan underneath the icebox amd emptied daily. Frozen foods were unknown, the contents of the box being mostly dairy products.

In those days income was not large and a job that paid a dollar a day was always taken by someone. When WPA started in 1935 the basic wage was $44 per month per unskilled labor, semi-skilled labor $50 and skilled (carpenter, etc.) $63. Foremen and supervisors went from $63 upwards. Besides the privy replacement project, WPA reconstructed school water supply facilities and upgraded almost all roads and streets by grading, ditching and surfacing.

Orville E. Pyle
DuQuoin, IL.

TWO DAYS OF HARD WORK
JUST TO DO THE LAUNDRY

Most of us experiencing those days of the thirties were all in the same boat. I guess it didn't seem so awful at the time. Since most of our folks didn't have fans, air conditioning or even refrigerators, we didn't know what we were missing.

To keep cool, children would spend the day at the neighborhood free pools in the parks. Houses would be kept cool by letting in the early morning cool air, then closing all the windows, pulling down the shades and closing the doors to keep out the hot sun. In the evening, when the sun went down, everything was opened again.

Washing clothes, washing dishes, and keeping one's self clean, with no hot running water, was a difficult and time-consuming chore.

To do the laundry, with no washing machine and no hot water tank, was an exhausting chore. The housewife had to heat huge buckets of water on the gas stove, filling them only half full, so she could lift them off the stove and not scald herself. She would put two chairs together, set a large tin tub on them, then pour in the boiling water, diluting it with cold water. Then she would put in some of the clothes and wash them on a wash board, wringing them out by hand. Thus she proceeded with each of the usual two or three loads.

For rinsing, she had to start the procedure all over, heating the water, diluting it. It was a job also to empty the tub after each washing and each rinsing. This, too, was done by hand.

Then she had to hang the clothes, outside in nice weather or on lines strung in the kitchen during the winters. At mealtimes the laundry would be hanging everywhere so you couldn't escape the smell of Fels-Naphtha soap.

Ironing the laundry was another huge chore, For those who didn't have electricity, the irons had to be heated on the coal or wood stoves. There was no such thing as spray starch so the starch had to be made and cooked on the stove, then cooled, and the clothes dipped into it.

Doing the laundry required two full days, one for washing and one for ironing. Looking back, I'm amazed that most of us looked so clean. Of course those two days was a huge piece of a week's available work time.

Taking a bath was also a big production, without hot running water or even a regular tub. The water had to be heated just as for the laundry. Some "bathrooms" only had a toilet in them, so one had to improvise and create a bath area. This usually consisted of putting up a clothes line behind the coal stove, with a blanket on the line and a tin tub behind it. Then, of course, one had to empty the tub, bucket by bucket, mop the floor, take down the blanket, put everything away. That's how it went to take a bath.

In spite of all this hard work to keep clean, there were small joys and happinesses too.

Movies used to cost five crents for children and ten cents for adults. We children loved the Saturday matinees. This consisted of a main feature, which continued each week. It would always end at a very exciting place, so we'd be thinking about it all through the week. Then there would be a comedy, a cartoon, coming attractions, and a news reel. A lot of entertainment for a nickel. For the adults, the Friday night movie would include receiving a free dish, every week. This was fun too.

In addition to all the activities at the neighborhood parks, the annual summer visits by the taffy-apple man, the hot dog wagon, and an organ grinder and his monkey, we had an assortment of inexpensive fun. Although some things were very difficult there were joys too. But we got through those years and really appreciate what we have today.

Esther Baranowsky
Chicago, Illinois

IN ORDER TO LIVE

Young Married Couple Fights Poverty
Dad Scrimped But Thought Mother Splurged
Those Were Hungry Times During The Depression
Subsistence Living
Aubrey And The Other Mules
There's An Art In Learning How To Be Poor
Roosevelt Gave Us Jobs And Kept Us Off Welfare
Hungry, Itinerant Family Has Problems
Mother Performed Miracles To Feed Nine Of Us
Thirty-Four Days of 100 Or More In St. Louis
Soap Opera Marjorie's Life Turns Around
A Buck A Day And Beans
The Depot Agent Moves Around
Didn't Eat Out For Sixteen Years
Hospital Admitted Three Heat Victims Per Minute
All The World's Against Us
Covered Crib With Dish Towels
I Have Lived On Potatoes And Home-Made Bread
Coming Close To Death
With Dignity And Pride We Stood The Test
Cornmeal Pancakes With Molasses And Meat Grease
We Mined Our Own Coal In North Dakota
Dad Had Many Ways To Bring In A Few Dollars
My Summer In A Tent
Nothing Was Discarded—We Used It All
Strained Honey Used In Radiators
Kind And Generous Grocer Extended Credit
I Paid A Dollar A Week For Mother's Washing Machine
Couldn't Sell Stark's Delicious Apples For Ten Cents A Bushel

YOUNG MARRIED COUPLE FIGHTS POVERTY

When I was fifteen I met a nice young man and fell in love. He was twenty-two at the time. We dated as much as we could for a year and then eloped. When I told my parents, my mother cried and my pop raged and raged. He said (and I remember the exact words) "You've jumped right out of the fire into the frying pan, young lady. You've made your bed and you can't come back home when the going gets tough."

My husband worked on a farm and made a dollar a day. We found two rooms in back of a vacant store and he had seven miles to walk to work and back. We had a cook stove, a table, one chair and a box for a second seat. I set two orange crates on end and put a curtain over the front—and that was my cabinet. With a wash pan and a water bucket on top, we set up housekeeping. The days were long and lonely and I was very homesick but I never let on to my parents. They weren't going to have the chance to say "I told you so".

We moved five times that first year. Hard winter came and farm work was scarce. A day now and then. We were broke and couldn't pay our rent so we finally wound up in a shack on the Mississippi river at Venice, Illinois. The shack was cold and had a big sheet of metal for the floor, which would spring up and down when we walked on it. It was one room and our big old cook stove kept us warm with the wood we picked up along the river bank. We carried our water from the Mississippi for washing clothes and baths but had a big jug for drinking water. Whoever came down there brought us water to drink. We ran out of oil for our one lamp and had no money so we went to bed when it got dark and got up at daybreak. We had left our one and only calendar when we moved and had no clock. We were even mixed up on what day it was until someone came and told us. We were really at rock bottom. But we loved each other and endured that very hard winter of '35 and spring of '36.

I remember when my folks came to see us one day and my mother cried when she hugged me. Pop never let on or made any comment. I know it must have hurt my mother to see us in such poor circumstances.

We were there for six weeks when I got pregnant. Then I realized we had to get out of there and back to Granite City, to try to get a job and a place to live that would be decent for our baby. We walked to town one day and I stayed with my oldest sister while my husband went to work on a farm. It was March and work was opening up and farm work was about all one could find. My husband was a good worker and could always find work. We moved into two rooms, small and dark and hot. One August day I was walking to my sister's house and saw some people papering and painting a little two room house in back of their house. To me it was beautiful. I asked if it was for rent. When they said yes I paid a dollar down on it till the end of the week and we moved in. The rent was five dollars a month.

I had worked on the farm with my husband that summer during threshing time. I saved all that extra money and by the time our baby arrived I had enough to pay for three days in the hospital ($15 total) and for the doctor ($35 total). My husband walked seven miles to work and back and was very proud of our son. We had no debts. We owed no one anything and we were happy.

In April, after our son was born, we moved to a clubhouse at Horse Shoe lake. It was a mile from my husband's work and thus was better for him. However, it was so cold in that shack. The wind blew across the lake and would lift the linoleum off the floor. My little boy, who was learning to walk, couldn't walk on that floor so he spent his days on the bed. The winters were terrible but it was pretty in the summer time.

I scrubbed on the board and boiled clothes in a wash boiler and wrung them by hand to hang on the line. I was proud of my work. The sheets, diapers and towels were white and very clean. We made all our soap out of lye and old meat grease. It didn't smell very good but it sure got my clothes clean. I even took the skin off my fingers. I would dream about a machine to wash the clothes and to have purchased washing powders. That would be real luxury. But I was happy caring for my little boy and my husband and I sang all day long as I worked. My husband finally got a raise to $1.25 a day and we stayed there for three years on the lake.

We had thin cotton mattresses on our beds and I sewed two old sheets together to make a big sack the size of our bed. We then went to the straw pile and filled it with straw. It sure made a warm and comfortable bed too. When the cold winds and snow came and ice was in the teakettle sitting on the cook stove, we were warm in our straw beds. After four years of using that straw we went to a sale and bought two feather beds for two dollars. We were progressing.

My first real knowledge of the depression had been when I was eight or nine years old. One Friday night my dad failed to come home for supper. We ate without him and I was sent to bed. After a while my dad came home and he was excited and talking loudly so I crept out of bed to see what was wrong. There he sat at the kitchen table and he was crying. I couldn't believe my eyes; he had never showed any signs of emotion except anger. I found out later that he had stood in line at the bank in Madison, Illinois a long time, trying to draw out what little money he had on deposit. The banks had closed and everything was in a turmoil.

We knew then that things were getting bad. We had to cut back on groceries and clothes and all our spending. Everyone else was going through the same thing so we accepted it. Our lunches at school were smaller and with no waxed paper to wrap our sandwich it was stale and hard by noon. Waxed paper became a luxury we could no longer afford.

Things kept getting worse. My mother became very ill and was in the hospital for a long time. My brother, who worked with my dad, got laid off and dad was cut to three days a week. A year later we lost our home.

We moved to Mitchell, Illinois outside of town. The house was terrible. It hadn't been lived in for several years. All the windows were broken and dad had to replace them. Then they put up new wall paper and painted things. Dear old mom scrubbed and scrubbed and cleaned and cleaned so we finally could move in. She never complained, but I know her heart was broken to leave our nice home in town. The pump was out in the back yard; the john was far back at the edge of a corn field. We all shed tears over that ordeal but we were taught to make the best of what we had and to be thankful it wasn't worse.

We fed many bums (as they were called back then). We were close to the railroad yards at Mitchell and they would get off the boxcars and walk across the corn field to our place. We had so many that mom finally fixed two old plates, knives and forks and two glasses and cups to keep on the back porch in an old ice box. They were for the bums. We no longer had to scald and clean our own dishes to keep from catching germs.

We truck farmed there and it was hard work. We all had jobs to do. My two oldest sisters got married and it made more work for me and my younger sister and two older brothers. We could never please pop. He worked on the job and came home to the farm and worked until he was ready to drop. And no one rested when pop was around.

Anyway, I was graduated in 1932. In September I took a job in Missouri, near Eureka. I had to rub on the board and set yeast to make all our bread and get up at 5 A.M. every morning except Sunday to get the man of the house off to work. Oil lamps to clean and fill every day. Carried water from a garage next door up on a hill by the hard road. It was quite a distance. I got paid two dollars per week and I was fourteen years old.

But, to get back to my married years: we used flat irons heated on the cook stove to iron our clothes. We also used them to heat our beds. We would wrap them in old towels and rags and put them in the beds by our feet. We even used bricks one year. Sometimes the cloths would get scorched or, if the irons became unwrapped, we would get a little burn when we touched them with our bare feet. But those hot irons were life savers on cold nights. You just haven't lived if you've never experienced the bliss of those hot irons at the foot of an icy bed.

My husband was offered a steady job on a dairy farm at Edwardsville, Illinois. He decided to take it since it was steady, year round work. We got two rooms and thirty dollars a month plus milk. That didn't turn out quite as stated because the man didn't pay regularly. One month all my husband received was ten dollars. We lived that winter mostly on biscuits and gravy. My folks came at Christmas and brought us some potatoes and some home-cured bacon and lard. It was a real treat.

My sister had given my son a little red wagon and it surely came in handy that winter. We lived next to a railroad track. The Green Diamond train came through there very fast and on our curve would throw off coal. I would bundle up my little boy in his snow suit and boots and we would pull the wagon to pick up the coal. We cooked and heated our home that winter on coal that my boy and I picked up. I was proud of the fact that I was helping out.

We finally left there and moved back to Granite City where our second son was born. My husband worked for several different farms and finally got a job at Maryville, Illinois on a dairy and hog farm. We got fifty dollars a month, a four-room house, two butcher hogs and all the milk, butter and cream we wanted. It was like a dream. We were so happy we were on our way.

We finally had water and electricity in the house. We got our first radio. How my husband enjoyed that. We were there for two years when the war came along and the boss was called to service as a captain in the army. He sold out and it was moving time again for us. All in all we moved sixteen times in our life time. Some good moves, some bad ones. But not a bad life. My dad always said hard work builds character so I'm glad we had the stamina to endure. Times were hard for everyone. Today we are retired and living on our own small farm. We've been together for almost fifty-three years. Our sons are married, have families of their own and have never had to experience the hard times we did.

I'm not sorry for the things we endured; rather it has helped us cope with life. In those days you married for love and love can keep folks together and help weather any problems that come along. I wouldn't want to go through those years again but if I were sixteen and in love I'd probably do the same things all over again.

Margaret Myers
Alhambra, Illinois

DAD SCRIMPED BUT THOUGHT MOTHER SPLURGED

I was in my teens at the time and had no idea I was surviving the terrible and unbearable.

We lived in Cairo, Illinois in a house set on brick pillars so high the front porch was four steps up. When indoor toilets had become mandatory, a room had been added beside the kitchen to accommodate the never-freeze toilet. This type of toilet had no trap. When the lid was down the water filled the round galvanized tank; when the lid was released, the toilet flushed.

In summer there was only the coal range for cooking and heating bath water. Of course sponge baths were all we knew and they required maneuvering, so most personal washing was of face and hands at the kitchen sink. It was helpful to believe washing hair more often than every two weeks was bad for it, but I found dirty fingernails and black nostrils impossible to avoid.

When the range gave out Mom traded a good heater and the range for a good range, paying off the difference in a few months. Dad was furious, but mother knew of a woman about a block away who had been scalded to death while heating water on a stove whose missing leg was propped up by bricks.

Dad was a coach cleaner for the New York Central railroad and made low but steady income of about $15 a week. Mom washed and ironed for a few people, including a family on relief. She wanted a dollar for the church offering and a little left over. When she made the stove deal, she had no doubt that Dad would buy a heating stove when winter came. How wrong she was.

With six people and no heat except a kitchen range, we were really crowded. It seems everything was in the kitchen. Mom pulled the washing machine out from the back wall on washing days and paired chairs to support two big tubs of rinse water. She ironed in that same space that winter and during rainy spells hung wet clothes from lines throughout the kitchen. In later years she looked back on these as having been hard times.

The floors were covered with linoleum. In spite of limited heat in the house, Mom kept to her schedule of housekeeping and fell on the ice while mopping the front room as usual.

The heaterless winter was unnecessary. We had less per person than households receiving aid. Mom sewed, making almost everything. Food, shelter, heat, light and medical care were the essentials in her life. Dad really wanted to build a savings account and feel like a man of worth. To do this, he contended that more than a main dish at a meal was unnecessary, that saving electricity was a good reason for early bedtime. Most people do survive sicknesses, he said, so most medical attention was a total waste.

Being without a heating stove was probably the result of marital discord. Dad didn't believe in squandering money on doctors unless a condition was obviously critical. Mom often told that Dad's family had lost a twelve-year old daughter who had been sick for so long that when finally she told her father that if he loved her he would get a doctor. She was dead by the time he returned with one. He kept money in his wallet or had secret bank accounts while Mom made sheets from unbleached muslin and tie-tacked new covers over worn out quilts to keep them together.

Nobody was constantly telling us that breathing could be fatal. Mosquitoes were still causing malaria. Measles, mumps, chicken pox and whooping cough were hurdles almost every child had to conquer. Tuberculosis was common but leukemia was so unusual that a child with the rare blood disease was reported in the press from diagnosis to death. Locally there was a flurry of diphtheria, colds were very common, and Mom had not missed a severe yearly bout with influenza since 1918. One year the flu caused fainting at onset, followed by extreme weakness. People passed out on the streets, behind pulpits, in their bathtubs—it was terrible. And infantile paralysis was on the rise.

A few years before that heaterless winter, we subsisted maybe three days on fried potatoes and white gravy, with oatmeal for breakfast, while Dad nursed five dollars in his billfold, determined not to go broke before payday. Mom sent notes to school, asking the lunch concession to let us have food on credit and we'd bring the money the next payday. The older children only racked up about a twenty-five cent debt but my brother and I had a ball. We charged a few cents over a dollar, with hamburgers a nickel and everything else priced similarly. It would have provided groceries for the whole family for two days or more, but Mom didn't care. Our potato and gravy diet had been unnecessary and had cost Dad as much as if he'd let her buy more food.

I remember that Metropolitan Life had visiting nurses who called on expectant mothers and advised them about nutrition, layettes and economics. Like—purchase your Ivory soap early so it would be dryer when the baby arrived and one bar would last many months.

A woman who lived near us had a flock of very blonde children. They received their weekly baths Saturday night and went to Sunday school fresh and clean. However, the school nurse did her inspecting Fridays, always finding these childrens' heads dirty. A little girl came home with the message that the nurse had told her she would give her a "P" for grooming if her hair were not clean next time. Her mama told the child "You tell her that I said your hair is going to get washed Saturday afternoon so it will be clean for church and that your mama said she could put a s–t on your report card if that doesn't suit her.!"

I was told that another family with three girls, always prettily dressed, never wearing faded or poorly fitted, used clothing, frequently had nothing on the table but fried potatoes and white gravy. The mother was motivated by the fact that people could see the outside but not the inside. In every way she appeared a faultless, loving mother, perfect housekeeper and I don't believe her children had any health problems traceable to nutrition.

I don't know when commodities were first distritubed but believe that was the first experience of integration for many people. A couple near us received these commodities and also had a son in a CCC camp. They were staunch Republicans and hated Roosevelt to the point that the missus practically frothed with rage when she spoke of him. Once, as her husband carried free commodities into the house, she told us how she had to stand in line And how the "niggers were given exactly the same things we received". White people received neither more nor better.

A photo of a statue was the closest I came to seeing a nude male before I got out of high school, after which I saw a tot who had shed his pants. Babies in our family were girls. I read nearly a thousand books a year by the time I got out of school and reread some suggestive passages with interest. Even pregnancy was spoken of with discretion; it was years before I heard the most common terms in current vocabularies.

Children today have awful things to overcome. I know one who has been sexually molested when five, another raped at seven. Because she was not avid for boys in the six grade one was accused by classmates of being a lesbian. Recently one, now nine, was accosted by a boy smaller than she, wanting to know if she were a virgin. Afraid not to answer, she finally said "Yes", upon which he chased her because he said he liked to kick virgins' butts. A very small boy comes down the street mouthing unbelievable filth. All of this from nice, white, professional type families.

This morning I hurt my fingers trying to grasp and pull off the plastic band of a gallon of milk. The cap was so tight that my daughter had to use pliers to open it. All the time our cereal and coffee got cold. Somebody is protecting me from random poisoning with cyanide but who cares if frustration gives me a stroke? If I lived alone, I'd never get into many of my "safe" containers.

Annie E. McAnally
Cahokia, Illinois

THOSE WERE HUNGRY TIMES
DURING THE DEPRESSION

Her name is Lillie Mabel Hall and she's seen the insides of more wild animals than your average wildlife biologist. "Honey, I've cooked every kind of wild game in the state, except a bear. And if somebody would bring me a bear, I'd cook it, too."

Lillie Hall was born and raised in St. Louis. The lone patch of green in her city block of apartment houses comes from pots of geraniums she's carefully tended and placed on the porch—otherwise her street is mostly brick, clapboard, asphalt and sidewalks. But Lillie can tell you about when Creve Coeur to the west was mostly woods and farms, and her father and brother went hunting—under the Grand Avenue bridge.

She lives just ten blocks from where she was born. Her former home was urban renewed, replaced by high-rises and high rent. "My childhood home was always open. Those were hungry times, during the Depression. But people knew the Clarks' house always had food, and most nights we had people in to share it with us."

She stretches out her walnut-colored hand, palm up. "My daddy used to say, "Keep your hand open. That way, things can come into it and go out of it.'"

Her father, Eldridge Clark, enjoyed a rare commodity during the Depression—employment. He worked for $1.25 a day for the railroad and supplemented the food for his extended family—Lillie's mother, two brothers, sisters, uncles and grandparents—by hunting. Or more correctly, chunking.

"Couldn't afford a gun, and anyway it was against the law for blacks to own one then. He hunted with a stick."

It was a common hunting method, Lillie said, and men got so good at chunking rabbits with a stick that they came to rely on rabbits as an important source of meat. Their main hunting ground during the Depression was the relatively untamed land on either side of the railroad under the Grand Avenue bridge.

Lillie has a deserved reputation as a superb ethnic cook. She has been selected as a Master in the Missouri Cultural Heritage Center's Master/Apprentice Program to pass along her knowledge of traditional cooking. Like most traditional skills, she learned to cook at the knee of her mother and grandmother.

"My mother says she can squeeze a nickle until the buffalo screams. And my daddy made us stock six months of food all the time." But it wasn't just quantity, it was the quality that made Lillie the cook she is today. Her father used his contacts on the railroad to bring in fresh oysters by the sackful from the Gulf. Neighbors contributed fresh produce and Lillie learned when to shop for fruit and vegetables when they were in season to preserve for winter's use.

Lillie says the family ate well even when times were lean. "I can make a chicken-foot stew that is perfectly delicious. In the spring my grandmother and mother and I picked wild greens—poke salad, lamb's quarters, sheep sorrel, crow's foot, three kinds of dock, pepper grass, plaintain and dandelion—wonderful! The secret for any food preparation is in the handling and the seasoning."

Eventually Eldridge Clark saved up enough money to buy a shotgun. "It was a double-barreled Ithaca, as I recall. My daddy didn't know much about guns and the first time he fired it he shot off both barrels at once. It nearly blew him out of his socks!" When Lillie's brother Steve took up marksmanship, the Clark menu began to include exotic fare like raccoon, venison, goose and duck.

Now Steve sometimes goes west to hunt larger game, bringing Lillie elk and deer to cook, but then they hunted mostly in north Missouri where Lillie developed a love for camping, hunting and fishing.

"I taught my husband to fish. My children were on a fishing bank before they were a year old. We never let children be a hindrance—we always included them."

Lillie was the designated camp cook on family trips that often included three carloads of people. "I'd cook five pounds of onions, some bacon and ten pounds of potatoes in my big black iron skillet, and gallons of coffee. When you play hard, you eat hard! And do you know anything that smells better than food cooking on a campfire? It's one of the most memorable smells there is."

Now widowed, Lillie has lots of good memories to sustain her. She has traveled all over the world, sampling the exotic foods of North Africa and Europe. "I've been to Nassau more times than I have fingers and toes," she says. But her experiences with her family in the out-of-doors remain one of the "pure joys" of her life.

"I taught my husband to love the outdoors. He didn't know about the beauty of the woods until I showed him how nature just kind of restores something inside of you—something everyday life will rob you of if you let it. It was instilled in me as a child, and I've tried to pass it on to my own children."

"These are the things so many children in the city are deprived of. They're so—what do you call it—'street smart' now, but they're really just robbing themselves by being closed off from nature."

Lillie has that combination—rare in the competitive "me-first" world of the 1980s—of education, down-to-earth good sense and compassion. For her work organizing a high school Red Cross volunteer group during World War II, she was offered a scholarship to St. Louis University and became the first black woman to be admitted. Throughout a life laced with the threat of poverty and unemployment, she remembered her father's example of extending the open hand.

"In those times if a neighbor needed help, people didn't say 'here's some soup.' They said 'fixed so much soup tonight the kids won't eat it. Why don't you take some?'"

Sharing is engrained in Lillie, whether it's soup for the neighbors or the love of the outdoors that's shared with her family. When rabbit was an important part of the Depression diet, Lillie's family shared this rabbit sausage with many people—black, white, Irish, Hispanic—whoever happened to need the generosity of the Clark household.

Field dress seven to ten young rabbits by removing the entrails. Skin under cold running water, and with a sharp knife, cut the meat away from the bone. Grind meat with one-half to one pound of salt pork, smoked jowl or bacon (eliminate added salt if you use salt pork) and season with sage, thyme, a little rosemary, freshly ground black pepper, salt and crushed red pepper (optional).

When Lillie's brothers began to hunt for deer, the same recipe was adapted for venison sausage. When they went waterfowl hunting, Lillie used the cooked sausage mixed with chopped apples or other fruit (raisins, apricots, etc.), pecans and cornbread to stuff the cavity of the wild fowl; she also placed uncooked sausage between the meat and the loosened skin for added moisture. "Most wild meat is lean and dry. Sausage adds moisture and makes the meat more tender." Lillie said.

The meat of raccoon is an overlooked delicacy, but care in field preparation must be taken, she advised, or the taste will be gamey. A freshly killed raccoon must be eviscerated and the musk gland removed while in the field. Lillie soaks the meat in several changes of salt water to leach away the blood, then cuts the animal into serving size pieces. She places the pieces in a marinade of apple cider, a bay leaf or two, chopped onion, garlic, cracked red pepper, coursely ground black pepper and salt, and refrigerates it overnight.

The next day the meat is removed from the marinade, dredged with flour that's been seasoned with salt and pepper, and browned in salt pork or bacon grease. Lillie reduces the marinade by about half and adds it to the browned meat in a covered roasting pan. "Cook it until the meat is ready to fall off the bones, then add slices of sweet potatoes and tart apples, like MacIntosh or Winesap. Ladle the juices over them and cook until they're tender. If you want, you can thicken the juices with cream and flour, or just cornstarch. Either way makes good 'soppins' to go with homemade cornbread or biscuits."

"Country cooking uses a lot of guesstimating. My recipes won't be exact because we just look at amounts and judge how much to use." She points to her cupped palm and say, "That's the best measure for a teaspoon or a tablespoon there is."

Lillie the angler has a special way for preparing fish, too, whether she reels them in or buys them in the supermarket. "I've used this recipe on shark, but it works just as well on catfish." She first soaks the fish in milk for 30 minutes to two hours ("takes away the fishy taste" she says), then she makes a mixture of fresh cracker crumbs and cornmeal seasoned with crushed red pepper, salt and black pepper. She dips the fish into beaten egg, then into the crumb mixture two times before chilling the coated fish for up to an hour.

With a raised finger, Lillie admonishes, "Now it's very important to use peanut oil to fry that fish. Peanut oil can be heated to 450 degrees without smoking. Get it good and hot and fry the fish until it's golden brown on each side. The coating seals the flavor and the egg makes it so it doesn't get greasy."

Lillie likes to serve fried fish with cornbread and spaghetti, dill pickles and ice-cold beer or tea.

Lillie, now in her 60s, sometimes finds herself wishing she had more to share with the world than recipes.

"Everybody has a row to hoe in life; some make their own handle short, where you break your back and never look up. But all my life I've worked with a long hoe. I can stand up, look any man in the eye and tell him all the good things in this life I know — the woods and the clean water and good food, all are gifts from nature- and the biggest gift of all is what comes from within your heart."

Kathy Love
Jefferson City, MO

SUBSISTENCE LIVING

I was twenty years old that summer, contemplating enrolling at the University of Arkansas, Fayetteville. I'd finished two years of college with a major in home economics at what was then a junior college, Arkansas Tech at Russellville.

Home was a 160 acre hill farm not more than ten miles from the Oklahoma line and about twenty miles southeast of Fort Smith, AK. My mother's family had been residents of the immediate area for five generations. Certainly all of those things gave me a sense of "place", of being "at one" with my environment. I could in 1936 have done with more self assurance. In retrospect I wonder how my parents managed to maintain sanity, much less survival for their family of five children.

Ours was subsistence living with no crops nor hay harvested to feed cow, hogs and chickens which provided food and a little produce for grocery money. My mother was a master gardener with any surplus carefully dried, canned or pickled for winter use. This procedure applied not just to garden truck but to early wild greens, home orchard and woodsy fruits. Waste not, want not.

My dad took special care with hog husbandry and was a master castrator of young piglets. He developed quite a reputation in the county and among drummers at Tatum hardware store, for his home ground, fabric sacked and hickory smoked sausage. He was also a good watermelon grower for home consumption.

Certainly the dry years of the thirties were not conducive to food production. When my mother's garden was reduced to scanty gatherings of odds and ends with never enough for a mess of anything, we ate a lot of stew or soup, plus cornbread of course.

I was the oldest and always felt pressured to be able to make a living for myself. There were family role models, such as my mother's sister. She and an uncle paid my college tuiton and I had on campus jobs through the National Youth Administration when in school. My total college debt for four years was $500. Owing that made me feel very obligated and bound by family expectations, so I never considered marrying my college love.

A summer job in 1936 would have been of great help, but there weren't any available. Traveling to work in every family consisted of walking or riding in a wagon. Of course a few families had cars but one couldn't regularly "bum" rides.

I recall one school event that summer — riding on a flatbed truck loaded with folk going to a "play party" in another community about ten miles away. Play parties consisted of games that ended with couples going for a walk down the road where the more brazen "made out" or attempted to. And did! As we returned home that evening a sixteen year old boy was thrown from the truck as it lurched around a corner. I recall being very concerned. Fortunately he wasn't seriously injured.

Life in those years was pretty primitive.

Katherine K. Hill
Springfield, Missouri

AUBREY AND THE OTHER MULES

There was no refrigeration but there was the cool cistern or the well into which milk and cream could be placed. If you were lucky enough to live in town there were iceboxes and men who delivered ice right to your door; you put it in the icebox with a drain underneath into a pan as the ice melted; some people even piped the drain through the wall to go outside the house.

Since there was no refrigeration, meat needed to be protected from spoiling, which it would do very rapidly. The most prevelant procedure was to butcher in the cool of late fall and to smoke or salt down most of the meat. Some of it was cooked and canned as were vegetables. Beef, pork and chickens were canned by cold packing in Missouri. In wintertime meat would hang in the smoke house and kept frozen or nearly frozen. Many a family kept a side of beef frozen outside, from which they cut chunks as needed.

Aubrey's mother had a pedal-powered sewing machine with which she clothed her family. In fact, Aubrey's wife used the same item when they were married and lived with the family on the farm.

Of course these are just a few of the inconveniences they didn't know they were missing. When no one knew of an electric icebox, when no one knew of an electric sewing machine, no one felt deprived. Mainly Aubrey's family thought of electricity as being "lights" and, as a result they spoke of "lights coming down the road" meaning the power lines were being strung. But that was years later.

Aubrey had been born on the farm, raised on the farm, spent most of his life on the farm or nearby. As we said, life lent ahead without electricity.

By the time he was a young man, the only labor-saving device on the farm was Aubrey himself; later on his younger brothers and/or a hired man, but Aubrey did most of it because he was the oldest son and his father was in town being a politician. Several different county jobs, but most noteworthy being a southern sheriff. So Aubrey did the work. He and the other mules.

They broke the furrows—he and the mules. They cut the trees and hauled them near the house to be cut up—he and the mules. They ran the threshing machine—he and the other mules. Little did they know what the gasoline motor and the "lights" were going to do to their world.

Time moved along. Lights came down the road and, gradually, changes came to the farm. The first, the very first, was a series of naked light bulbs hanging down nakedly in the middle of farmhouse rooms. Soon Aubrey's family realized they could hook up other things to the electricity and, as money permitted, these other things gradually came about.

But Aubrey found himself moving into his middle years without having to adapt to all of these new items. He didn't need them. He left the farm and worked in town. He tinkered with a home-made radio set and people came around to hear Arb's radio pick up Kansas City, a hundred and eight miles away.

Soon came the depression and then the years of the drought. Now there was power in town and he started hearing about some of these fine new electric items, like an electric stove (Can you imagine!) but who had money for things like that? It was very difficult just to keep food on the table and there were times when he missed all the food available on the farm. His siblings had fresh eggs, chickens, fresh pork, a lot of things that he and Mary had to buy with the few dollars they could scrape together. Others tell us how difficult it was, but Aubrey knew first hand. He had a tough time making enough to live on. He found it humiliating and defeating, just as did millions of others. And then there was that awful heat that burned things alive and turned green to dead. The best years had been on the farm.

Eventually that damnable depression passed and Aubrey started making some money again, meaningful money, but he still worked like the mules. He finally was able to retire and move back to the farm for some of his last years. But then Mary died, he eventually remarried and moved back to town again. He enjoyed electric thermostats, his beloved radio for baseball games, some television, an electric mixer in the kitchen and an electric sewing machine for his wife, but those were enough gadgets to make him happy. The air conditioner was mainly for visitors. He didn't need it most of the time. He'd always liked hot weather.

And then one day when he was in his eighties he visited in his son's house, hundreds of miles away. He noticed that all the windows were closed and the air conditioner was usually running. When his son came home from work, Aubrey heard the garage door open automatically, as the motor hummed. Two refrigerators in different parts of the house would gently turn on and off, but Aubrey could hear them. A dehumidifier operated to control the moisture level in the lower level of the house, while clocks all over the house kept up an almost imperceptible hum, as they kept everything on time.

"Damned", said Aubrey, "something is always running in this house. I can always hear at least two or three motors going. What are all of those things? What are they all doing?"

Aubrey never really received an answer. It was man's old complaint that the world had changed, perhaps too much for any one lifetime to have to absorb.

So Aubrey never used all of those newer conveniences. Born in '93, he died at 93 — years that is — in 1986. And, most of all, he didn't want to be kept alive uselessly by machines. He got his wish.

William H. Hull
Edina, Minnesota

THERE IS AN ART IN LEARNING HOW TO BE POOR

As a Georgia native I recall most vividly the summer of 1936. The sky was full of dust and it was awesome here.

In 1935 I had been on a train passing through Texas. One moment it was daylight and the next utter darkness. My panic was relieved when someone said it was a dust storm.

In April 1936 a vicious tornado killed more than two hundred people in Gainesville, Georgia, about thirty miles from where I resided, on the brink of the famed Tallulah Gorge. We moved to a safer location.

The crops in north Georgia were not much affected by drought but to look upward and see western land blowing toward the Atlantic ocean was depressing. (Our awful drought came later, in 1985–1987). Add to that the pests an aged woman called "seven-year locusts"; there wasn't much comfort. She said their weird song was "Pharoah" and it was fae-roe day after day. Also, according to her, the doves sang "Old Noah...saved ...you...me" in their mournful way.

My husband found a job away from home at $12 a week; many men were far less fortunate. In his absence that same aged lady taught me how to gather wild greens, berries and fruit. I learned to make dyes and to quilt. But fishing became my recreation and dining-out passion. Fish on a green stick broiled over an open fire and eaten beside a stream was too delicious to describe. And the precious silence of the forests, after having lived in asphalt jungles for most of my life, was a joy.

We didn't have a single utility bill or any rent to pay. Our home was a two story log house with a porch spanning two sides. It dated back to 1816 and had been dismantled and moved three times, probably on ox-drawn wagons. I found it marvelously cool in summer and warm in winter.

If I were not now age seventy-five, I should like to return to the simple happiness of 1936 and the great depression era. If one had no money, so what? One needed so very, very little and one learned to make do — and had fun doing it.

There is an art in learning how to be poor, just as coming into sudden wealth must be mastered. It takes grit and gumption to be happy in either situation. In those days the poor seemed to be far happier than those more well-off. They had nothing to lose and thus were carefree regarding loss.

Today, so many of us are hostage to our own possessions. We forge our own chains.

Isabelle M. Coffee
Baldwin, Georgia

ROOSEVELT GAVE US JOBS AND KEPT US OFF WELFARE

We were married on November 24, 1930 in Watseka, Illinois; he was twenty-one and I was sixteen.

Then in the spring we went to live in Colorado. First we lived up in the mountains at West Creek, where my husband worked at a saw mill. His dad and brother and my husband and I went out every day to the forest and cut down trees, trimmed them and cut them into eight foot logs. Then we hooked them together with logging chains and with an old mare pulled them down to the truck at the foot of the hill where we loaded them on the truck to go to the mill.

We cut a hundred logs a day, for which we received ten cents each, so the two of us made $10 a day; that was good money in those days. My husband's dad and brother made the same.

We moved to Colorado City and my husband worked for the forest reserve making parks; he cut stones to make out-houses in the park. In those days Roosevelt was president and he put people to work to earn their money. That's what we ought to have now — another president like him so everybody wouldn't be on welfare. All the years my husband and I have been married we never were on welfare — because Roosevelt gave jobs during the depression.

We lived fifty miles from town and once a week went to get groceries. We would buy a case of eggs at nine cents a dozen, bread for five cents and half a hog for $5.00. One day a week we went to town to eat out. Hamburgers were only five cents each and we would take in a show which was twenty-five cents. This was living high on the hog, as the saying goes.

We bought our first house for a hundred rabbits — which we had raised.

We have three sons. The first one was born in Colorado City; he cost $45.

The second one, also born there, cost $75 and our third son was born in Illinois. He cost $25.

We moved back to Illinois in 1938 and my husband worked on farms until 1947 when we moved to Farmer City, Illinois and he worked as a contractor. We built our own home, as did all of our sons.

I hope you get as much enjoyment reading this as we did in living it, back in the depression days.

Angeline Reynolds
Farmer City, Illinois

HUNGRY ITINERANT FAMILY HAS PROBLEMS

Born on a farm in 1925 near Boxholm, Iowa, I am the eldest of nine children, my father being a tenant farmer. Probably the most vivid memory I have of that era happened during early September 1936.

The day dawned as so many that year, hot-dry-miserably boring. It was a Saturday so we kids we up early to do the chores and, afterwards, with no school, we would figure out something to keep us occupied.

For three or four days we had noticed an old truck parked in a field driveway about sixty rods from our house, with a man, woman and small girl herding about six cows along the road ditch. This was not completely unusual but there was precious little grass growing in the ditches and any green that existed came from the more tenacious weeds. But it was forage and ditches were public property with no restrictions against herding cattle.

About 10 A.M. the woman and girl walked up the driveway to our front door where they knocked. I was in the house, standing just inside the screened door and answered the knock. The woman asked if my Ma was home who, by this time, was at my side, asking what she could do for the woman.

I'll never forget her answer.

"Mrs," the woman replied, "My man don't had nothin'' in his belly for over three days and I'm wonderin' if you could spare a cup of coffee for him? We come from down in Missouri with our cows lookin' for some grazin' grass, and we run out of money and gas just down the road, and the cows is all we got left.'

Mother invited them in the house, had them sit down and immediately poured the woman a cup of coffee, gave the girl a glass of milk and started poking up the fire in the old kitchen stove. The woman got up from the table and started for the door carrying the cup of coffee, thanking Mother every step of the way for the coffee she had poured for "My man." Mother said not to go yet, because she was going to fix some egg sandwiches for all of them, and that coffee was for her. She also said she'd pour a fruit jar full of fresh coffee for the man.

I believe Mother fixed a dozen sandwiches, giving the woman and girl the first half dozen while they sat at the table and putting the remaining six in a sack to carry back to the man. The woman and daughter ate ravenously and even I, with seldom any thought of table manners, realized that here were two people who were damned nearly starved.

I remember Mother asking if they had any bed covers or quilts, or any pans to cook food in. I also remember the woman's reply, "Yes, Mam, but we've got nothing to cook."

I remember the look of pity in Mother's eyes, and the anguished look when she glanced at the little girl. Mother told the woman to wait a minute and, grabbing a handful of newspapers, disappeared into the outdoor cellar where she kept the hundreds of quarts of canned goods she had put away and where was stored the salt pork barrell during the warm months. She came back with her arms loaded with jars of canned goods and a big package of salt pork.

"Oh, no, Mrs., we ain't beggars. Something will turn up. Maybe my man will get some field work from one of the farmers around here, and we can get some gas for the truck and get movin'."

Mother insisted she take what was offered; she knew they were not beggars, and maybe some day they too could help out someone. The woman was crying when they left the house, but she took the food.

They continued camping at the same spot for a few more days, although they never came back to the house. I remember also seeing them gleaning wild plums from a thicket in the roadside.

About three days after the woman's visit, Dad came in from chores and announced that we would all have to delay eating supper until we had all helped move all of our milk cows to an isolated pasture some forty rods down the road, the opposite direction from where the itinerants were camped. Mother asked why and Dad replied "Because I think that man has Bang's disease in his cattle."

Bang's disease at that time was very serious, causing cows to sling their new born calves, milk from infected cows was suspected of carrying human ailments, and when it reached a certain level a mandatory testing of all cattle was demanded. Such infected cattle had to be slaughtered, with the government paying for testing and reimbursement for any lost catle.

As it turned out, the fellow's cattle were infected. Dad saw to it that they were tested. Our cattle did not contract the disease but the poor itinerant left the area with nothing but his old truck and his family.

I have thought of them many times.

C.L. "Gus" Norlin
Monticello, Iowa

Dust storm in Liberal, Kansas, April 14, 1935. (*Courtesy The Kansas State Historical Society, Topeka.*)

Dust Storm in Kansas. (*Courtesy The Kansas State Historical Society, Topeka.*)

Hauling water from an emergency well near Overbrook, KS 1930s. (*Courtesy The Kansas State Historical Society, Topeka.*)

Dust bowl scene near Reydon, Oklahoma. (*Courtesy, Oklahoma Historical Society.*)

Civilian Conservation Corps (CCC) men working sloping sides of gulley and planting grass to prevent further erosion during dust bowl days. (*Courtesy Oklahoma Historical Society.*)

Praying for rain near Beardsley, MN July 1936. Members of the Holden congregation of the Norwegian Lutheran Church. (*Courtesy, Minnesota Historical Society.*)

Lighting a lantern suspended from a chandelier. (*Courtesy, Minnesota Historical Society.*)

MOTHER PERFORMED MIRACLES
TO FEED NINE OF US

Cold! Cold! Cold! Then Hot! Hot! Hot! and even Hotter. If you ever thought it couldn't get any hotter, it did, in the summer of 1936.

I was fourteen and had just been graduated from the eighth grade and been confirmed. Actually, my family was lucky because we lived on the north side of Hydes lake about three miles north of Young America. If there were any breeze, it came across the lake and maybe cooled things by a degree or two. When the thermometer read at least 100 degrees day after day a little cooling didn't mean a whole lot. The whole thing was that we didn't know any different. Even if there had been air conditioning, we couldn't have afforded it. When there were nine of us at the table three times a day my mother performed a lot of miracles with bread and milk.

I remember that it was so hot we couldn't do any field work during the day but waited until the sun set. Then we'd go to the field to shock grain and haul hay if there were any to haul. I remember that the cows would stay in the wooded pasture because the barnyard was too hot. It was my job to bring them in each evening and dad would let them stay in the yard overnight because of the lake breeze.

In the front of the house we had a big screened porch with a tin deck and a railing around it. When we knew that my mother was asleep, my oldest sister and I would crawl through the window with a sheet and pillow and sleep on that porch. We had to be very quiet because that tin roof was noisy; the rest of the children slept downstairs on the dining room floor.

We had little money. My oldest sister worked in the local grocery store for $30 a month. She would give some of the money to my father so he could buy sugar and flour. Mother made lots of bread. At that time everlasting yeast was used. She'd have to get a start from a neighbor; she'd use some of the yeast and then add sugar and water so the remainder would ferment. At times the yeast would spoil and she'd need to get another start from a friend.

When we went to church on Sunday — and we did go — heat or not — the men wore their suits, jackets and all. Ladies wore long cotton stockings and hats. Bare legs or being coatless was unthinkable.

When the potatoes were ready to harvest we gathered them by hand. It was like picking up marbles because they were so small. But we were glad to have them even though we kids hated crawling on the dry ground.

As for the cold, it was bitter. My father would put the truck in the barn with the cattle and horses so we could get to school. There was no antifreeze or plug gadgets and no public bus service, so he had to be able to start the truck in the morning.

To pass the time my mother and eldest sister made lots of quilts and we all played cards. We had a radio but that was used only for the news and a church service.

I'll take today. The heck with the good old days.

Mrs. L. H. Hoeft
Young America, Minnesota

THIRTY-FOUR DAYS OF 100 OR MORE IN ST. LOUIS

Consider 1936, the year the thermometer blew its top, the summer the temperature rose to or above 100 on a record 34 days, including 12 straight days through mid-August.

How about a 118 degree reading at what is now Lambert St. Louis International Airport? It was reported Aug. 14, 1936.

Although record keeping methods were suspect, officials said 470 people died and that daily death tolls ran as high as 90 during the 1936 heat wave, which drove thousands of people from their homes in a search for cooler air in city parks and the St. Louis County countryside.

Francis O'Brien, who was staying in a rooming house in the 3700 block of Olive Street, indirectly blamed the heat for a fractured hip, according to a 1936 Globe-Democrat newspaper report.

The roomer told police that he moved his bed to the roof of the building in an effort to get cool "and apparently rolled off the roof in his sleep. He fell 40 feet to a brick pavement."

Newspaper casualty lists sprawled over columns; hundreds of patients suffering heatstroke and exhaustion filled hospitals, and the St. Louis coroner was working around-the-clock. Seventy heat deaths were scheduled on the coroner's docket on a single day and Calvary Cemetery set a one-day record with 44 burials.

The treatment for City Hospital patients who had suffered heat attacks included intravenous injections of salt water and a bath in a tub of ice water. In those days before air conditioning, some motorists placed containers of dry ice on the floor of their cars in an attempt to keep cool. Overcome by the heat, some drivers collapsed at the wheel of their cars as they drove along steamy St. Louis streets.

A shortage of ice — which was used in iceboxes to preserve food — developed as ice plants worked overtime in an attempt to keep up with the demand.

At one point, the Mississippi River stage at St. Louis was 1.3 feet, compared with a normal of 17.3 feet.

After 23 days of 100-or-higher temperatures that summer, newspapers began reporting that it was a "day of relief" if the high was 97 and "mild" if the mercury rose no higher than 94.

A headline in the July 18, 1936, edition of the Globe-Democrat read: "Only 19 Die of Heat Stroke and 8 Overcome in Day of Relief."

The summer of 1936 — the hottest on record here — also scorched outstate areas including Brookfield, Mo., where a thermometer hit 131 degrees and burst.

The average temperature (in St. Louis) for the summer of 1936 was 83.4 degrees. In 1934, the average was 83.3 degrees and in 1901, the average was 82.7.

Edward L. Cook
St. Louis Globe-Democrat, July 23, 1983

Reproduced with special permission.

SOAP OPERA MARJORIE'S LIFE TURNS AROUND

We were so poor that my mother and I owned one pair of silk stockings between us and one dress coat. I started a new fashion wearing my ski pants to school and pushing them up to just below my knees, like knickers.

I was in my senior year at old Chi Hi, right here in Lindstrom, Minnesota in 1936. There were only twenty-three of us in that class, not like the huge classes in the Chisago Lakes school district today.

I received free milk at noon and $6 a month for working in the superintendent's office. I saved that to buy material for my graduation dress, hitchhiked to St. Paul and back for the material. Mother made the dress of white moire taffeta, floor length, with white net over it and an applique of fleur-de-lis cut from a table cover embroidered by my grandmother. My great aunt Helena bought me a pair of silk stockings and I have snapshots that showed me looking elegeant. I had a nose-gay bouquet from Holm & Olson, sent me by my brother Norman who was a cook in Denver.

I started school in Duluth where Dad was with Minnesota Power and Light and we lived very well in an eleven-room flat — and took trips in our Marmon touring car. I was ten years old when my mother's dad became ill with cancer. My step-grandmother was in a rest home. Mother and my brother and I went to our family home, Villa Cape Horn, in rural Lindstrom to look after Grandpa. He died early in the summer and Dad was out of work, so he joined us at the resort which Grandpa had deeded to my folks, complete with a $4,000 mortgage. It consisted of sixteen acres on South Lindstrom lake, five guest cottages, summer kitchen, barn, a fifteen-room house and a small cottage where my parents had lived briefly when first married.

The state highway department decided to change the course of highway eight and blocked our driveway. Business was at a standstill and the lakes receded. Finally the bay dried up completely and we could walk across it. The poor turtles started migrating north in search of water and so many were squashed on the roads, causing hazards, that special crews were sent to shovel them up. Friends in Detroit thought we made up this story. Wells dried up, lawns were just burned brown grass, dust was so thick the sun could barely shine through it and I think every tumbleweed in both Dakotas blew over to roll around and plague us.

We would not have eaten were it not for a good friend who found Cape Horn a good place to hide out with his girl friend. She also gave me clothes after the banker's wife died; they eventually were married.

Dad couldn't get any work and he and Mother fought constantly, our electricity was cut off; we had no money to pay the bill. No money for the mortgage either.

Dad and the father of my classmate tried picking up scrap iron to sell. Dad got arrested for taking some off the railroad company's property but the other man was let off scott free. Now when Jim, my youngest brother, and I went down the street we were called "Scrap Iron Picottes!" That name stuck until we left town.

But we kids skated, went sliding and ice boating, swam in the summer and I know now never realized how poor we were. None of the other kids lived in a big house with oriental rugs, oil paintings, imported china and sterling silver, but they were lucky, especially the farm kids, because they had food.

My friends used to bring me meat sandwiches for lunch — a real treat. I still have the same friends here and why not? The milkman brought the milk every day even though we could not pay him. He told my mother that the cows had to be milked anyhow. Dear old Mr. Danielson.

One day when Jim and I were coming home from school, Dad drove by us, never even waving. That was the last we saw of him for some time; he just couldn't take it anymore and left. Eventually he went to Michigan where he had relatives.

Mother wrote letters searching for him, but nothing ever happened. Finally she divorced him. I testified for her, feeling like a traitor to my dad. No one else got divorced in those days.

The mortgage was foreclosed, we were forced to vacate, there was an auction and we went to Minneapolis to stay in an old apartment building owned by one of our former resort guests.

Mother finally located my dad living in Detroit with his sister's family and she made a bus trip to see him. He didn't want to see her because he was going to marry a 28-year old girl. I don't know what Mother said or did but soon we were on a bus going to live in Detroit. It seemed like a solution. At least we'd be anonymous there. From fifteen rooms to a one-bedroom furnished apartment was a real shock.

In retrospect it was the loss of everything and the stark reality of the move that made us push on. Jim went to Lawrence Tech and I went to Wayne university, quitting to go into show business. I was a well-known circus performer for many years. Dad became a maintenance electrician at U.S.Rubber. Detroit was good to us. Michigan was still a common law state and Dad refused to re-marry Mother but we lived as a family. They continued to fight all the time about everything and did so until he died at 86. She died later at 93.

In the fifties I built a beautiful home on several acres of lakeshore, back home, and my daughter was graduated from Chi Hi twenty-five years ago. It was my way of showing the kids who called me "Scrap Iron Picotte" that I'd made it— also wearing mink and diamonds.

I'm sure this story would have been very different had it not been for that terrible drought.

Marjorie J. Hackett
Lindstrom, Minnesota

A BUCK A DAY AND BEANS

I was graduated from high school in a little town in eastern Montana, name of Ekalaka, in 1933. Farmers and ranchers in my county were abandoning their homes and mostly heading for the west coast.

I was offered a job herding cattle for a buck a day and beans, and the buck a day was very iffy. I had skills as a typist and could take shorthand and wasn't about to stick around the old home town.

I got a ride to eastern Iowa tending a carload of horses late in the fall of '33, beat my way down to Peoria, Illinois and tried to get on with Caterpillar. My math skills were a little shy so, being in a crack, I joined the Civilian Conservation Corp (CCC) in the spring of 1934. They promptly shipped me to Jefferson Bar-racks in St. Louis for basic training and indoctrination. Then I was sent to a state park in southern Illinois for about a year. Back at Jefferson Barracks in 1935 where I met my future wife, married her in July 1936 and found a job with a local steel producer.

Both of my parents were dead when I was only thirteen years old. Before FDR rescinded the 18th amendment, I even sold used bottles to bootleggers, five cents for half-pints and ten cents for pints.

A wonderful way to grow up! Now I am retired, have my own little place for weekends in the country, and spend a lot of time doing volunteer work. Married fifty-one years last July. Wouldn't trade my life style for any one I know.

W. E. Vedell
St. Louis, Missouri

THE DEPOT AGENT MOVES AROUND

I lived through that drought. My husband was a young depot agent for the Great Northern railroad. He was working his way up the line toward better hours and a location near my home, the Twin Cities, or his home, Willmar.

The lack of rain and accumulated dust really started for us in Johnson, Minnesota, about 1932 or 1933. It blew from the prairies of South Dakota and was so bad we had to cover our young child's head and face with wet towels at night. In 1934 we moved to Clontarf, Minnesota, getting closer to home. The dust followed us.

By 1936 the drought was so bad that we were forced to sleep outside on the big yard at night. There were no bugs, just dry grass. Our house was too small for any breeze. We had no fans. I spread sheets on the grass as soon as it was dark and the sun awakened us in the morning. Another day of heat. Outdoor plumbing. I can't remember when the rain finally came.

We moved from there in 1939 to Darwin, Minnesota. Lakes and trees and dust storms forgotten. By that time we had lived in five towns, moving our own furniture each time.

I well remember the time about which ALL HELL BROKE LOOSE was written. (Editor: this book was also written by William H. Hull and is currently in its tenth printing.) We left Minneapolis for our home in Darwin and just made it before the rain turned to snow. My husband turned on the depot light and left the door unlocked because he knew people would be stranded on the highway. It took weeks before the streets were cleared for cars. I was spending some time in Minneapolis with my mother who was recovering from a stroke. I would get off the midnight train from Minneapolis and walk on the high peaks of snow before I reached my house. The man who collected the mail from this train was instructed to turn off the town lights as soon as the mail was put in the post office. I remember asking him to leave the lights on for ten minutes so I could find my way home.

Alice Hanscom
Minneapolis, Minnesota

DIDN'T EAT OUT FOR SIXTEEN YEARS

I have lived through two depressions in my eighty years. When I was a child corn was selling for ten cents a bushel. We burned it in our stoves because we couldn't afford coal.

I married James Jeffryes in June, 1930; our first son was born August 17, 1931, our second on May 8, 1933, and our daughter on March 8, 1936. That was the year of a dust bowl or the drought.

We lived on a farm north of Genoa, Nebraska.

When the wind came up the dust blew so badly we couldn't see the church a half-mile away. We couldn't afford storm windows so the dust came in so badly that when you walked across the floor you could see your tracks.

We didn't raise any crops. My husband drove a neighbor's truckload of hogs or cattle to Omaha, then on south of Omaha for apples. They were selling cull apples for twenty-five cents a bushel while good ones were a dollar. My husband brought home ten bushel of cull apples the neighbor gave him and I canned those. That winter there were times when all we had for the evening meal was apple sauce and home made bread.

We had to sell all our live stock except one cow which was a wedding gift and we kept her for milk. We had no meat and no telephone. Our brother gave us a hog to butcher which we did, then hung it between the corn crib and oats bins. Dust and wind came up strongly during the night and blew it so full of dust that we couldn't use it. We never had money to eat out like people do now; even those on welfare eat out.

All those years from 1931 to 1947 we never ate in an eating place. We bought a package of cinnamon rolls and some cold meat to eat in the car if we had to go to the county seat for business.

We made do with what we had. I made the children skirts out of colored feed sacks, pants for the boys out of the backs of grown up pants.

Every time the dust blew into the house I had to wash windows and curtains all over again. Usually at least once a week.

My younger son once asked me "Mom, didn't you have a dollar?" I replied "Son, we didn't even have a nickle."

Our second son became very ill one day and we took him to the doctor. When we came home we forgot to drain the radiator in the car and as a result it froze and broke the block. There was no way we could afford to fix it so it was parked on the south side of the house for four or five years. Folks wanted to buy parts from it but I said no — I'd fix it some day. I ordered a new radiator on time from Wards; by then we had borrowed money to buy cattle and horses.

Our cream checks were $9 a week; one week I sent the whole $9 to pay on what we owed on the car. That week we didn't buy food. You see, on top of it all, the bank went broke and we had to take our loan to a different place.

Things began to look better. I raised turkeys one year, sold a hundred of them for $3.95 each and bought a used car. We did fix up the other one, having it welded and adding the new radiator. That put it back in running shape again.

I've been baby sitting the past twelve years and it's far easier than cleaning barns and chicken houses.

We have no complaints. My children are all married. One teaches in Hawaii and has four children and I have the girls, whose husbands are teachers.

I remembrer a lot about the dry years. Now, when I hear about the food pantries I can't understand why people are hungry.

Lillian H. Jeffryes
Columbus, Nebraska

HOSPITAL ADMITTED THREE
HEAT VICTIMS PER MINUTE

For a while I was living in Fennimore, Wisconsin, working for the Soil Conservation Service. I remember the darkened sun and dust settling everywhere. When it rained, which was seldom, it rained mud.

I understand that when the heat was at its worst in Minneapolis there were some days when Minneapolis General hospital admitted three heat cases a minute.

I know that here in Missouri we had no crops in 1936. It was so dry the corn reached about six feet tall but the tassels couldn't make it out of the whorl, so we put ten acres of corn in the basement of a small silo. I Believe the chinch bugs about ate another field alongside some wheat.

We used government creosote, made a trench and kept it powdery by dragging. We limed about the first in the county, using a small spreader pulled behind the wagon and scooped the lime into it as the horses pulled the wagon. That was also the year we built our first terraces; they were just large sweet potato ridges but they worked and helped hold some of the soil.

My Dad said if we could only raise something we might make it. He had seven children, two in high school. One, my brother, was just out of the University of Missouri with a major in chemistry and no job. He helped on the farm until a job opened up in St. Louis.

Finally President Roosevelt's New Deal started to pull the country out of the depression and in 1941 World War II fired it up.

I worked the Soil Conservation Service from 1935 until March 1951 in summers all over the country. I was in the army from 1942 to 1945, then back to the SCS. I worked C.C.C. camps in Missouri, Wisconsin and travelled as a soil scientist, taking soil inventories, doing soil erosion work—trees, crop rotations, strip cropping, contouring, wire dams, stream bank erosion, and control.

John R. Harness, Jr.
Montgomery City, MO

ALL THE WORLD'S AGAINST US

We were married in 1935, William Henriksen and I, in a double wedding ceremony with my brother, Robert W. Golitz, and Gertrude Week. I was seventeen and Bill was twenty-one. We've now been married 52 years. My father and mother had to sign for me and my brother to be married since we were both minors.

We were married in the Dells. That evening there was a dance and a reception at the Beaver building in Wisconsin Dells. We didn't have a honeymoon. None of us had any money.

Work was very scarce and we were determined to do what we could to exist. We both went to work for a farmer in Lewiston, Bill doing the farm work and me doing the housework. Bill received a small salary and we had our room and board. It was quite a job for me because I had to feed silo fillers and threshers with no help. I was interested in cooking so I could fix varied meals. I took cooking in high school but quit school in my junior year. Anyway, these men were hungry and there were probably ten to twelve of them at every meal. The owner had a brother-in-law living with him so I had two bachelors and my husband whose laundry I had to scrub on a board, then boil in a double boiler on a wood-burning cook stove. The bachelors wore long underwear summer and winter so I had my work cut out for me—a lot for a kid of seventeen. We soon had to leave the farm and became caretakers for some people.

I didn't go to a doctor until about two weeks before our son was born. The doctor wouldn't use instruments so I almost died—and also our son. He was a black baby and never cried when born. The cord was around his neck three times and he laid on the kitchen table all afternoon. He was born at one o'clock and started to show some life about five that afternoon. My mother and grandmother and husband were there. It took the three of them to hold me down on the bed. I was eighteen years old. He's now fifty-two years old and is a tall, good looking man.

We had to move from that cabin because it was so cold and this was a bad winter—that one of 1935–1936. So we moved out of the cottage, moving in our 1929 Model A Ford. We moved down the road to a hotel to be caretakers. Bill had worked for them as a teen-ager, working from 5 A.M. until 9 P.M. These people went to Florida and left us to care for the hotel and animals. It was a terrible winter. They didn't leave us enough coal so we were very cold. They had a hot water heating system and the radiators froze and broke. Also the hot water heater in the hallway froze; there just wasn't enough heat—this was a summer hotel and not built for winter.

There were cows my husband had to care for. The water cups in the barn froze and he had to carry water from the house. He also worked some in the Dells, walking two and a half miles sometimes when the Ford wouldn't start; there he worked for a lumber company, hauling, shoveling and delivering coal.

It was so cold in that hotel that I got the chil-blains; it's a wonder we didn't freeze to death. We did this for nothing but it was not appreciated because the owners weren't very happy about all the things that happened that winter.

In the spring of 1936 we moved to a farm to work for the same kind of deal as before.

The temperature was miserably hot—106 to 111 degrees. One hot day my husband was walking behind a horse, plowing. The horse was hot and over-worked, so he keeled over. They tried to revive him but they put the wrong packs on him and he died right there. The boss had no sympathy for anyone so, as hot as it was, he ordered my husband to bury this horse right then and there. Bill couldn't dig a big hole so he had to break the horse's legs with a sledge hammer to get him into the hole. What a terrible thing, to expect a man, and a small man of 117 pounds at that, to bury this horse by himself.

We did get through that terrible summer but I don't know how. We moved back to Wisconsin Dells that fall. No fuel. Not much work. My son got pneumonia in this upstairs apartment and I got a strep throat. So we moved out of there and into a small cabin on Superior street. My husband helped our landlord tear down an old house on a corner, for our rent. That 1936 winter Bill cut pulp and skinned it and had other small jobs, plus hauling coal.

These were two bad years in our lives. We haven't had it easy. My brother's wife passed away a couple of years ago but we've been married fifty-two years.

Edna Henriksen
Wisconsin Dells, Wisconsin

COVERED CRIB WITH WET DISH TOWELS

It was in 1932 with the depression upon us when we moved from Union, Nebraska, where I had been in the radio and electrical business to Brule, Nebraska. I was to take over the radio/electrical business of a shop left vacant after my older brother had died.

There are at least three different experiences with dust storms which left lasting impressions on me. The years of the worst storms were from about 1933 through 1937.

The first such storm we experienced was during the summer of 1933. I was working in my shop early in the afternoon when it started to get very dark. The sky seemed nearly black at a great height and apparently we were about to have a severe thunderstorm. It was nearly as dark as night, which caused my wife and two small daughters to come down to the shop. Naturally they were concerned. We then had some lightning, high winds and some rain.

Back of the shop was a cave which we decided to go into because we were uneasy. We came out later, after the storm had subsided, and found everything covered with a reddish dust. During this storm a small tornado had hit south of our town but didn't do much damage. This was just the first of many dust storms we experienced and we wondered if they would ever subside. And would the drought and the depression ever be over?

Another such storm occurred in 1935 when our son was about six months of age. We had a clothes basket type crib in which he slept and when we had these dust storms the dust was so fine that it would sift through the windows and doors so badly that his mother would cover his crib with damp dish towels or sheets to keep the dust from settling on him. There would be small drifts of dust on the window sills and floor around the doors after these storms.

We also had a small flock of chickens and laying hens on this place where we lived; they were a food source. So, whenever we had one of these storms, and the sky got dark, the chickens would go into the chicken house and go to roost, just as they did on ordinary nights.

Huge drifts would form along fence rows where the dust was caught in tumble weeds and would accumulate.

Another experience I will never forget happened when I was called to repair a radio on the North Table Land for a farmer. This Table Land was about 600 feet higher than the land along the South Platte river valley. After I had the radio working and we were listening to it, the static was getting stronger and weird whistling sounds were drowning out all radio stations.

I had heard these sounds before whenever a dust storm was approaching, so I told the farmer that I was going to try to get home. When we went outdoors we could see the heavy clouds of dust reaching from the ground to high in the sky, with clouds rolling as they approached from the northwest. I tried to keep ahead of the storm and, descending a long hill, I had nearly reached the bottom when it caught up with me. The dust soon got so thick that it was like midnight. I turned on the car lights which did no good, so I had to open the car door and drive very slowly in order to see the side of the road. I managed to drive the remaining mile or so back to town.

These were some of the many dust storm days we went through in these Dirty

Thirties. They finally became lsss frequent and soon they didn't appear any more.

Raymond F. Fahrlander
Plattsmouth, Nebraska

I LIVED ON POTATOES AND HOME-MADE BREAD

I lived through the dust bowl years of 1935 and 1936 in Kansas City, Kansas, alone most of the time because my husband worked out of town. At age seventeen I spent weeks wetting sheets to cover windows to keep out the dust. There was no air conditioning then and it was very hot inside and out.

At times the wind would be like a blizzard. For weeks it would blow steadily, never ending. When it would quieten, even for a day, people would try to get clothing and sheets washed and dried, groceries laid in for a week. I have lived on potatoes and home-made bread. We, the working class, usually cooked on coal oil (kerosene) stoves. If you ran out of kerosene you had to borrow from people in the apartment house or starve. I saw men get lost for hours trying to find some kerosene.

Dust piled up on the railroad tracks until trains could barely get through. Highways were completely lost in some places. People put up strings to guide them around their own yards. Our apartment manager tied a small rope to the porch and laid it across the street, tieing the other end to a small grocery store. That helped us find our way.

In 1936 the land had all blown away, then the weather decided to burn everything else. It broke all records and those records haven't been equalled today.

I had a baby girl and many a day and week I wished I had no baby; it was so hard to keep her cool and dust free. Many a day I'd hang wet pieces of sheet over her crib.

There was no relief at night. Yards and parks would be full of people trying to get some sleep. It was hell on earth just trying to survive during that time.

Mrs. Harry E Griffith
Boonville, Missouri

COMING CLOSE TO DEATH

We started our days in those years by cleaning up the red Oklahoma dust from our Nebraska floors. It was if someone had dumped a load of soil in our house. We had taken down our shades and window curtains and hung wet sheets to help keep the dirt under control.

We had very little rest because the nights were so hot and there wasn't any grass to go out and sleep on outdoors.

We prepared and ate our meals as quickly as possible, before our food was covered with dirt.

One day at lunch I left the table to go to the bathroom (it was an outside one) and came back shortly. I had just gotten inside when the south wind changed to the northwest. There was a vacant lot back of our house which was filled with metal grain bins. As the wind became a gale, the bins broke loose and came blowing across our land, smashing everything in their path, including the little outhouse which I had just left. They didn't hit the house but took trees, fences and everything in their path. I would have been killed if I'd been in their path. I'll probably never come any nearer to death.

Mildred Budler
Columbus, Nebraska

WITH DIGNITY AND PRIDE WE STOOD THE TEST

I was born Lois Varnell one mile south of Cheyenne, Oklahoma, in 1927 and I well remember the thirties. I remember President Roosevelt gave the farmers five dollars a head for their cattle, then shot them. They let people have what they wanted of the meat. I remember my mother and aunt set up all night canning beef.

We had greens to cook but no flour to make bread. Dad worked on W.P.A. work and made $2.30 for eight hours of work. The government furnished shells and the men killed rabbits which were eating up the crops. I never could eat wild meat so I ate the greens.

Then there was the lunch the government gave us at school. We had two tin cups, one for soup and the other for wheat pudding, which sometimes had raisins in it. We were very thankful for the warm food. Some people went to the soup line in another town if they had enough gas to make the trip.

My mom and dad had twelve children to feed and raise but, with lots of love and courage, we made it—and it made fine people out of us. We are one big dirty thirties family; with dignity and pride we stood the test.

That's what an American style family is all about—sticking together through good times and bad times. And the Good Lord saw us through the bad times.

I also remember the sewing room where the women would sew for eight hours at a time, making clothes for children and families. We were so proud of those new clothes.

President Roosevelt set up CCC camps; my brother went. He sent home part of his pay for which we were very grateful. Then there was work for teen agers, training jobs, which were also good. That was through the N.Y.A. (National Youth Administration.)

I remember putting cardboard in my shoes to keep out the cold snow, and making sure I kept my feet on the floor in school so the others couldn't see the holes in my shoes.

Those were rough times but it made better people out of us. Now when we get something we appreciate it and make a dollar go a long ways. Some people may call us stingy but the thirties made us that way.

Lois Marshall
Sayre, Oklahoma

CORNMEAL PANCAKES WITH MOLASSES AND MEAT GREASE

In 1926 the Bill Casey family moved from Longmont, Colorado to Okfuskee county, Oklahoma. We arrived in a 1922 Model T Ford, there being six of us including we four female kids. Dad had $125 to his name and our belongings were in a trunk tied to the back of the car. We kids had to watch the trunk constantly after it fell off somewhere near Bristow.

It was April and had been raining, leaving the roads with deep ruts in the red clay. We had been travelling for six days and were anxious to arrive in Welty, Oklahoma, where daddy's two youngest uncles lived. It was dark and daddy drove witth a lantern on the front of the car to show the way. At last we saw a light far away and when we reached it, it wasn't much brighter; we tried to make out the features of our relatives.

Daddy rented the old Cox place southwest of the Mason school. It had an old house with two rooms and a porch. Here he raised cotton, corn, some sweet potatoes and a garden. He bought two old mules, Pete and Jack, and a milk cow, Bessie. They had to watch the kids because old Bessie was a fighter; they soon learned to stay on the other side of the fence.

By the fall of 1927 an aunt left her husband and with her two kids piled in on us. Grandpa Hayhurst also came to stay. That made six kids and four adults to sleep in one room with two beds and pallets all over the remaining floor. As I look back I think what a mess it was and what a good man my daddy was to put up with it. In the spring they left when my aunt went back to her husband and grandpa went to Arkansas.

I started school at Mason at age six. We had a chart class at first and then used the blue book reader. I didn't have a book until almost spring when we found one for fifteen cents. I sat near the end of the class and memorized the page before they got to me to read it. We read about The Ginger Bread Man, The Bee in the Bag Swallowed By the Rooster, Little Black Sambo and The Three Goats.

After two years on the Cox place daddy rented a farm near Rock school from J. Walter Long. We lived there from 1928 to 1937 when I was a high school junior. This is where I grew up. We walked one and a half miles to school and were urged by our parents to do well. A whipping at school meant a much harder one when we got home. Teachers visited the home about once a year and parents attended school functions.

Daddy worked on the road some with his team for the WPA. Sometimes when flour was scarce we had cornmeal pancakes for breakfast with molasses and meat grease. Molasses mixed with meat grease was delicious on hot bread. Since we raised a lot of sorghum for sweetening, we made our own candy from molasses, butter, vanilla and nuts, the more nuts the better.

Mom made drop dumpling possum grape pie and cinnamon dough pies— real treats. Too much cinnamon made the dumplings slick.

Uncle Fred High ran a tomato canning factory in High, Arkansas, where he was the postmaster. He sent us a case of canned tomatoes for the postage, which daddy was happy to pay. As we used the cans, daddy filed the rough spots on the tops of the empty cans and gave each of us our own can from which to eat cornbread and milk.

By this time daddy had kept the heifer calves and we had cream to sell; now we could buy the things we couldn't grow but which we needed. Flour came in beautiful print sacks. One sack would make a small girl a dress. More were needed for larger sizes. Women would save and swap sacks to get enough of one color or one pattern to meet their need. Mom used the print sacks to trim the white floursack dresses. They were beautiful.

In the fall we worked hard to pick our cotton so daddy could repay the bank for money he had borrowed to make the crop. We would then pick for other people to buy our winter clothes and for money for school needs. We learned early how to sew on the old treadle machine and ordered material from Chicago Mail Order, paying four cents a yard for it.

Things were cheap during the Depression. A neighbor gave daddy his car for payment of a five dollar repair bill. Daddy bought two 125 pound hogs for three dollars and daddy and Uncle Mart went together to buy a box of 22 calibre shells to kill Hoover Hogs (rabbits) and squirrels. Believe me — they seldom wasted a shell at that price!

Since we lived near the Deep Fork river in Okfuskee county, our next adventure was taking care of the pecan harvest for Cecil and Atchinson. We were to earn one-half of what we picked. At first pecans sold for four cents a pound so we received two cents for each pound we picked up. Daddy got high-line climbers and learned to climb the highest and biggest trees. He didn't use a belt because of the limbs on the trees. Although he never got hurt badly, he slipped a small distance a few times; once a rotten limb broke off in his hands when he was standing on a large limb. He slowly squatted down and cooned the limb back to the main tree trunk. During the season wagons were used to haul the pecans but scrap pickers had to carry theirs on their backs. A forty to sixty pound sack got heavy after carrying it a mile or so; many rest stops had to be made.

Working in the pecans was hard work but also a savior in disguise. It paid for this old place where we live and helped send us girls to college. Mom and dad saw to that. We were given a chance they never had.

Nola Casey
Castle, Oklahoma

WE MINED OUR OWN COAL
IN NORTH DAKOTA

We went through the drought and depression. We farmed in North Dakota and had a very hard time getting seed to farm. When we did get it and planted it, we had no rain for several years. The seed did not grow. The wind would blow every day and night. Dust piled up on fences, covering them. We couldn't grow a garden because, again, there was no moisture. Hence, food was scarce. We often wondered what we could prepare for the next meal.

We were unable to pay our taxes on the land which was about $59 for 160 acres with a barn and sheds and a not-too-comfortable house. We had to mine coal for heating, getting it from a river bank. Maybe three or four farmers would get together trying to mine enough coal in one day so each could take home a wagon load. Day after day they would each get a load in order to have enough for the winter. We cooked with a cook stove, where we also heated water for washing, hauling that water from the pump; we had to wash clothes by hand, for all of us, including four children.

We felt lucky to have a well of good water. We pumped the water by hand for the few cattle we had—a few milk cows—and we raised chickens for grocery money. We sold eggs at eight or nine cents a dozen and sold the cream in five gallon cans.

Time went on and when we couldn't farm any more we moved into town. My husband worked at almost anything he could find. He worked for the undertaker for ten cents a day; he also worked digging graves. Sometimes it took a year before we collected that six dollar fee. He also hauled grain for the elevator for our flour for baking bread. He worked many days for $1.00 a day but for that $1.00 we could buy these items for twenty-five cents each: a pound of coffee, five pounds of sugar, or five pounds of flour. So the dollar went quite a ways.

We moved to town in the fall and on December 21 we had a house fire. It was caused by a kerosene stove. It took all of our clothes and the food we had stored for the winter. Thank goodness that people, as poor as they all were, found us an apartment in which we could live and brought us clothing and food.

My husband worked enough to save $8.00 to buy a house lot. We built a basement there and lived in it that winter. In the spring (1938) times were so bad we started back for Wisconsin. We had $20.00 when we started and three five-gallon containers of gasoline which he salvaged from a gas leak; we put the cans on the running board of the car, emptying a can as needed. We made the trip fine, pulling a trailer my husband had built. It had a few furnishings, clothing and some household items. We had left our furniture and other items for which we didn't have room.

We had ninety cents left when we arrived here in New Glarus, neither a job nor a place to live. But he found a job and a house in the country where we could live for a few days only, because the rats were so bad. We came to town again and he was lucky to work for Pet Milk, driving the big semi trucks for ten years. We paid only $5.00 a month rent but earned about $27.00 a week. He took out accident insurance with the company, which we were glad he had done because when he was cutting wood he injured his knee. He was laid up from October to April and the insurance paid the expenses. Again people were so helpful. In 1956 he obtained a job with the state, which meant being away from home about nine months of the year. He drove the Historymobile for ten years. It was an interesting time but we were on schedule and found some days heckish when the roads were bad and the weather unpredictable. We enjoyed those years, though.

Irene Tschudy
New Glarus, Wisconsin

DAD HAD MANY WAYS TO BRING
IN A FEW DOLLARS

Between 1929 and 1945 there were nine of us born in our family. I was 1931.

I always felt the depression ended in 1941 which was the first year Father had a regular job, and we started to live nearly normal lives.

My father always had ways to bring in money. They were small amounts, but there wasn't any public aid at that time.

He borrowed some money from his father and bought an old car. At that time produce came to the chain stores in bushel baskets and burlap bags. He would go to these stores and buy the empties—baskets for two and one-half cents each and sacks for one cent each. He would take them to the farmer's market and get five and two cents each, thus doubling his money. I used to go with him and the farmers liked to see him come in. Occasionally he would buy a bushel of apples for fifty cents. They were a great treat for us kids.

We received our allowances on Sundays. The big kids got three cents and the little ones two cents. I was in the top money bracket at that time witth three whole pennies.

Tuition at the Catholic school we attended was two dollars a month for two or more children. We made out pretty well because there were always several of us in school. At the end of the year the nuns wouldn't give you a passing slip if tuition was still owed. Although it was only a few bucks, most of us had to sweat out the summer, wondering if we would be held back.

The nuns were in bad financial shape also. About twice a year some brownie girl in each class would suggest a shower for our nun. It meant that each student would bring a can of food and we would surprise her and sit around screwing off all afternoon. I suspect the nun put the brownie up to this ploy.

Everyone had a cash (pay) telephone in their home, which required a nickle to work. Many times Mother didn't have a nickle and one of us would hammer a penny on the sidewalk to make it nickle sized. When the phone man collected the box, these were called slugs and you had to pay up. We lost our phone once and got it back in my uncle's name, where it remained until 1970.

We always rented a flat (apartment) but had to move every year because of inability to pay the rent and because the landlord would find out how many kids there were. We would go in with two children, but they would notice a lot more around. Cousins, we used to say.

For several Christmas seasons my older sister and I sold Christmas wrappings, ornaments, tree lights, twine, etc., door to door. My Dad knew a wholesaler and got them on consignment. Dad also sold some of them. He was also a milk-man but only worked vacation routes in the summer when the regular men were off. He didn't get a steady route until about 1940.

When it snowed heavily Dad would go around shoveling sidewalks for about a quarter. I went with him on these excursions also and on the horse-drawn milk wagon some times.

Every summer we each got a new pair of tennis shoes for fifty cents and a new pair of socks for ten cents. The shoes had to last all summer. We put on the new socks at the store before trying on the shoes. The socks we got for Christmas were full of holes and rather gamey by this time, maybe a little offensive to the poor clerk.

The show was ten cents but then went up to eleven cents. Talk about inflation! A ten percent increase.

There was a family of neighbors who were cousins. Twelve children and they were in the same boat financially as us. Our summer vacation was to stay at their house for a few days and vice-versa. Thus not much travel time was involved.

We would all get together about twice a year, along with other cousins, for a huge picnic at the zoo or forest preserve. We all jammed into street cars at seven cents for adults and three cents half fare. The streetcar men always looked thrilled to see about thirty of us waiting on the safety island, waiting to board and destroy their car.

All my brothers and sisters are still alive, all married, good jobs and typical middle class people. We are all probably happy to have come up so far from those so-called hard times — good times.

But everyone was in the same boat, so we didn't know we were (I can't say "poor") anything but normal. If I could do it over again, it would be the same way.

Robert J. Schmidt
Chicago, Illinois

MY SUMMER IN A TENT

During the depression my husband was laid off from his job as a railroad conductor. This was a terrible blow because jobs in our home town were hard to find. Also, we had small children to feed and dress, along with payments on our house. We struggled along, really having a tough time, until a friend came along. He was head of road repair on another railroad and gave my husband a job as conductor of a small crew operating a crane.

Our children were two and four years old and we decided to go along with my husband during the summer. We had a Model-T Ford coupe so we added a box-like addition to hold our equipment. A small umbrella tent became our home that summer.

We prepared our meals daily on a camp stove. Wherever the crew worked, I drove our truck. The highway ran atop a high embankment along the Mississippi river in Iowa while the railroad tracks were below along the river. One time the road down the hill was so rocky that we awaited at the top for my husband to drive us down the grade. I was glad not to attempt that steep, rocky road when I once saw it.

One night we made camp on the banks of the Mississippi, caught a few catfish for our supper and were about to retire when the sky looked ominous. In fact, it was so threatening that we took the tent down and moved into the old depot where there were rooms for an agent. It was a good thing we moved; during the night there was a bad storm and there was ten feet of water where our tent had been. During the night the children were so restless that I turned on the lantern and behold! Bed-bugs scurried to their hiding places. There was no more sleep that night.

The next day my husband moved the machinery up the road where they were needed to lift sandbags in an attempt to save a railroad bridge. We went to a home higher on a hill where we stayed until he returned that evening. He and that crew worked sixty hours but they saved that bridge. The river was full of trees, boards and other debris.

After the flood subsided, we walked to the only store and the river had been so high, there was still sand over the counters. My first experience in a flood. Railroad tracks were clear by this time.

This was a summer to remember, the summer we spent in a tent.

Leona M. Curry
Adams, Wisconsin

NOTHING WAS DISCARDED. WE USED IT ALL.

When I hear people complain that they don't have any food and are hungry but they won't eat this, that and the other, my mind turns back to really hard times.

We were married and just started our family when the depression started, and it grew worse. People either learned to cope or went under. Sad to say, some could not face it and committed suicide.

We learned to use only one light bulb for the whole house, by changing the bulb from one room to another, or by using candles.

We learned that cardboard boxes had many uses. They made good house insulation and they could be used inside shoes when the soles wore out.

A razor blade could be sharpened by rubbing it on the inside surface of a glassful of water. We used dry salt or soda to clean our teeth.

And it was surprising how warm water would become when left out in the sun for a while.

We could not afford to go to a doctor so we learned to make do with what we had. Plantain leaves, the same pesky ones we fight in our lawns now, were crushed and the juice and pulp rubbed into sore tired feet. And cattails could be made into a great poultice when the fluff was pulled off; they helped heal burns. We could use a poultice of fried onions, applied to the chest, to relieve a cold.

Most products came in cloth bags. Sugar, salt, flour, tobacco. The bags were unravelled And the string saved for sewing. The bags were carefully washed and bleached by boiling in soapsuds, then carefully rinsed. They were then spread on the grass where they bleached to snow white. They were used to make different articles of clothing; the tobacco sacks were used to make quilt blocks.

Nothing was discarded. Old clothing was made over for another family member. There were no foods for pets; they ate table scraps and hunted for themselves. We hunted wild foods, berries, dandelions, and found abandoned farms with orchards. There were always apple trees. We ate the food fresh and canned and dried the surplus. Not a crumb was wasted.

Potatoes were cooked in the skins because we could eat the skin or we could peel it with much less waste.

Not a scrap of fat or a bone was wasted. When we were lucky enough to have a chicken, the bones were saved and cooked with vegetables for another meal.

In order to use no fat, we cooked our bread Boy Scout style. It was rolled out, then wrapped around a stick and cooked over a campfire. It was very good.

We enjoyed being together. We told stories, made up plays, and went on hikes. Through it all we stayed together, kept clean physically, spiritually and morally. We tried always to keep our humor.

Finally things began to get better. My husband's first job paid S25 a week. There were eight of us in the family and with wages like that we felt we had nothing left for which to wish.

Elnora Harris
Atchison, Kansas

STRAINED HONEY USED IN RADIATORS

I had received an inheritance of $500 from my grandmother's estate, had graduated from high school, and decided I didn't want to be a farmer like my dad, so I went to Wright's Airplane Mechanics school at St. Elmo, Illinois. That was the summer of 1929 and by the time I completed my studies the depression had struck and the school could not provide the promised employment at good wages. They only promised that I could stay and work without pay.

My finances were about exhausted so I went back to the family farm and got involved in the work there. I was given the job of taking the eggs to Hume, our nearest town, and trading them for sugar, flour and salt; these were the only things we needed.

We ground our own wheat in the coffee grinder for flour and breakfast food. We raised barley which we parched and ground as a substitute for the coffee we couldn't afford.

We fed the hogs ear corn and then raked up the cobs and burned them in the cook and the heating stoves. They had a certain amount of manure on them and, although they made a hot fire, they sometimes smelled rather badly. Some people were burning their ear corn which was only worth eight to eleven cents a bushel at the local elevator. When it got up to twenty cents a bushel dad sold some corn so we could pay our taxes.

Some people used strained honey in the radiators of their vehicles because they couldn't afford antifreeze. It certainly attracted bees whenever they parked.

Of course we had plenty of pork for meat and lard for cooking. Farm women made their own soap from the hog fat and kept the clothes sewn up and patched.

After FDR became president, we sold the first load of hogs for two cents a pound, which was more than they had been.

Charles Lange
Hume, Illinois

KIND AND GENEROUS GROCER
EXTENDED CREDIT

The most difficult period for our family was between 1931 and 1937. The depression was in full swing and we lived in the near northwest side of Chicago. My parents immigrated here in 1895 from the southern part of Poland which was occupied by Austria.

My father lost his job working in a dairy. Being illiterate made finding new employment impossible. My older brother, Joe, was working part time, two or three days a week as a truck driver. Finally he too lost his work. With no money coming in, my sister, Marcella, age 15, left school and found work in a candy factory. She earned ten dollars a week. Like my mother, she was our heroine, so selfless and courageous. Mother, in desperation, found night work with the telephone company, scrubbing floors and cleaning spitoons.

Still the going was rough. The little insurance my father had was cashed in to supplement the meager income. Having money in the bank was unheard of in our family at that time. We barely were able to pay the $22 rent for our six room apartment. The grocer carried us for a long time by selling us food on credit, intending to receive the money when the family was financially solvent. What a kind and generous man.

Even with commodities priced so low, there was little money to make purchases. I remember a one pound loaf of rye bread costing ten cents, postage stamps two cents, sugar five cents a pound. A two trouser suit cost $40 at Sears Roebuck and the movie houses charged ten cents for kids.

It got so bad that there was a six month period when we had to ask help from the Chicago welfare department. We were eligible to receive food aid and, since there were six school children, we were given an astounding amount of food. Four quarts of milk a day plus a large box of dried and canned food which was delivered once a month. To expedite the delivery, a large trailer truck was parked at the intersecting street on our block, the recipients' names were yelled out and the people would claim their box of food at the truck. It was a blessing but so embarrassing to disclose our desperate plight.

Slowly conditions changed. I left high school in the third year and found work in a box factory as a stockroom boy. The NRA was enacted, guaranteeing a minimum wage. I then earned $12 for forty hours of work. By 1936 my father and older brother began to work regularly. My sister found better employment and I continued in the stockroom. I also was attending high school in the evenings.

Much has happened since then. My father at 59 and my mother at 80, have passed away. All the children married, having modestly successful but very happy lives. That six year period was an experience we all look back on with dread, yet with many fond memories. We cared for each"other, sharing what little we had. Mostly we acquired a keen sense of frugality and a respect for the value of money. Knowing that many fine, generous people were concerned about us was an added blessing.

Edward A. Wronski
Mt.Sterling, Illinois

I PAID A DOLLAR A WEEK FOR MOTHER'S WASHING MACHINE

I was lucky to have a job.

I worked at Marshall Field's store in Chicago and ran an Elliot-Fisher billing machine. I received $14 when I first started and then was increased to $16. Work hours were from nine to five-twenty six days a week, except in July and August when it was only five and a half days. (Ed.: that calculates at twenty-eight cents per hour and this editor remembers having a twenty-five cent an hour job and being the envy of his friends so this was a going rate.)

We worked on the tenth floor where it was very hot, so hot that we would go to the drinking fountain to wet a handerkerchief to wrap around our wrists. There was no such thing as a coffee break.

My room and board cost me $5 a week and my weekly "L" (Elevated) pass another dollar. I could get a blouse for fifty cents and a skirt for an equal amount.

When I rode the south side "L" to and fro work it was usually so crowded that I had to strap hang all the way.

At night I would walk east to Jackson Park near Lake Michigan and, if it were cool I'd go to to White City. There for ten cents I could enjoy a ride and for a nickle eat an ice cream cone on the way home. There were also dance marathons at White City.

During the World's Fair I would have my family come to Chicago and in some way I was able to get them to the Fair. They lived in Chillicothe, Illinois, where I live now.

My father always had a nice garden and it was surprising how many people were fed from his garden. My uncle from Peoria would get a truck and people would go together to get a dollar's worth of gas and drive up to dad's to get garden produce.

I never went hungry and never had a bank account. We were paid every other Monday and the second weekend I'd stay home to wait to get paid Monday. I bought my mother a washing machine and I paid a dollar a week for so long — and then after that a Philco radio at a dollar a week. I never knew what arthritis was and remember having a really good time in my twenties. I am almost seventy-eight now and back home in Chillicothe.

Frieda Fisher
Chillicothe, Illinois

COULDN'T SELL STARK'S DELICIOUS APPLES FOR TEN CENTS A BUSHEL

We bought a used Model T Ford for $35 and made a trip to South Dakota with no trouble. We had a total of $60 among my husband, his brother, niece and me. We couldn't stay in a hotel so we saw an old school house with the door open. We spent the night there. Our food was sandwiches; we had purchased sausage and bread. We had to go easy on the money.

Finally we arrived there, stayed with my husbsnd's brother and wife on a farm and worked hard. We had our room and board but no pay. We stayed there two years; then I got lonesome so we came back home. We decided to go to St. Louis; we had $40 which we thought was a lot of money. We said if we could find a job, we could get some furniture and rent a place. No job so we took one caring for an apple orchard for a man who lived in St. Louis. We barely had furniture. One bed, an old black range which I highly polished, bare floors and an orange crate for the dishes.

Half the time we didn't know what to eat. It was summer so we had turnips in the garden and a few chickens. To this day I hate turnips. If we had company, they either bought food or we had eggs and biscuits, which we all enjoyed. There was a little lake there, and one day my husband got a wild goose; that was a big treat.

Then a nice lady gave me a kerosene stove and an icebox which was nice in hot weather. It got so hot we had no fans and we would go to the basement to put our feet in cold water.

I had to get the water from the lake on wash days and heat it on a little stove in a shed. I had a hand wringer. We didn't have a lot of clothes. Al had two pairs of stockings. I hung them on the fence to dry and the goat ate them.

It's a good thing we were young and things didn't bother us too much.

One day I was sick and needed to go to the a St. Louis free clinic but I had no way to get there. We asked the milkman who passed our house daily if he would take me, which he did. When I was through there, I stayed with my mother, until the people who owned the farm picked me up and took me home the next weekend.

The only way we ever made a little money was to kill a few chickens, clean them and take them to market with a few dozen eggs. In St. Louis we could only get twelve cents a dozen for the eggs. We took Stark's Delicious big red apples there also and couldn't sell them for ten cents a bushel. To avoid taking them home, we gave them to a policeman who said he would take them to the Little Sisters of the Poor.

Al's sister in St. Louis would buy eggs and chickens and also gave us a few dollars.

We worked hard on the farm, spraying the trees and working the fields. Then one lovely day the mailman brought a letter and there was twenty dollars in it from Al's brother in South Dakota. We thought we were rich.

That night we went to the store to buy a few items which helped a lot.

We made apple butter because we had so many apples, making it outside in a large copper kettle. Relatives would come out and help us stir the apple butter. Later we sold it for twenty-five cents a quart.

One day we decided to go back to St. Louis. I got too lonesome and tired of that kind of living. In St. Louis Al couldn't find work so I got a job doing housework for four dollars a week until they found out I could work and gave me a one dollar raise. I stayed with them for a year and got together with Al on weekends. For his room rent I gave him the five dollars I made and he got his meals at his siter's. He went to Procter and Gamble for a long time and the story always was that they were not hiring. He usually walked there. Finally one day he called me and said he had a job there so I quit my job. He made nineteen dollars a week and later received a bonus.

The people where I worked didn't want me to leave but promised me a job as soon as the husband opened a few restaurants where he catered at factories; later he had cafeterias so he called me and we both had jobs. We bought a Chevrolet coupe for $610 and later we both got jobs at McDonnell Aircraft where we worked for sixteen years, both on the night shift.

We then got ourselves a nice home but I lost Al five years ago. We had everything going for us finally. Years ago on the farm if someone had said that some day we'd have what I have now, I would never have believed it. There were times when we didn't have money for a two cent stamp and Al had to take in two dozen eggs and a five cent piece to get a haircut. No telephone, no radio, no nothing. But we had our love and stuck it out and it all ended well. Hard to believe one could ever have been so poor.

Ann Whitehouse
St. Johns, Missouri

DIRT AND DUST

Varnish Peeled Off The Furniture
Our Old House Was Full of Dust
Natural And Man-Made Calamities
We Learned Lessons About Going In Debt
Dust As Pulverized As Face Powder
Drought, Dust and Depression
Dad's Asthma Caused By Dust Storms
No Need For a Gym Workout in Those Days

) OFF THE FURNITURE

ry bad in western Kansas. I remember looking from
:nt in the court house in 1935 and being unable to
:ross the street, because of the dust in the sky.

Mother stuffed rags and paper around the windows to keep the dust from sifting in, but it still came in. Every morning everything was covered with fine dust sometimes one-fourth inch deep. Cleaning house was a constant job.

The air was so dry that varnish peeled off furniture. We had a very good piano that was the pride of the family. Mother had sold her pair of matched bay horses in order to buy it when we three girls were small. She wanted us to take piano lessons. At the beginning of the drought a gunsmith advised mother to use on all our furniture the same linseed oil and root mixture he used when making guns. She did this, particularly to the piano, and even kept a pail of water in the bottom of the piano so the wood wouldn't dry out. To this day the piano is in remarkably good condition and has never been refinished. I know because I was the one who turned out to be the family musician and was given the piano in 1958.

Yes, although it has been over fifty years, I vividly remember the drought and dust storms that caused such desolation in the plain states during the nineteen thirties.

As I recall, Oklahoma and the pan-handle of Texas were the first to start having dust storms. Those storms were caused by the top-soil blowing away because of lack of moisture and improper farming methods. In 1933 or 1934 it became apparent that western Kansas was in a serious drought also. The soil was so dry that when the ground was worked for planting, the rich soil and seeds were blown away by the winds. Young wheat plants and stubble left after the harvest were blown from the ground. Most fields were bare and the sky was a pinkish brown. Many people left their homes and came to California, but all of my relatives stayed except my uncle Fred Kisner and his family. They left their farm east of Garden City and came west in 1935 because Fred had lung trouble.

I was the youngest daughter of James C. and Beaulah Mae (Kisner) Standley of Finney county, Kansas. Before the drought my father had been a successful wheat farmer eleven miles south and six miles east of Garden City, Kansas. The farm was owned by Jesse N. Kisner, my mother's oldest brother. For many years there had been sufficient rain and snow to produce excellent crops.

In addition to that rented land, my father farmed other land and had over 200 head of cattle he kept in the sand hills just south of Garden City. During harvest time he employed as many as twenty-five extra hired men. He no longer worked in the fields himself, being a gentleman farmer, wearing expensive business suits, white shirts and neckties, buying a new car every year. Such a farming operation as he had constantly needed supplies of some kind, which he procured on trips to town practically every day.

Our life style was extremely good. We lived high on the hog as the old expression goes. It didn't seem possible that anything could change our way of living but then the area gradually started getting less rain each year. The farmers were always optimistic and looked forward to next year, being sure thaat conditions would become favorable again. Kansas wheat farmers are the world's greatest gamblers.

Like many farmers at that time, we lived on credit, paying the bills for the preceeding year when the wheat was harvested. As the crops diminished it was impossible to pay all the bills so it was necessary to cut back expenditures in every way possible. The herd of cattle was sold. The papers purchasing farm land were never finalized.

In order to support and educate his three daughters, my father took a job with the Finney county wheat allotment committee of the Agricultural Stabilization Conservation Program (A.S.C.P.) which had been formed to help drought-stricken farmers. Farmers were then paid not to farm all of their land and to strip farm.

My parents rented a small house at Tenth and Saint John street in Garden City. It was close to both the court house where Dad's office was as well as near the schools. With a monthly check, we were better off than a lot of people but there wasn't any extra money. My older sisters' spending money came from the milk bottles they returned to the market. Being an excellent seamstress, Mother was able to dress us well by making our clothing.

An election was coming up in 1934. Sheriff R.S. Terwilliger had been in office two terms and could not run again. People encouraged my father to run for that office as a Democrat. Being a very friendly respected person he had made a lot of friends all over the county, so he was elected and took office January 1, 1935. An apartment on the fourth floor of the court house, next to the jail, was the sheriff's living quarters. My father had no experience as a peace officer but he learned quickly; my mother cooked and served the meals for the prisoners.

It was while we lived in the court house that we fought the serious battle to save the piano, as I mentioned earlier.

The shortest way to school was north through the alley. My sister, Maxine, and I would tie scarves peasant style around our heads to keep the dust from our hair, and scarves over our noses and mouths bandit style for obvious purposes. We could see only a few feet ahead of us and many times couldn't see the fences along each side of the alley. By the time we reached school our faces were covered with dust where the scarves hadn't been. We'd go to the rest room and wash our faces before class.

Conditions were bad in town but not nearly as severe as in the country where fields were so close to the houses. Farming equipment left outdoors was soon buried and ruined; reservoirs were filled; rows of trees which had been planted as windbreaks, were buried under a hill of dust. At times the dust settled on patches of the road, even covering the ditches, until you couldn't locate the road. The wind was so strong and dry that it often produced electricity which jumped from one barb to another on a barbed wire fence.

In addition to the lack of rainfall, the wind and the dust, farmers had to contend with invasions of giant grasshoppers three to four inches long. They ate the few seedlings that sprouted. And there were thousands of jack-rabbits. In order to get rid of the pests, men would form huge circles and drive the rabbits to the center of the circle, clubbing them to death. It was a horrible sight but the rabbits had to be destroyed because they ate the crops.

The people who stayed in that area during those dreadful years showed great fortitude and deserve the highest commendaation.

Verna Mae Standley Bartok
Fair Oaks, California

OUR OLD HOUSE WAS FULL OF DUST

We farmed 360 acres with horses. We were coming home from a trip in Missouri the last of May, 1936. Nearing Des Moines the dust was blowing so badly we turned on the car lights. By the time we neared Fort Dodge, our home, we could see only three-fourths of a mile ahead.

My husband said he had to harness the horses and hitch them to the cultivator, to cultivate every few rows to prevent the small corn from being destroyed by the dirt and sand that was blowing across the fields. My job was to get our two small children inside the house and to unload the car.

Having an old unmodern house, the dust was on everything. I had to get water for the chickens in the coops. As I pumped water to bring in the house, it had to be covered immediately with a cloth. Pans and dishes had to be washed before they could be used. They were covered as soon as washed. Dust even got into the cupboards. The beds needed to be covered by extra sheets each morning. It was awful.

Linoleum covered floors needed to be swept with the electric sweeper to pick up as much blown-in dirt as possible. We had only one wool rug in the living room. The piano was covered with sheets at all times—as was the davenport.

When the rains came, more grass grew and the dust storm was over for a few days. You can imagine how much there was to do in those brief times—washing clothes, cleaning inside the house—cupboards, closets—all in an old house.

At times I even sucked dust into the electric sweeper from the walls. The house actually smelled of dust. We had electricity but it was the only modern convenience we did have, until the land was paid for. And I was grateful for that luxury.

Many people wonder why I still like winter months best. I'll tell you.

As a farmer's wife in the winter, there was no more gardening, canning vegetables and fruit. No more baby chickens to tend. No more hired men to board, etc. In winter months we women could sew, read, entertain and accept invitations. We could enjoy all the canned vegetables and fruit, the soups, the meat that we had prepared.

Winter was meat canning time. Butchering in the winter and canning beef, pork and chickens made meal preparation easier in the summer months.

What a luxury when our land was paid for. We built a lovely five-bedroom house. Deep freezers came into use. Not much more canning. Refigerators were a joy to have in our kitchens. Oh! Airtight windows and doors! Air-conditioning in summer now.

My husband was known as the National Champion Corn Husker. He won four national honors. Also the Kingsweepstakes.

Being conservative years ago paid off. I'm seventy-eight now, widowed, live in the city. I still drive my car, play bridge, have nice clubs and churches. I plan to go into a retirement home. Life has been good to my family and me.

Mrs. Fred Stanek
Fort Dodge, Iowa

NATURAL AND MAN-MADE CALAMITIES

I was a young lad in my early and middle teens during the era of the Great Depression and the drought. I was raised on a farm in south central Minnesota and speak from knowledge and experience.

It seems that natural and man-made calamities built up earlier and the summer of thirty-six was to be the knockout punch. Man-made calamities included bank failures, unemployment, farm foreclosures and very little money.

Natural calamities primarily involved the weather. A number of successive years of hot and dry weather began in the early thirties; the springs were windy with dust storms and I can recall seeing minidrifts of dirt along the fence lines as I walked home from country school.

One night when we were talking with J. C. Frase in his haberdashery store, he ran a finger over one of his shelves and, when looking at the dust on his finger, exclaimed "I wonder if some of this dust came all the way from Oklahoma and Kansas."

Successive years of hot weather and low annual rainfall were taking their toll on our lakes and trees. In 1934 the bed of our local Clear lake was bone dry. Trees were dying in our grove from lack of rain. Severe wind storms in the summers before the era of hybrid seed corn insured us that we would have to bend over to pick our corn off the ground in the fall.

No, the natural calamity of weather was not confined to the summer of thirty-six. The coldest recorded spell started January 18, 1936 and extended for twenty-three consecutive days with the mercury at zero or below all day. Snowstorms were frequent and heavy and combined with the subzero temperatures. The high snow drifts across the roads froze and isolated our town for two weeks. Not a train, car or truck entered the town. Food supplies and heating coal became scarce. An attempt to clear the big drift west of town by the Caterpillar was unsuccessful and the driver had to turn back.

On April 30 a tornado coursed for about seventy-five miles through northern Iowa and southern Minnesota and passed within five miles of us. It took the life of one man. I recall that my brother and I were walking home from school during that storm and took shelter under a cottonwood tree. What a foolish thing to do, but we didn't know any better.

Again the summer was very hot and dry. It took its toll on animals and crops. Many horses were lost to equine encephalitis (sleeping sickness) and heat prostration. My father would get out of bed at ten or eleven o'clock at night, harness the horses, and plow corn by moonlight.

The pastures were parched or burned and I remember my brother and I herding our cattle into the roadside ditches so they could get enough to eat. At harvest time my father commented that we had the poorest small grain and corn crop ever. Soon came the rumblings of war in Europe and we had prospects of a better market. The demand and price increased as the Great Depression was lifting and with it the drought.

One wonders how we survived. With the strong fiber of the American people, the basic drive for survival was never lost. Togetherness played a big role.

Nowdays we seem so fragmented and isolated with the amenities of an affluent society. We have our televisions, stereos, boats, cycles and many articles of pleasure to keep us home. During the depression we had our radios and ourselves. We would sit or recline in front of the old Majestic or Atwater Kent and listen to Jack Armstrong, I Love a Mystery, Gangbusters, Jack Benny and Fred Allen trading insults, Admiral Byrd and his Saturday night broadcasts from the South Pole. Families and relatives visited each other. There were Wednesday night band concerts or free movies on Saturday nights sponsored by local merchants.

Frequently, after Sunday morning church services, where the sermon lasted an hour, we went to relatives' home for a fried chicken dinner, followed by an afternoon of visiting until it was time to go home and do the chores.

Summer Sunday afternoons were different from the winter ones because it was the golden era of amateur baseball. Almost every town, however small, fielded a team of home bred and raised ball players. The pride was great, the competition was keen and the teams battled it out on the ball field. Needless to say there were many enthusiastic fans to cheer on their boys or indulge in a little friendly needling and ribbing.

The fiber and determination of our society to get through the hardships of the Great Depression paid off during a later and greater man-made calamity — World War II.

John R. Fischer, M.D.
Frontenac, Missouri

WE LEARNED LESSONS ABOUT GOING IN DEBT

Another cloudless day dawned. You could hardly see the sun, however, because of the dust in the air. My parents lived at 1002 Lincoln avenue, here in Platsmouth, Nebraska. We had no refrigerator, no air conditioning, and even a fan was a very rare luxury. It was very hot that 1936 summer and we had to leave the doors and windows open to let in what little breeze existed.

My father and my husband worked on the river and left very early in the morning so they could quit before it became too hot. The road or street in front of our house was not paved and when a car passed, it was just like a dust storm. My husband I lived in a small house behind my folks, being happy that we had several trees to catch a lot of the dust. My mother would wash the night before and hang out the clothes at 4 A.M., bringing them in by 6 A.M., before cars stirred up the dust on the street. That dirt was clay and the clothes would get yellow colored.

It was hard to keep the house clean because this dust penetrated everything. Wells all over town were going dry so we preserved water every way possible. We used wash water to scrub and wet down the porch and walks. We wiped everything with a damp cloth once or twice every day and even then the house wasn't very clean. Everyone suffered from the heat, much less the poverty.

Obviously the depression had set in and there were very few jobs available. Even those had very low pay. My folks lived in a rented house costing $7 a month which my dad paid with work. He cleaned rugs and wallpaper, sharpened scissors and knives and did any odd jobs either in or out of the store owned by our landlord. Sometimes he worked all day for fifty cents which he said was better than nothing.

There was no Social Security, no pension for old people, most of whom had to live with relatives to have anything to eat. Farmers were destitute. The ground was too hard to work and had large cracks in it from lack of moisture. There were no government programs for them. They helped out each other and pooled their machinery and resources, trying to hang on. Of course some of them didn't make it and had to try again later on. Some became the big farmers they are today.

Everyone was touched by the drought. Many lessons were learned. Those who lived through this experience became very cautious about going in debt. This same lesson is being learned today by many people. It's a hard lesson to learn because so many banks, lending institutions and stores make it easy to get loans and credit cards.

Finally, after all the years of drought, we started getting rain and with it our faith in the Lord was strengthened.

Ruby Sheldon Gochenour
Plattsmouth, Nebraska

DUST AS PULVERIZED AS FACE POWDER

I was a teen-ager during those years and lived in Kit Carson county, Colorado, near Bethune, Stratton and Burlington being our shopping towns. My father had moved there in 1927 and had about three good farming years. Then in 1930 the dust storms rolled in clear across the west from north to south, mostly during the evenings.

A few times we were sent home from school early with lights — and sometimes we stayed overnight in the school. My mother hung wet gunny-sacks by the windows to hold back some of the dust which was seeping into the house. That dust was as pulverized as fine face powder.

So often I can remember my dad walking the floor, wondering if he should return to Nebraska because there in Colorado it was impossible to raise any crops.

My brother and I helped dad stack tumbleweeds into a large stack for winter feed for our cows. Also, we gathered cowchips for heat or baking.

Each year we return to Bethune where we exchange memories that now seem somewhat fond. We're hoping for a happy alumni reunion this year because it's about time for Denver Pyle to join us.

Irene L. Theewen
Columbus, Nebraska

DROUGHT, DUST AND DEPRESSION

Drought, dust and depression — that's what I remember about life in the thirties. There is no one left among my family and friends to talk over those days so I am glad that someone wants to record that period of history.

I was living in DeSmet, South Dakota, where I was born and at that time I was teaching a rural school about four miles north of town.

The first really severe dust storm I recall was on a Sunday. We have plenty of wind storms in South Dakota but this one was very strong and blew not only along the ground but high in the air. It was carrying all sorts of debris in addition to large quantities of dust. We were accustomed to tumbleweeds blowing across the ground and down the roads but these were flying high. The wind was also carrying branches, pieces of wood and paper; it was frightening.

Since we had not received much rain, the houses were not as tight as they get when moisture causes the wood to swell. Our house must have been very old because the dust penetrated every nook and cranny. We were kept busy dusting and sweeping until the storm subsided. Before long we became used to constant fighting of the dust — it was to be with us for a very long time.

But that storm was only the first of many, so many that I don't recall any specific one except that just described. I drove to school each day and many times I could barely see the radiator cap. That was when all cars had them. I had trouble only one time- when the back wheel of my Ford slid off the road into a ditch filled with soft soil. Now I had been stuck in snow many times but this was diffeerent. I had three pupils riding with me, so we all piled out and with our hands and empty lunch buckets removed all that loose dirt; then I was able to drive out easily.

It wasn't pleasant but we learned to live with those storms and I wish I could remember more details. I know I vowed never to complain about rain again even if it upset my plans. Now I live on the Pacific ocean in southwestern Oregon where it rains very often. If I catch myself starting to fuss about it, I remember my vow. We have a saying here which applies when it seems the sun is never going to shine again — 'Well, at least we don't have to shovel it.'

It was tough just living during the depression. My wages had been cut in half so I was earning $45 a month for nine months. How did we live? No one else had money either.

Prices were down and we learned to make things last and to do without. We never were anywhere close to starving. Some people received surplus food from the government but we were Republicans and Republicans weren't too popular.

We didn't fuss about our low teachers' wages because we knew people didn't have money to pay their taxes. Now, when teachets strike I sometimes blow my top. When I see young people throwing money around and having everything they want, I often remark that "It would do young people good to have to live through a depression but I don't want to see it happen again." I served my time.

Elva Lindsay Johnson
Port Orford, Oregon

DAD'S ASTHMA CAUSED BY DUST STORMS

My father was an asthmatic, the problem being caused by the dust storms of the thirties. He was the late Reverend John J. Vander Schaaf, pastor of the Emmanuel Reformed church of Springfield, South Dakota. There was so little treatment for this disease in the thirties that we suffered along with him.

On the fourth of July, 1936, the temperature was well over one hundred — even in the shade. In Yankton, 35 miles away from us, it was officially 102 degrees that day and 113 the very next day. The all-time high was set on July 18 with 116 degrees while the all-time high for the whole state was set that month with 120 degrees at Gann Valley. (These facts from Jerry Oster at WNAX News in Yankton.)

My Dad was suffering intensely. I stayed home from our annual Sunday school picnic (at the age of nine I hated to miss this annual fun day) to help mother care for dad.

He was in such misery that we placed a chair in his bed upside down with the legs pointing upwards. We put pillows on the back of the chair to give him a comfortable sitting position to help his labored breathing. Mother and I together hung wet sheet blankets over the curtain rods to act as air-conditioners to filter the air. It was the best we could do to alleviate his discomfort.

Amy R. Breisch
New Glarus, Wisconsin

NO NEED FOR A GYM WORKOUT IN
THOSE DAYS

I remember well the old days of the thirties. You notice I didn't say "the good old days". The times were really rough. Our three children were born in 1931, 1934 and 1937; they actually cut their teeth on a bacon skin stripped clean of the fat.

My husband grew up farming aand since there were no jobs to be found we thought we could at least raise our own food, but we were very young. My father-in-law had a team of mules he said we could use; we rented an old run down farm and house, on shares, in an area called Sand Prairie. Rattlesnakes were everywhere. The first time my husband plowed up a rattler while walking behind a plow, he decided to look for a riding plow.

We tried hard but when the crops came in we couldn't sell them. Corn was eighteen cents a bushel if we could find anyone to buy it. The smaller ears we kept and used as fuel in the cook stove; they made a quick hot fire.

The cook stove was used winter and summer and we made a fire in it only to cook meals because we saved fuel for heating. We often parked our old Ford truck near the railroad tracks and, while the baby slept in the truck, we walked along the tracks, picking up lumps of coal which had fallen off the coal cars. We would fill our sacks, drag them to the truck and then drive to another location to continue. We saved that precious coal to add to our wood supply, which we sawed with an old crosscut saw. Believe me, I did develop muscles.

We made a large garden and also raised tomatoes to sell. We couldn't sell them, even for twenty-five cents a bushel, because many people didn't have the quarter. A government agency opened a small cannery in the area where we took our produce to be canned. For each five cans of our produce, we received four cans, with one being kept to give to those who had no gardens.

My parents gave us twelve brown leghorn hens so we had fresh eggs. I made a lot of egg noodles which I used with our canned tomatoes to make a meal.

There was no electricity and no refrigeration. We used the food we cooked since there was no way to keep it in the summer. In the winter we had a window box, a box nailed to the outside of the window, which we could access by opening the window. In cold weather, it kept food from spoiling.

I remember the old washboard, the large tub and the sore knuckles from the lye soap my mother made, the aching back that went with it. No need to go to a gym for a workout in those days.

My husband worked for the area potato farmers for a dollar a day, picking and sacking potatoes from sun up to sun down...a long day.

We finally had to ask for help as did almost everyone else. We were given a grocery order worth $2.85. It bought a large box of the most needed staples. I remember many meals made from a can of mackerel to which I added eggs and cracker crumbs to make a big plate of fish cakes.

We patched clothes and took the old worn out ones and cut the best pieces from them. These were sewed together to make comforters for the beds.

In the summer there was no way to keep cool and many nights when it was too hot to sleep I would sit by the childrens' bed to fan them with a newspaper.

When our oldest son wanted a kite to fly we made him one out of newspapers, flour and water paste, and strips of thin laths from an orange crate. We used orange crates for storage cabinets by stacking three or four on top of each other.

When we finally gave up farming and moved to town my husband went to work for the WPA; he received $12 a week or $48 a month, out of which we paid $15 for rent. We finally managed to save enough to have electricity turned on. How happy we were when we had a small radio and could listen to the evening programs. It was our one and only luxury. We also bought an old ice box and in the summer we could buy a chunk of ice on special occasions.

We were as poor as the proverbial church mouse but somehow we survived.

I am now a widow with great grandchildren and hope and pray that we never have another depression. I would know what to do to exist, but I'm not sure I would have the strength. Some call the old times the good old days, but I for one would not want to go back.

Anne (Granny) Schiber
Worden, Illinois

FIGHTING HEAT OR COLD

We Cleared Road With Scoopshovels
The Start Of '36 In Iowa
Sleeping In Yard Was Talk Of Town
January Blizzard Records Vs. July Heat Records
Sleeping On Fire Escapes
Minnesota Heat Worse Than Solomon Islands
Thermometer Burst At 120 Degrees

WE CLEARED THE ROAD WITH SCOOPSHOVELS

I'd like to start with a comment about 1934. It was a very hot and dry summer, pastures were very short and the cattle kept the grass eaten to the ground.

We cut the corn stalks, which were about a half to two-thirds normal height, placed them on a platform about seven by fourteen feet, on a wagon, and hauled them out to the cattle for feed. We had counted the rows of corn and knew how long it would feed the cattle. When the leaves started turning brown, we filled the silo. The remainder of the crop was cut and shocks were built to preserve the leaves.

This leaves the winter of 1935–1936 to talk about. It was a long and very cold one. There was a period of thirty days when the temperature was zero or below night and day.

Roads were blocked with snow. Everyone had horses and bobsleds and that was the means of transportation. There were no snowplows then; when the roads were opened, if at all, it was done with men using scoop shovels. One day when we opened a road with shovels the snow was higher than our heads; the next morning it was all filled in. After that we went through the fields with teams and a sled.

John J. Cunningham
Sigourney, Iowa

THE START OF '36 IN IOWA

I have lived in this same place over 52 years. My husband moved here in 1932 but he was killed in 1969 when a tractor upset on him.

I was a young bride. . . married on October 2, 1935, so I went through horse farming, hired men, washing on a board. We did have a car, though, a Chevrolet for which we had paid $500.

The October 11 storm started on a sunny day; then, about 12 A.M. snow moved in. Cold winds. The chickens that didn't make it back to the henhouse froze to death.

That summer of 1935 each day was hotter than the one before. I never got so tired of dust and heat—no refrigeration, no electricity. I especially hated ironing, using a wood cook stove to heat the irons.

The winter of 1935 started on Christmas eve. We left for midnight mass and the big snowflakes were sort of dancing. We didn't have gravel roads then either. The priest was sort of long winded with his sermons going on for an hour and a half. Someone told him to quit because the weather was getting bad.

We started home, hitting the first drift about a mile south of Norway. We dug out since we had a scoop shovel in the back seat. It kept snowing. Others kept getting stuck. When we got home a couple with three boys had broken in and were sitting in the kitchen with the fire going. They had carried one of the boys a mile; he had frosted ears which were white. We put rubbing alcohol on them and they never even peeled.

Before morning there were 21 here for breakfast. It was Christmas day. We ate eggs, fried down meat and my Christmas hickory nut cake made from scratch. (There were no cake mixes then.) During the morning the men worked on the snow and they all left, going in a group.

Of course the mail carriers didn't make their runs. About once a week someone walked to Norway and brought the mail home for the entire route.

The young went as far as they could go—they can go a lot further now. I can remember my great grandmother who was born in 1826, always saying "My, my, what's the younger generation coming to!"

My husband's cousin, a young man, died. I guess from a heart attack. They couldn't get a doctor. They kept him at home until the funeral. They took his casket out in the back of a pickup truck. Sixty-five men dug out the road, among them was Hal Trosky, a Cincinnati ball player from Norway. We couldn't see over the snow tunnel we were in when we went to the funeral.

When we went to town we went over fences with the bobsled and two horses. It's 3½ miles to Norway but it was 5 miles the way we went. We picked out the best routes behind groves of trees.

That was the start of 1936. For 21 days the temperature averaged 7.7 degrees below zero.

I still have a wood cook stove. I had a woman move in for three days during an ice storm as she had a six months old baby and two other children—and no heat. So the old cook stove comes in handy sometimes.

I feel bad about locking my doors when the weather is bad; we never used to do that.

I'm still here. The boys are all gone—no farmers. One lives in California, which has its earthquakes. Florida has its alligators—they are in most if not all the lakes. Nevada doesn't have grass. I gripe about mowing it but I miss it. The east and west coasts have too many people. It's hard to pull up your roots. Every place I've been has been a good spot. When I was in Europe I was the odd ball and glad to get home for a glass of water.

I live near Amana and vote there. My fire truck is from there. Mail and school is from Norway. I worked at Amana for twenty years finishing furniture and breaking in the new help.

My prediction for the future: instead of other countries coming to our level—we're headed for theirs.

I've been a widow for years and have to make my own decisions. That is hard for me to do, yet I get lots of advice. Advice without deeds is like a garden full of weeds.

Geraldine Schulte
Norway, Iowa

SLEEPING IN YARD WAS TALK OF TOWN

The nights were unbearable that summer of 1936, after we had been married on June 1. I moved from a large farm of 190 acres and a big square house with plenty of windows to an upstairs apartment in town—Fonda, Iowa.

My husband decided to convert a malted milk mixer into a fan. It worked so he decided I should sleep next to the window since I weighed 110 pounds and wouldn't stop the breeze from reaching him. We had just gone to sleep when the fan burst into flames. Not being accustomed to electricity in the country, I was gone like a flash out of that bed and the room! He often remarked that in our 49 years of marriage I never really trusted his mechanical ability after that.

A few nights later it was so hot we decided to carry our studio couch down the stairs and sleep in the back yard. I made him promise we'd awaken early and carry it back upstairs before the neighbors would see us.

It was comfortable, covered by a sheet. We slept well, you might say too well. In the next block a neighbor's barn caught fire. The fire engine came—neighbors came across our lawn to witness the fire—and we never heard a sound.

We hurried our nest back into the apartment early but when my husband went downtown to work he found that everyone in town knew about our overnight yard sleeping.

Mrs. Jim Witcraft
Fort Dodge, Iowa

JANUARY BLIZZARD RECORDS VS. JULY HEAT RECORDS

I grew up on a farm northeast of Washington, Iowa. After high school I taught country school for several years; that was during the years when one could take Normal Training courses in high school and could teach country school upon graduating.

During the school year of 1935–1936 I taught five miles north of our place and, since none of the roads were improved, I had to go by horseback or wagon when weather was bad. We teachers had to build the fire in the potbellied stove and carry water from the nearest neighbor's. There were no rest rooms, just the two cold little buildings out back. There was no electricity so on dark days it wasn't easy to see our work and our books.

In January snowstorms hit with a vengeance. By January 22 there was so much snow on the ground that Dad had to pick me up in the bobsled drawn by two draft horses. The drifts were four feet high and more. On January 24 another storm hit and schools couldn't open for several days. Even bobsleds had problems getting through the stuff. Temperatures had dropped to 25 and 30 degrees below zero. The snow was fine and hard-packed so we went over fence tops with Blanch and Maude, not sinking in at all. Neither did the bobsled sink.

Dad would go to town in the bobsled to get groceries for us and the neighbors. Coal became so scarce that it had to be rationed to 500 pounds per family.

On January 26 the roads were opened but because of high winds they blew shut almost at once. Four days later another big storm hit and the drifts were even higher. The mail carrier could not get through again. On February 11 a woman died about four miles north of us. The snowplow went through as far as the Boyd Foster corner with the hearse following, to meet another bobsled carrying the woman's body. Then the snowplow led the hearse back to town.

There was even talk of closing Iowa State college in order to save coal. Many schools and public buildings across the state were closed. There was much sickness among the livestock but too often the veterinarian could not get through and the animals were lost.

February 12 to 14 we had the worst storm in 117 years. It really was terrible. All that snow.

Eventually the weather eased up and snow started to melt, resulting in lots of flooding. By March they were predicting a hot, dry summer and warned of problems with chinch bugs. Most of that spring the schools were kept open on Saturdays to make up for the time lost during the winter.

By July 1 crops were drying up and chinch bugs had hit in full force. On July 13 Washington, Iowa, recorded a temperature of 115 degrees and we were launched on the hottest heat wave ever on record.

During that summer I was enrolled at Iowa State Teachers college (now University of Northern Iowa) and, needless to say, without air conditioning, the heat was unbearable. I was continuing with piano lessons there and when we did our practicing in our little cubicles, there wasn't a dry thread on us. Many students were ill from the heat. On July 22 a tornado hit the campus at 11 P.M. It sounded like a freight train coming, broke windows, uprooted trees, damaged the football stadium. The dust was terrible. Of course we girls were always washing things and hanging them in our rooms to dry. When the tornado hit, it sucked things from one room into another. Afterwards we had to go up and down the hall hunting our belongings.

At home it was too hot to sleep in the house so Dad and my brothers pitched a tent in the yard and slept there at night. With no electricity on the farm and, of course, no air conditioning, it was the only way they could get a little relief.

By September we were getting a little rain.

I wonder if we could survive such weather now without all of our conveniences? I, for one, would not like to try.

Even though we didn't have much money or many conveniences, it was not a bad time to be growing up. Of course, there were no drugs then, and there was no drinking among our friends. Without television and other entertainment, we made our own. We had many house parties, coasting and skating parties in the winter. When there was plenty of snow on the fields, we would all gather at the top of a hill on my Dad's farm, build a big bonfire to keep warm, and with the sleds would coast down the hill, through the gate, and across the bridge over the creek. At the end of the evening, we all went to the house and had hot chocolate, popcorn and apples.

During the summer we had lawn parties, where we sang the music for games, which were a lot like square dancing. After refreshments. we gathered around the piano and sang till the evening was gone. It was wholesome fun.

Jane Marsh
Hiawatha, Iowa

SLEEPING ON FIRE ESCAPES

I was employed as a clerk in a grocery store in Renville, Minnesota, the summer that was so unbelievably hot. Of course very few stores had air conditioning in those days and the brick buildings never cooled off, even over night.

The farmers had a few chickens and the farm wives used the eggs to buy groceries. For their crates of twelve to fifteen dozen eggs they had lists which might include a box of Rinso for ten cents, five pounds of sugar for a quarter, hamburger at two pounds for a quarter, Wheaties at two boxes for a quarter. When it was so hot that the hens didn't lay as many eggs, it became a serious survival problem for the farmers.

Everyone canned their own fruit for winter in those days. That summer was a good year to buy cheap fruit. Since most warehouses and trucks didn't have refrigeration, the peaches were rushed to the stores where they ripened quickly. In the store we received fourteen pound crates of peaches several times a week, a hundred at a time, selling them quickly at sixty-nine and seventy-nine cents per whole crate. A partly spoiled crate sold for less. Most people would buy two or three crates at a time and then come back for more as soon as those were canned.

Canning was another hot, miserable job for the women. It was done on a wood range or a kerosene stove.

The trucker who brought our fruit to the store told us people in the Twin Cities were sleeping the parks or in yards. Those in apartments slept on fire escapes or any place they could find outside the hot brick buildings. I'll never forget how everyone suffered in that intense heat that went on and on during those years— 100 degrees or more day after day.

Sylvia Kronlokken Shafer
Le Sueur, Minnesota

MINNESOTA HEAT WORSE THAN SOLOMON ISLANDS THAT SUMMER

Sometime in the early thirties one of the Minneapolis newspapers ran a boxed editorial to the effect that, in conformance with regional usage and contemporary trends, the applicable word would be "drouth". As a matter of fact, my memory tells me that Minneapolitans and South Dakotans said "drouth" and I believe that such was the general usage in areas affected by it. (Editor: I'll stick with my Webster's that lists "drought" as the first spelling).

1936 was one of several drought years in the Upper Midwest. I spent the summers of 1933 and 1934 in Perkins county, South Dakota, where it was my duty to drive Herefords from one Russian thistle patch to another, there being nothing else green for them to eat.

During the summer of 1936 I spent brushing in the piney woods near Park Rapids, Minnesota, and I have never been more quickly exhausted by heat, even in Quantico, Virginia, or in the Solomon islands, after moderate physical effort. I have been bitten by grasshoppers who also roughed up hickory pitchfork handles and ate out the underarms of my shirt.

L. L. Cavanaugh
Brandon, Minnesota

THERMOMETER BURST AT 120 DEGREES

I remember the year 1936 very well. We lived in northern Wisconsin, eight miles from Merrill. We had lost our farm there two years earlier, had moved to Washington and then back to Wisconsin the next year[1935], living on a small farm which had been my grandfather's. My father was a carpenter and worked away from home much of the time; hence we were not farming.

That winter, early 1936, it was extremely cold. One morning our thermometer dipped to sixty degrees below zero. We had a cow and I usually had to chop a hole in the ice on the creek for water for her, since the place did not have well water. I had to take a sled and milk can to a neighbor's for our drinking water. We did not have electricity. We used wood for heating and cooking.

The summer of 1936 was so hot and dry that our thermometer rose to 120 degrees and burst. The chickens walked around with their mouths open. My mother, whose health was not good, couldn't do anything except the most necessary housework. She had to spend a good share of time lying down. I was fourteen at the time and probably not as helpful as I could have been.

In August 1936, we moved to western Oregon and here we've stayed, enjoying the much milder climate. The first fall in Oregon we earned money for school expenses by picking prunes and nuts: we continued doing this through all of our high school years.

Ruth Reese
Forest Grove, Oregon

THE LIGHT SIDE

THE HUNGRY REVIVALIST

The special memory that I have of the summer of 1936 may be different from others, although it will never be forgotten.

My husband was an Evangelist minister and was very dedicated to his work. We had more calls for revivals than we could fill. Many ministers were afraid to go because of the drought. When we were called, my husband would look at me and say "Let's go by *faith*." And we would go.

We travelled many miles throughout northeast Louisiana and Mississippi. I recall one time when he went to check the tires, coming back saying "I had to put a boot in the bad tire but, as we said, we will go by faith." We were supposed to be in north Mississippi that night and as we travelled the tire would bump at each rotation. The preacher looked straight ahead as if nothing were wrong.

We crossed the Mississippi river on a ferry boat and drove up the steep hill. After going about five miles we passed a little boy rolling a tire. My husband said "Look! That tire will fit our car." He stopped and asked the boy if he would sell the tire; the boy was very happy to sell it for twenty-five cents. However, my husband insisted the boy's father approve the deal but the father told the boy to give the preacher the tire. My husband thanked him but made the boy take the quarter. We drove on that tire one year.

That night the pastor took up an offering for us and got seventeen cents. But the next night brought in thirty-four cents. My husband gave the whole fifty-one cents to a young minister and family who were hitchhiking to another town for a revival. My husband said they could buy their lunch on the road, for the four of them, with that money.

This, too, was farming country. It was so dusty you could hardly get to church without getting filthy. But in spite of the drought, we had a good revival.

When it came time for us to leave for another revival, my husband sold a gasoline lantern in order to buy enough gasoline to get to his mother's grocery and service station. I well remember that when we got there she said "Son, stay here and help around here until the drought is over" but my husband replied "Mother, I've got to be about my Father's business."

She filled our Model T Ford with gas and we had enough to get to the next place, still in farming country.

That night we started another revival. They gave us a place to stay that looked like a barn. It had a makeshift stove and bed. We had nothing to eat all day and went to church hungry, asking God to give us strength. We went to bed hungry that night.

Early the next morning I heard my preacher praying "Lord, David said that one time he was young and now old and he had never seen the righteous forsaken, nor his seed begging bread." I stood in the doorway, crying.

After he finished praying, there was a knock at the door. He opened it and there stood a well-dressed man who had the largest basket of groceries I have ever seen. He said "I know everyone on the farms is having a struggle and thought you could use some groceries." My husband was in tears but before he thanked the man he looked up and said "Thank you, Jesus." The man also was in tears—and he was in church that night. After this good man had left us, I cooked the best meal we had ever eaten.

That wonderful preacher of mine passed away ten years ago. He built a lot of churches. Sometimes I visit some of them and when I get home say "My dear husband, you are now resting from your labors but your work still follows on."

When I think of some families going hungry now, and I have plenty to eat, my heart cries out "Lord, how long?"

Agnes Ladner
Winnsboro, Louisiana

A WHITE CASTLE HAMBURGER FOR A DIME

The summer of nineteen thirty-six was indeed a time many of us are not liable to forget. The time of the stock market crash definitely led to the lean years of the thirties.

I had been married in thirty-four and discovered what the word "depression" meant. Somehow we struggled through, with the help of soup lines and menial work to survive. A week after we moved to Minneapolis the trucking firm my husband worked for went on a three-week strike. It was a devastatingly difficult period.

The weekly wages were $25 and the rent was also $25. Many weeks my husband walked to his job five miles away because we didn't have enough money left for him to ride the street car, even though the fare was only ten cents. I thought nothing of walking 25 blocks to purchase bread at five cents a loaf. A cup of coffee or a bottle of pop or beer was also five cents. A real treat was a ten cent White Castle hamburger. For 25 cents we could go watch a dance marathon, or a roller derby. Many times I would get on a streetcar and, with transfers, ride all over the twin cities, just to find my way around, and to visit with other riders. For a dollar we could take in vaudeville and see such stars as Fred and Gracie Allen or Edgar Bergen and Charlie McCarthy. The big bands were there, too—names like Glen Miller, Rudy Vallee, Guy Lombardo and Tommy Dorsey.

Luckily I found part time work in a fruit and vegetable stand, for which my pay was some of the produce. I also ironed a nurses starched uniforms and her husband's white shirts. I loathed that job but it meant a few dollars and the chance to go to a ladies day bonus ball game for only ten cents. That was to see the Saint Paul Saints.

My parents saved the day when food was low. They would drive 160 miles with their Hupmobile loaded to the hilt. They brought canned fruit, vegetables, fish, meats and canned wild game. Also jams and jellies of all kinds, plus such treats as home-made bread and pies and cookies. Somehow baked goods and foods have never tasted as good as the ones baked in that "Ideal" cookstove.

The only clothing I purchased came from The Women's Exchange. It was all nationally known brand names from those who were more fortunate than most of us.

With Christmas coming, I went to the Dayton company and made such a pest of myself they finally hired me part time for special sales and for the holidays. How sweet it was to receive that check for a first good "giving" Christmas in a long time.

When we attended church, we dressed for the occasion. Hats were a must, along with gloves. Slacks and jeans wer unknown commodities. The dresses and skirts were ankle length. Occasionally we ventured to the hairdressers and submitted to that monster of a permanent wave machine; more often than not we came out frizzled and frustrated. We shampooed our hair in rain water and sometimes set it with liquid boiled down from flaxseed.

It was difficult to survive but, to sum it up, we learned how to do so with initiative and the family bringing-up our parents had provided.

It was so hot we frequently had to go to Elliot park at night with blanket, pillow and alarm clock to try to get some sleep. Imagine doing that today! We still had ice boxes then but the ice would melt almost before the iceman left the apartment. We looked forward to Sundays at one of the city parks if we could find a space to sit or swim. Wall to wall people were all trying to savor one of the good things that summer of thirty-six.

The one thing I regret about those times was that I discarded a letter I had received from President Franklin Delano Roosevelt. As a teen-ager I had written him complimenting him on initiating the March of Dimes which was in 1931, I think. I had stated that I would like work with polio patients, specially children.At that time my handwriting was hardly readable because of the polio effects on my right hand and posibly someone on the President's staff thought it was a hoax. In any event, the President sent a note that a staff member would come to Minneapolis to see me. When that person came and requested I produce the presidential letter I couldn't do it. Being naive, young and down-right stupid, I didn't handle the situation too well.

The polio had affected my right side, particularly my right hand. With my mother's initiative, I did overcome much of the problem. She always kept ninety-proof brandy on hand for colds. She would pour this on my back and the effected muscles, and somehow it loosened the muscles. Also each day, as my fingers my fingers loosened, she would have me key the piano, and sent me to a chiropractor. They immersed me in water using electric pulsations to enhance the poor circulation. The typewriter brought me around and was very helpful.

Eventually I was able to work for the March of Dimes.

Evelyn R. Erckenbrack
Verndale, Minnesota

MAN BROKE BACK CARRYING DIME'S WORTH OF OATS

The year 1932 had been a good year with good crops of grain, fodder and hay, but the prices were very low. If I remember right, Red-Durum wheat sold for 26 cents a bushel and oats for only a few cents per bushel. The story went around about a man who broke his back trying to carry ten cents worth of oats. One elevator had a sign—Shelled corn eight cents per bushel...Ear corn, 10 cents less. Some people burned corn in their stoves instead of buying coal.

So the Dirty Thirties really started in 1933, the first really dry year. Some crops were harvested that year. I harvested some corn for feed. There was almost no hay, but everyone had a carryover from 1932 so all got by that year in pretty good shape.

When 1934 came along it was really dry. Most of the grain that was seeded did not even come up. The only crop that I seeded was some millet and sudan grass late in the summer, after a little shower. It did come up but grew only enough to furnish a little pasture. The Russian thistles did very well and everyone cut a lot of them for feed. They were not the best feed but did bring the livestock through until grass was available next spring.

1934 is remembered mostly for the dust storms. All the plains area from Texas clear up into Canada was bone dry, and all was blowing. Some days folks had to light their lamps in the daytime, the dirt made it so dark. One day it was so bad that we took our noon meal down in the cellar to eat it. We could at least eat without our food getting all covered with dirt. It wasn't so bad down there.

Some of the things we remember so vividly were the drifts of dirt on the window sills and by the bottom of the doors. If and when a still day came along so the washing could be hung outside, the clothes line had to be washed off real good. The sky was watched very closely so the wash could be brought back in before the wind and dirt came up or the clothes would have to be washed over again.

In the fall of 1934 the U.S. government bought a lot of livestock and most of them were killed and buried. If I can remember correctly, I think the farmer was paid $12 for a cow and $6 for a calf. Most farmers kept only the best of their herds so they could start over when things would get back to normal.

There was the WPA (Works Progress Administration) which started in the fall of 1932 and continued on until sometime in 1935. Each family was allotted so many dollars to be worked out on various projects. Building Amsden, Pigors and Tollefson dams were some of the projects in this area. Others were grading and graveling roads and for the women there were the sewing projects, making garments and mattresses to be given out to the needy.

Some of the families without an able-bodied person to work were given direct payments of a few dollars a week. My wife remembers that she was paid $2.80 a day for sewing and she was allowed to work one and half days a week, or $4.20 for her and her mother to live on.

Another story that went with the dust storms was of the gopher that was digging a hole. When the wind went down, he found that he was six feet in the air.

Along with the poor prices, drought and dirt came the grasshoppers by the millions. They ate everything that had survived the drought. The men soon learned to stick the handles of their pitchforks into the hay so the grasshoppers wouldn't chew on them and make them too rough to use.

In 1935 there was a good crop and folks rejoiced.They thought the drought was over, but it wasn't. Most of the late 1930's were still very dry. Lots of no more than four-bushel to the acre wheat was harvested and it was worth around 50 cents per bushel. The land still blew, making for more dust storms.

After things got back to normal in the 1940's, a lot of farmers took a tractor and a road grader and bladed the dirt away from their fences, which had been completely covered with the drifted dirt.

One thing that I remember about the "Dirty Thirties" was the eagerness of all the people to help one another. There was a feeling of concern and sharing that through the years of more abundance seems to have been lost. There were good things about the "Dirty Thirties."

Edwin C. Cunningham
Conde, South Dakota

(Originally written for the Redfield (S.D.) Press)

HOW TO DROWN CRICKETS

Pre-teen-aged son came into the kitchen. "I've played every video game I have," he said, "and now there's nothing to do." He made a glum face and hung his head.

Son can be so exasperating. I thought of the fun things I did when his age, back in the summer of 1936. Remembering that summer, the drought and the garden we raised by carrying water in buckets from the windmill, reminded me of crickets.

"Why not drown out crickets?" I asked.

He looked up. "That sounds groady. What is it?"

"Well, when I was a kid..." I began.

"Do you have to start that far back?" he grumbled.

"Yes. We had to raise or grow our own food or we didn't have anything to eat."

Son grinned like the light had just dawned. "That was before grocery stores, huh?"

"No, but it *was* before computers. My family raised gardens, chickens, hogs, and cows." I tried to explain.

"Where do the crickets come in?" He sat down and drummed his fingers on the table.

"The garden was full of crickets," I replied.

Son's eyebrows went up. "You raised crickets too! I didn't know they were edible." He made a face and started to get up.

I pushed him back. "Wait. I haven't finished. If we didn't get the crickets, they got the garden and we didn't have vegetables to eat."

Son perked up a bit. "What a neat way to get rid of vegetables. You didn't like them either, huh?"

"I liked them. We got rid of the crickets. I was the champion cricket-drowner of my family. Armed with only a teakettle of water, I drowned more crickets in less time than any of my siblings."

"No, you don't" I stopped him as he was about to walk away. "You said you didn't have anything to do, so listen. Cricket hunting is fun. Here's how it's done."

So I told him. You take a teakettle of water and a quart jar with a lid and go tto the garden. Look around under the bean and pea vines, up and down the rows until you see a small hole in the ground. That's most likely a cricket hole. Pour water into it and wait for the cricket to crawl out, then grab it, slap it in the jar and screw on the lid. If you're still there after dark you can get the crickets that come out voluntarily. All you have to do is listen for the chirps and soon you'll have a quart of crickets. Son's eyes lit up. *He finally understands* I thought. "Now I see," he said. "In the olden days there was a market for crickets and you sold them by the quart. I bet you made a lot of money, mom" and he patted me on the back.

"Actually we fed the crickets to the chickens," I said. "You should have seen those biddies go after the crickets," I laughed, remembering the excited clucking.

Son looked glum. He paced and waved his arms. "Gross to the max. What if everyone spent their time drowning crickets? Soon all the crickets would be gone and there wouldn't be a cricket on a hearth anywhere. What would the Japanese do without a market for their little cricket cages? What a mess the world would be in."

He paused as he turned toward his room. "I guess I'll re-program my computer. Maybe I'll make up my own video game." He slammed his door.

I shook my head. At least he found something to do. But there's the generation gap. Computers or crickets? I still think drowning crickets is more fun.

Doris Crandall
Amarillo, Texas

THIS HOUSE NEEDS ONLY ONE THING – A MATCH

A few years ago my son asked how we survived the depression. I replied it made little difference in my family life amongst my parents and nine children. We had no stocks or a bank account. We were poor before, during and afterwards.

My father worked as a common laborer for the railroad, placing railroad ties. Work was never steady so when a child graduated from grammar school, he or she had to find a job. One sister cried because she was not sent to high school and, even as an adult, she still mentioned it at times. Those of us who were younger were able to go to high school only because the older ones were working. I was eighth of the nine.

We lived in an old wooden two-flat we owned. Tenants rented the top flat. But the building needed so many repairs we couldn't afford to make that we had a standing joke: "This house only needs one thing – a match." The rent money paid the water bill and the real estate taxes. My parents grew vegetables and herbs instead of a lawn, which helped the food situation. My father used a homemade cart to bring discarded railroad ties to be cut up for fuel. He used a large two-man saw (nothing electric) and was always looking around for one of the kids to help man it. We usually took off because it was a hard job, especially for girls.

Only once did my parents try to get help from the government, for food. The government people sent a letter asking my parents to appear personally with an older child to help translate if necessary. Mom picked a sister who would lose the least money by taking time off. But at the office they were told we could get no aid because we had tenants in our building and that rent was considered as income.

Only two pairs of shoes could be purchased each week. If yours were worn out or outgrown and it was not your turn, you simply stayed home from school. Public schools and the Catholic church where we belonged gave no help in any form. Some of us younger ones belonged to an after school social club run by wealthy people. They helped make arrangements when we needed our tonsils removed.

Although we never starved, most meals were filling and tasty. My mother worked hard to achieve that. She believed that food was the most important item to survival and without it sickness was sure to develop.She was right too because we had no serious illness among our large brood.

Being one of the youngest, I still remember many of the thoughtful deeds my older brothers and sisters did for the younger ones. One Christmas the eldest brother cut down an old small table not in use, painted it bright red and bought two little red chairs to match. This was for use by the four younger kids. A pair of roller skates was used by two of us. One skate for each.

Did we feel deprived or were we unhappy at our way of life? Probably not. All of our relatives and neighbors were in the same boat. The struggle to survive was hardest on my mother since she ruled the family; she died at an early age from overwork.

Evelyn Socha
Chicago, Illinois

AMALGAM

Kentucky Tobacco Crop Poor
Cannon River Ran Dry
We Never Once Called It A Depression
Beating The Heat In Iowa
We Created Our Own Entertainment
Thinking You Would Die
Best Answer: Joined The Navy

KENTUCKY TOBACCO CROP POOR

We lived three miles from Drennon and Drennon creek in Henry county, Kentucky in 1936. Dad (Owen A. Shaw) had rented a farm from Les Courton who lived in our county seat, New Castle. We raised a tobacco crop, such as it was that year.

There was no grass for cows or sheep. My dad and brother would drive them three miles to Drennon and by the time they got back they were just as thirsty or more so than when they left.

It was so hot we slept in the yard on quilts. The ground cracked open so wide that dad could put his hand in the cracks.

We also had a bad electrical storm that year. I am sixty years old and have not seen anything like that since. The sky was completely covered with streaks of lightning going in every direction. It seemed to last all night. The sky was so bright we could see anything.

The only thing that grew was a weed with a blue flower. I remember pulling them and feeding them to the chickens which would eat every bit of the weed. Dad sold the tobacco in the barn and we moved to Pleasureville before winter. Dad worked at the tobacco warehouse in Shelbyville that winter.

I still live in Pleasureville and we are having a drought right now in 1987 — not as dry as 1936 — we still have some green grass.

Helen Shaw Bond
Pleasureville, Kentucky

CANNON RIVER RAN DRY

The drought really started in the early thirties. The winter of '31–'32 probably recorded the least snow ever recorded in Minneapolis.

I opened my office as a dentist in 1933; there were dust storms all the next spring of 1934. No water ran in the Cannon river in that spring. I had an upstairs office in a brick building and when the temperature reached above ninety degrees, I just locked up the office.

Lowell Rieke
Waterville, Minnesota

WE NEVER ONCE CALLED IT A DEPRESSION

We had two years without rain and hadn't enough crops harvested to pay for the seed we had planted. This was on our farm in Hardin county, Iowa.

Hogs were ten cents a pound, or less, and corn ten cents a bushel, or less. My dad burned some corn to warm the house, saying it wasn't worth anything, but he had tears in his eyes when he did it.

Luckily, we had milk and eggs and vegetables canned in the cellar. We herded our cows in ditches along the road to eat grass but we sat for hours to keep them out of the road.

We six children would go barefooted all summer and, as for clothing, our mother made most of it and I, being the youngest, mostly wore hand-me-downs. Our overalls would have patches over patches. We had only one change of clothes which we'd wear a week when our mother washed them on a scrub board and tub. We had to change to work clothes after school.

Of course there was no electricity and we had to pump the water by hand from the well and carry it to the house, unless there was enough wind for the windmill to do the pumping. The water would freeze in the pail in the house at night.

Our boots would get holes and our feet get wet going to school. We'd sit by the pot-bellied stove to get dry.

In the summer our upstairs was so hot we would sleep outside on a blanket in the grass. In the winter the snow would sift through the windows onto our bed covers. The only heat was a stovepipe going through our room but the fire would always die down before morning. We slept three to a bed to keep warm. Our feet would get frost biten (called "chilblains") doing chores and we had to soak them in Epsom salts.

For cereal we'd grind popcorn and pour milk and sugar over it.

Mother made a mixture called "starter yeast" which she used to bake bread. We tapped our maple trees and boiled the sap to make syrup; we raised navy beans and threshed them on a tarp with a carpet beater. We saved our seeds from watermelon, potatoes, seed for cornmeal so we ate much cornmeal mush and navy bean soup and vegetable soup.

We rendered our lard in a big iron kettle outdoors and made our own soap with lye and lard. We didn't buy shampoo, just used soap. We didn't buy toothpaste, but used salt and soda. We made our own butter; I recall that a neighbor put extra salt in her butter to keep her boys from eating too much of it.

The only toys we had was a coaster wagon and a sled so we invented games. We used branches from trees for stick horses in the summer and would stand on barrels to roll down the hill. In the winter we cut animals from cardboard and used boxes for buildings and played farm. We made a checkerboard and used buttons for checkers. We put a button on a string and twisted it just right until it would spin and hum. We put tissue paper over a comb and blew so it would make a tune.

We never once called it a depression.

We respected our parents and it made us a closely knit family which, after fifty years, left us a loving group.

Elsie Reed Nehring
Iowa Falls, Iowa

BEATING THE HEAT IN IOWA

I am a seventy-six year old widow, who was married to Everett D. Severns of Callender, Iowa, in Fort Dodge, in that hot, hot summer of 1936. My parents were farmers between Gowrie and Callender in Webster county. My husband managed the H.E. Rhodes lumber yard in Jamaica for over twenty-three years going there in 1935. When we were first married I'd go with him to try to collect from his customers but it wasn't easy in the middle of the depression.

That winter was a bad one and Everett couldn't get through the roads to come from Jamaica to Gowrie, for three weeks. I have a photo showing the drifts being higher than the car. Everett would plan to drive up every weekend but the wind always blew up and the roads were filled again.

As I said, my folks farmed about three miles north of town and my brother would walk to town to buy food; the roads were closed for many days that winter.

When we went to buy furniture before we were married it was unbelievably hot. Few places even had fans. This fellow lived in Fort Dodge and they ran a fan blowing on a large hunk of ice placed in a dishpan. It kept the house fairly cool. We bought all of our furniture wholesale through the company and it was of good quality.

To beat the heat Everett and I went to old Coon river near our town almost every eve after work I'd grab a sandwich and maybe coffee in a thermos and off we'd go.

Ethelean Severns
Jefferson, Iowa

WE CREATED OUR OWN ENTERTAINMENT

You should know that I made one big mistake in my life: I started a detailed diary two weeks before Charles Lindbergh made his epic flight to Paris—then made a helluva mistake when I quit keeping it up in 1950 when I was moonlighting to finance making railroad movies.

(The author goes ahead to tell how he spent several years filming railroads and created a big file of such film which is becoming increasingly in demand for use by others.)

Our entertainment in the evenings was cheap as no one had any surplus money. We played cards, ping pong, listened to the radio, told "new" dirty stories. If we were flush and had a dollar we'd go to the movies. Note that the boxing champs didn't make much money and had to fight quite often to be self sustaining. We also ate a lot of popcorn and peanut butter sandwiches, while shooting a BB gun at a target in someone's basement. Ten factories here in town had baseball teams playing each other twice weekly. We also spent a lot of time going to meetings because the woods were full of union activities.

1936

Wednesday, January 8: Went to a meeting tonight. The union electricians want us power company employees to join, since the Wagner labor act is now in force.

Friday, Jan. 17: Joe Louis, a negro, and a North Dakota farmer named Retzlaff fought tonight. Louis won in 1 minute, 25 seconds in the first round.

Sunday, Jan. 19: It was 16 below zero at 7 A.M. today.

Tuesday, Jan. 21: King George of England died yesterday at 5 P.M.

Wednesday, Jan. 22: It was 31 below zero today—the coldest in the past 25 years.

Thursday, Jan 30: Was only 6 degrees below today. While in the grocery store a lady rushed in and said a fire was burning between the walls.

Monday, Feb. 3: Grandma Ackerman died at 10:55 A.M. During a terrible snow storm.

Tuesday, Feb. 4: Had Grandma's service here in Cedar Rapids this P.M. and then sent the body to Waterloo.

Wednesday, Feb. 5: Buried Grandma at Waterloo. It was 28 degrees below zero. Came back on the Interurban (train) and the snow was so high I couldn't see out the coach windows.

Friday, Feb. 7: Took out of state relatives through the giant Quaker Oats plant this afternoon and then to Bishop cafeteria.

Saturday, Feb. 8: Had another terrible snow storm at 25 below zero. Street cars quit. Those who had cars couldn't get them started. Factories closed down.

Sunday, Feb. 9: Still storming. It is now reported this winter of 1936 so far is the worst since 1887. Snow is 2½ feet deep on the level with drifts up to 25 feet.

Monday, Feb. 10: Ordered coal today. Was told they could deliver only one-half ton, fearing a shortage of coal since the railroads are at a standstill.

Thursday, Feb. 22: Washington's birthday. Tonight we stacked 538 wooden matches on the neck of a beer bottle.

Wednesday, Mar. 11: The ice went out of the river today, after a big ice jam broke loose upstream.

Wednesday, Mar. 18: Went down to see what is called a "Streamliner" train go through town. It had five ritzy coaches and wasn't pulled by a steam locomotive.

Wednesday, Apr. 1: Bruno Hauptmann (Charles Lindbergh baby kidnapping case) was saved from the electric chair today on a 48-hour extension.

Friday, Apr. 3: Bruno Hauptmann was electrocuted tonight at 7:45 P.M.

Friday, June 19: Max Schmelling knocked out Joe Louis in world championship heavyweight fight, in the twelfth round at New York.

Wednesday, July 1: We went downtown to see the new fang-dangled streamliner go through a town.

Monday, July 13: It was hot today. 112 degrees with lots of humidity.

Tuesday, July 14: The newspapers reported that yesterday's high temperature (in the country) was in Cedar Rapids.

Friday, July 31: The Spanish are having a rebellion and civil war.

Tuesday, Aug. 4: I cut weeds in the back yard. The grass out front is so badly burnt there was nothing to cut.

Wednesday, Aug. 5: We had a third inch of rain today. Our first in six weeks.

Tuesday, Aug. 18: Joe Louis knocked out Jack Sharkey in the third round tonight.

Friday, Aug. 21: Governor Alf Landon, Republican candidate for president, spoke to a big crowd from the rear coach of a train at the depot.

Wednesday, Aug. 26: Our fifth wedding anniversary. I married a farm gal.

Thursday, Sept. 3: Got a 10% pay raise notice today, effective September 1.

Sunday, Sept. 6: Drove to Minneapolis, 267 miles in eight hours, on the way to a fishing trip.

Tuesday, Sept. 22: Joe Louis knocked out an Italian fighter in the fifth round.

Tuesday, Nov. 3: Democrat Franklin Roosevelt carried all but two states over Republican Alfred Landon in the presidential race.

(It's easy to see Mr. Billings' interest in railroads and heavyweight boxing matches as one reads his diary.)

Harry A. Billings
Cedar Rapids, Iowa

THINKING YOU WOULD DIE...

What was it like living through the drought of the dust bowl days?

Words can't describe it. Memory tries to shut out those horrible times. Dust filling the sky, obliterating the sun, making the world an eerie place, every day all the time. Dust everywhere, sifting into the house, closing it up tight until you thought you couldn't breathe, wearing wet handerkerchiefs over your face when you went out, which you had to do.

Life had to go on. The dust was gritty in your mouth when you ate. Water was scarce, carried from the windmill. Men were forced to leave the fields because they were choked and blinded. Red dust from our own fields.

Never again must there be soil erosion. Save the trees.

Mrs. Ida Belle Sands
Cedar Rapids, Iowa

BEST ANSWER: JOINED THE NAVY

My Dad, J.R. Burklow, and my Mother, Elsie, did all they could to keep us in food and clothes. My mother even washed clothes by hand for other people to get enough money for seeds and groceries.

We had a nice home and a barn in Zalma, Missouri, but we couldn't pay our property tax. The two-story house where I was born still stands near the Zalma school.

People who could find jobs worked from sunrise to ssunset and were paid only fifty cents a day or they could take it out in trade. When I learned that the Navy paid twenty-one dollars a month plus room and board I signed up; I would have signed up for twenty years without a raise if I'd had to do so. I appreciated that Harry White and Earl Bennett helped me to get in; Earl took me to St. Louis so I could take the test.

We moved from Zalma to Wapello, Iowa, in 1923 and to Puxico, Missouri, in 1925, from which I left to join the Navy.

I joined the Navy on March 1, 1936, stayed in for twenty-three years and missed out on most of the hardship others people experienced.

I have a brother, Oren, and two half brothers, Cletis and Roy, plus three sisters, Iva Mae, Lora Edith and Bessie Bernice.

James A. Burklow
San Jose, California

INDEX

You'll Like William Hull's Other Book Too

Although three of William Hull's books are out of print, his two newest ones are going strong and are highly recommended.

ALL HELL BROKE LOOSE contains experiences of young people during the Armistice Day 1940 blizzard in Minnesota which killed 59 people. 167 Minnesotans tell how they coped with the storm that killed so many neighbors. Over 500 people were interviewed and selected experiences were included. Best seller in Minnesota. About to go into its tenth printing. Paperback, 236 pages, illustrated. ISBN # 0-939330-01-6. $8.95 retail.

> "Get a copy for yourself. This is a keeper."
> *St. Paul Pioneer Press and Dispatch.*

THE DIRTY THIRTIES. A brand new book which has young people telling how they stayed alive during the depression and drought years of the nineteen-thirties. The author shares with you the experiences of 147 people from 21 states who lived through these terrible years. People who tell 151 different stories. Some humor and photographs. Paperback. 262 pages. ISBN # 0-939330-03-02. $9.95 retail.

> "These stories are invariably laced with good humor and provide a testimony to the durability of the human spirit...natural eloquence."
> *GRIT* Magazine, Dave Wood

Both books are handsomely covered in color with an appropriate illustration and are 5-3/8 x 8-1/2 inches in size.

You may obtain either book through your bookstore by furnishing the ISBN numbers shown above or, if you prefer, you can order directly from the author using the following...

— —

ORDER FORM

Send to William H. Hull, 6833 Creston Road, Dept. 22, Edina, MN 55435 along with check. No books shipped without payment.

_____ copies of ALL HELL BROKE LOOSE at $8.95 each = $_____

_____ copies of THE DIRTY THIRTIES at $9.95 each = $_____

_____ Plus 6% sales tax to Minnesotans = $_____

_____ Plus $1.50 shipping for *each book* = $_____

Total Enclosed: $_____

Name: _____

Address: _____

City: _____ State: _____ Zip: _____

Prices subject to change.